Johnnie Cooper

Collages 1992–1997

Fractured Light

■ ■■ ■ black dog press

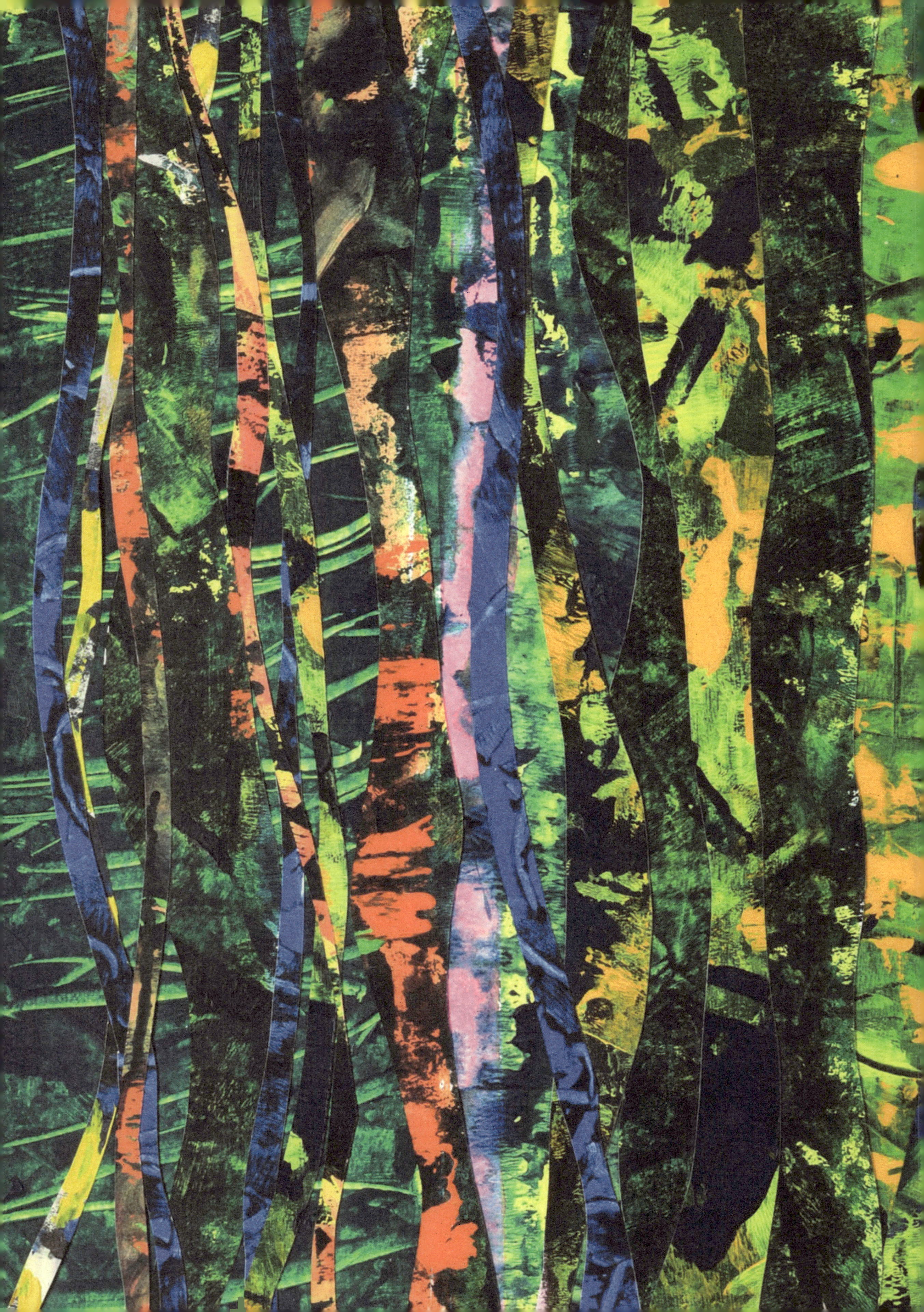

Contents

Time, Place, Light

'Sensation, revelation.'
(Georges Braque: *Cahiers*)

I *Time*

Each day is different; every day is the same. Painting is a means to the revelation of this daily paradox. Revelation of the everyday as marvellous is the work of art.

II *Place*

There is a wood in Gloucestershire. Aspects of the wood – daybreak, diurnal, noontide, afternoon, crepuscular, nightfall, nocturnal – are discovered in this book of days and nights. Art is the lens that refracts this spectrum of time and light. As the seasons turn, so each day's own seasons merge. Every day the wood changes; every day the wood is there; every minute the wood changes, every minute the wood is different. Every morning the wood is revealed by light. During every day the wood registers every quick and slow change of light and shadow. Always, quick and slow are simultaneous. Every night the wood is there. There is no utter darkness; the night wood contains glimmers of light, slivers of gleam. There is no absolute light: every dawn a lightening, morning a brightness, at noon, shadows at our feet, and in the afternoon, at evening and at nightfall darkening, there are shadows and shades, tones and nuances. No image here records a moment; each registers rather the passing of moments, just as the wood is a timepiece that suffers no pause. This denial of stillness is a reflection of the endless flicker of nature. Each image is a colour clock face. Time inscribed on a place in space: a wood in Gloucestershire.

III *Light*

These arboreal landscapes splinter space and time in two ways: vertical and lateral. The trees, and the magical spaces between them, receding to light or darkness in varying degrees, are vertical. The air that weaves its colours between the warp of the receding trees is lateral. (In the wood there is no horizon.) If we concentrate on that envelopment of air-colour, light and shade, our eyes lose sight of the trees and are beguiled by the fabric of the wood as a whole: painting as gestalt. Looking at the vertical trees we delight in the fleck and smudge of bark, its reptilian variegation, its brilliance at dawning, sunlit moss-green, afternoon turquoise, night-time blues, its dark against darks, its night-light gleams of star and moon: painting as sensation.

Mel Gooding

Arcadian Fantasies
and Dripping Embers

Gabriella Pounds

British Abstract Painting
in the 1990s

A thin layer of purplish acrylic paint glides across paper to convey an early morning sunrise. Horizontal swathes of magenta and violet, flecked with dribbles of cerise pinks, feign a peach-drenched sky at dawn. *Silver Birch Shadow*, 1995, belongs to a body of collages created by the British artist Johnnie Cooper during the 1990s. Over a five-year period, Cooper made over 100 collages from within his rural Gloucestershire studio at Brook Farm, overlooking the Malvern Hills. Perpetuating the artist's research into abstract landscape painting – and employing a ceaseless emphasis on, and fascination with, colour and light – a typical collage would be dictated by the season, weather conditions and time of day. Three or four sheets of paper were usually stretched up to work on in one sitting, while only one would receive an application of the uniform foundation colour. The remaining three would be painted in an array of similar shades: complementary and secondary colours lifted directly from a pristine landscape, which were then cut into strips and arranged into mood boards. Cooper recalls surveying the woodland and carefully noting the darker areas, the spaces blotched with sunlight and the verdant hues of foreground foliage. In *Silver Birch Shadow*, for example, collage strips stained with coral, royal blue, turquoise and metallic, earthen tones are layered over the mauve backdrop, attesting to the hallucinogenic rainbow of tinctures glinting in the distance. The undulating, serpentine shape of the collage pieces are inspired by the gnarled bark of, in this case, a silver birch tree. Other formal influences would often include trees, plant stems and branches, in order to retain the illusion of gazing through a forest.

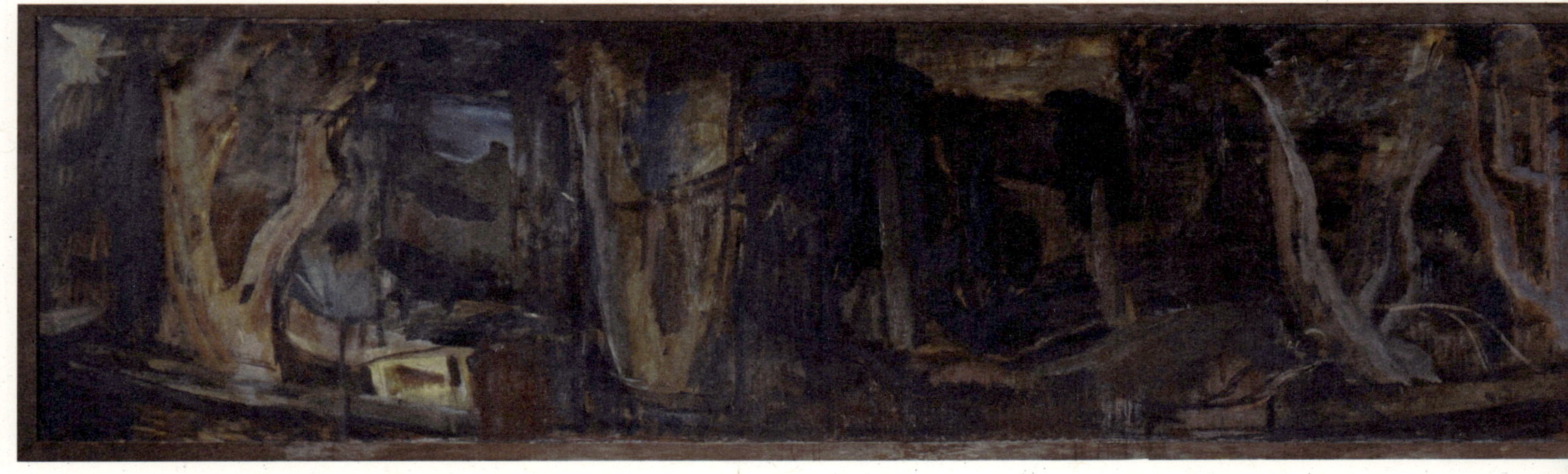

Morning

Although Cooper adheres to this formal process for each work discussed in the following pages, like many of his contemporaries working with abstraction, he notes awaiting the unexpected. He recollects eagerly anticipating "a moment of serendipity", when two or more colours melt into one another to create a sensation, a burst of hues he had not foreseen. Spontaneity, which undergirds much action-based and non-figurative practices, was simultaneously generated by the medium of collage. Creating a large collection of cut-out shapes to work with facilitated a rapid transmogrification of an image: a piece's resulting finality became a delicate collision of colour and shape, where the slightest alteration could have resulted in its loss for eternity. In the darker, and comparatively dense composition *The Green Man*, 1992, crimson and pink flames erupt through lashings of navy blue and taut scratches of forest and emerald green. The work rhymes with the Arcadian fantasies of Ivon Hitchens (1893-1979), one of the pre-eminent British painters of high modernism. In particular, the sombre pallet, its bruises of acrylic, recalls Hitchens' painting *View from Terrace: Ashdown Forest*, 1938-1941. Glimmers of lilac and sky blue emerge from the autumnal backdrop. It's as though Cooper revivifies Hitchens' knack for gently eluding the bones of a landscape with an older, longer tradition of gracefully snaring chromatic 'illumination'. In a manner akin to British Pre-Raphaelite painters such as William Holman Hunt (1827-1910), *The Green Man* pulsates with patches of colour visibly affected, changed, by their surrounding tones and the reflections of nearby objects.

Cooper created this body of work within a landscape of British painters radically altering a well-established national tradition of painting the countryside. He cites Ivon Hitchens as having the most profound impact upon him, and, as we shall elaborate on later, noting the ways in which Hitchens' combinations of colour and shape taught him much about the emotional potential latent in art. But similarities can be drawn with other painters captivated by the awe and terror of the British countryside. Peter Lanyon (1918-1964), Patrick Heron (1920-1999), Bryan Wynter (1915-1975), John Hoyland (1934-2011) and Howard Hodgkin (1932-2017), for example, were each melding tropes of abstraction with the formal qualities of foundational landscape painting. These forms were defined a century earlier by artists

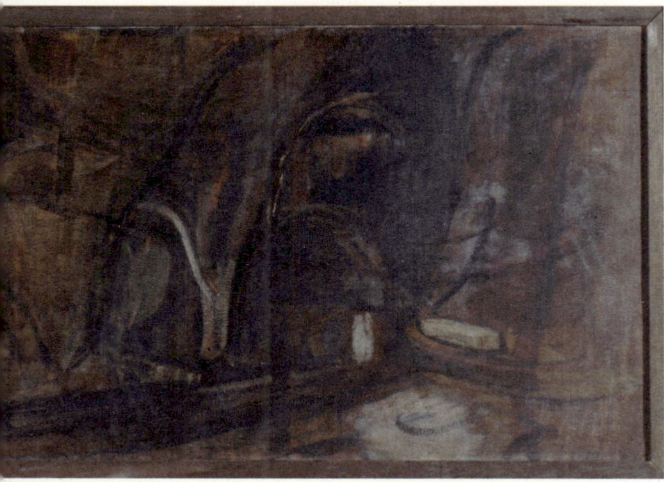

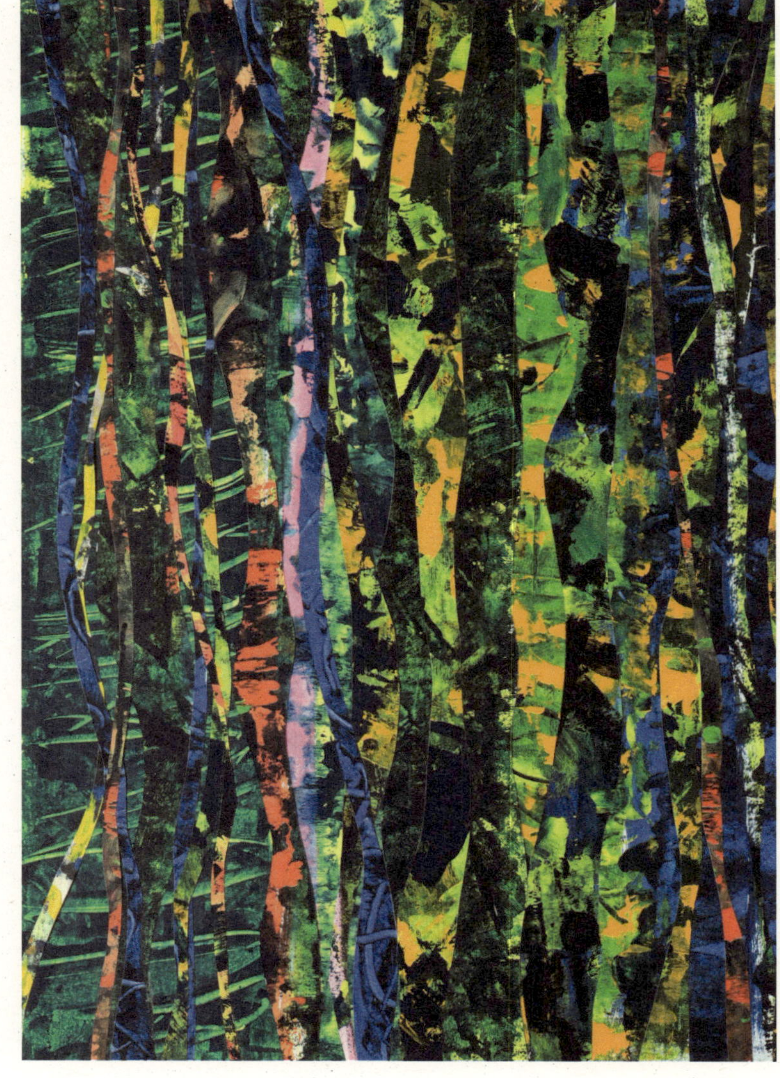

Above
Ivon Hitchens
View from Terrace: Ashdown Forest, 1938–1941
© Tate

Right and page 4 (detail)
Johnnie Cooper
The Green Man, 1992

Below
Johnnie Cooper
Tannery Pond, 1996

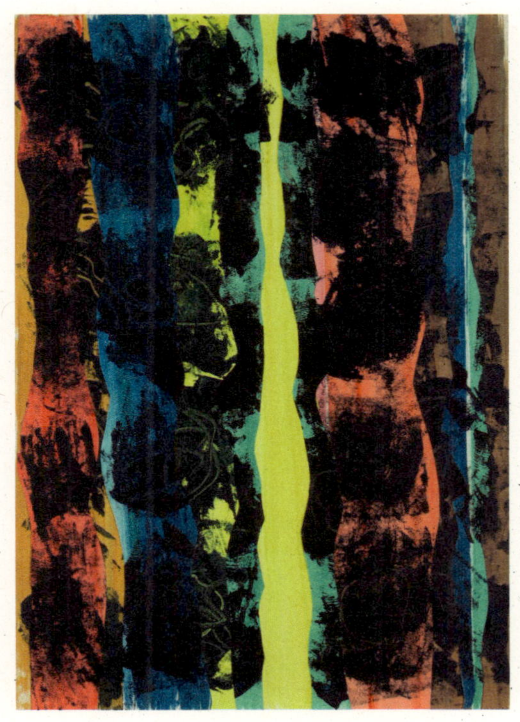

such as JMW Turner (1775-1851), John Constable (1776-1837) and Samuel Palmer (1805-1881). The work of Lanyon et al. formed a notable grouping within British contemporary art of the post-war era. During the 1980s, and the 1990s - when Cooper began making these collage works - the British art scene radically dispersed. The experiments in landscape and abstraction of the 1960s and 1970s gradually fell by the wayside in the presence of punk. It was not until the Young British Artists of the late 1990s emerged, bearing their bleak and sardonic explorations of death and sexuality, that a congruous movement within British art was felt again.

Nevertheless, the thick smudges of Cooper's *Tannery Pond*, 1996, and wide, slick strokes that cut vertically across the picture plane of *Fallen Bough*, 1995, evoke the generous mark-making of Howard Hodgkin. Furthermore, Bryan Wynter's dramatic, vertical arrangements of trees (some of which are especially haunting, exuding a malevolent atmosphere) in oil, for instance, chime with many of Cooper's assemblages. The dense arrangement of the slender, towering ribbons of colour in Cooper's *Stoney Beach*, 1994, and *Summer Solstice*, 1994, are reminiscent of Wynter's works, such as *Torrid Zone*, 1958, and *Impenetrable Country*, 1957. Although Wynter morphs views of the Cornish landscape into geometric forms, recalling earlier abstract traditions of Futurism and Cubism, parallels remain visible in both artists' use of brushy textures and naturalistic palettes (blues are used to signify rivers and skies, while yellows, golds and browns, the earth, etc).

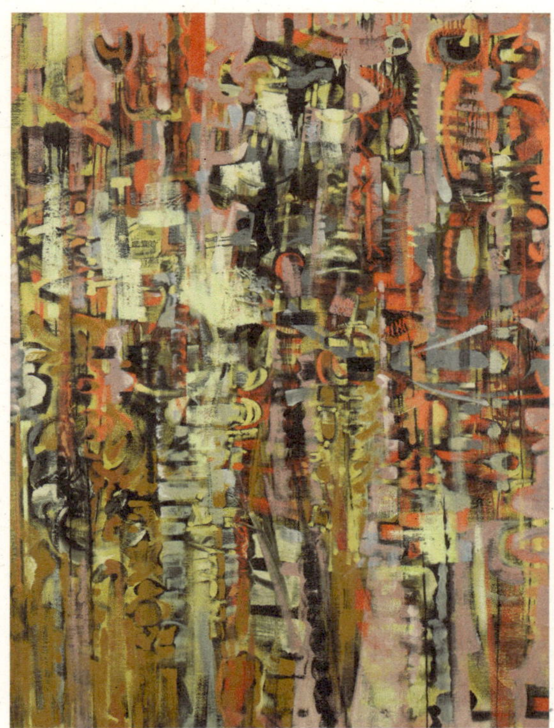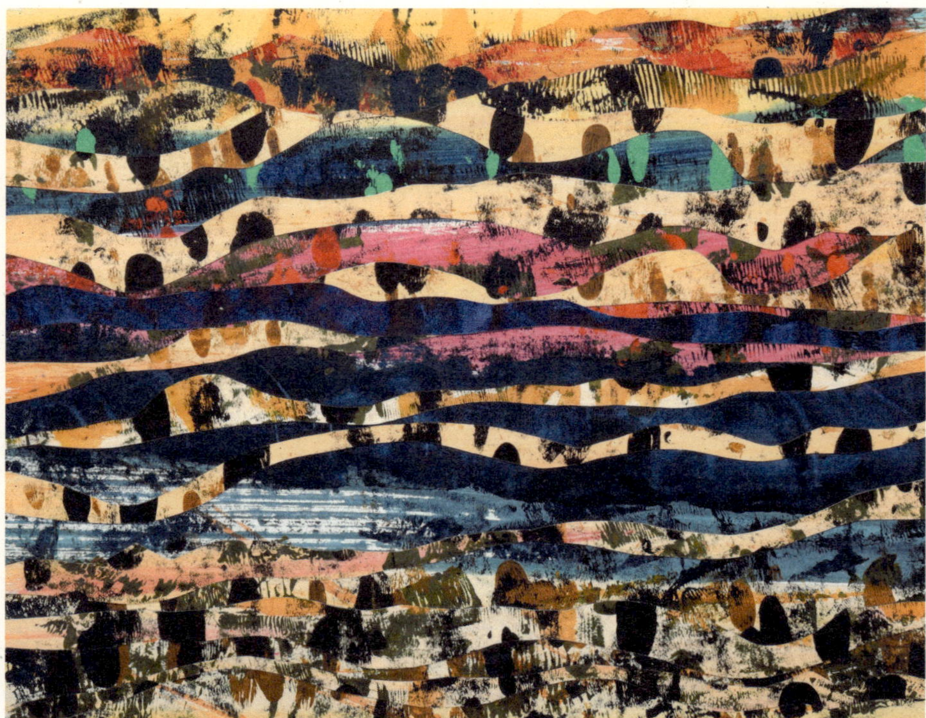

In the years prior to developing this body of work entitled the 'Brook Farm' series, when Cooper was mostly producing sculptures and paintings (other elements of his stylistically versatile oeuvre), he became interested in Minimalism. This offshoot of abstraction extended the idea that art should have its own reality and resist being an imitation of something. In the Minimalist canon – which includes the work of artists such as Sol LeWitt (1928–2007), Carl Andre (b. 1935) and Richard Serra (b. 1938) – no attempt is made to represent a real form: a Minimalist artist wants the viewer to respond to all (and only) what appears in front of them. Of all the painters working in this genre, Cooper considers the American painter, sculptor and printmaker Frank Stella (b. 1936) to be the most relevant to his practice. In particular, by the mid-1970s, Stella had begun to break away from the confines of the frame. In a nod to this distinctly Stella-esque pictorial innovation, in many of the collage works, Cooper allows the compositions (the strips of colour) to spill over the edges. Moreover, Stella's freeform assemblages notably played with combinations of effulgent hues. This greatly informed Cooper's break with the rigid bands of tones he had previously incorporated into his works, and gestures to the emphasis on blending and bleeding: the chameleonic transformation of colour that seeps into every corner of the collage pieces.

Left
Bryan Wynter
Torrid Zone, 1958

Right
Johnnie Cooper
Stoney Beach, 1994

Noon

Scatting from the morning to the middle of the day, many of the collage works also reference non-visual inspirations, such as the music of jazz. Like the mid-century Abstract Expressionists (working from studios based, predominantly, in the USA), who skewed and emulated the lyricism and spontaneity of jazz music in their works, British artists of the post-war period continued irreconcilable iterations of this trend. Creator of mind-melting canvases, Willem de Kooning (1904-1997), once quipped about the legendary jazz trumpeter Miles Davis (1926-1991) that he "...bends the notes. He doesn't play them - he bends them. I bend the paint." Looking at Cooper's works on paper with de Kooning's observations in mind, we can see that the rhythmic splatters, painterly 'bends' of zestful lemons, limes and oranges, which comprise works such as *Solar Stream*, 1996, emanate with the improvisation typical of a jazz song. Cooper recalls that, despite being influenced by all styles of popular music, the shimmers of brilliance from a jazz saxophonist and/or drummer - such as the heart-jolting solos of Gene Krupa (1909-1973) - informed the musicality of his paintings. Speaking of Cannonball Adderley Quintet's 'Umbakwen', Cooper notes how it "sparkles like the white brushstrokes on John Constable's painting *The Hay Wain*, 1821". At the same time, *Solar Stream* exemplifies a shift into a more vibrant palette, which occurs in tandem with the changing light throughout a typical day in the Cotswolds countryside. There are exceptions here, however, with notably gloomy works such as *Bull Rush Pond*, 1993, featuring smears of charcoal black, smouldering crimsons and flashes of yellow.

Below
Johnnie Cooper
Solar Stream, 1996

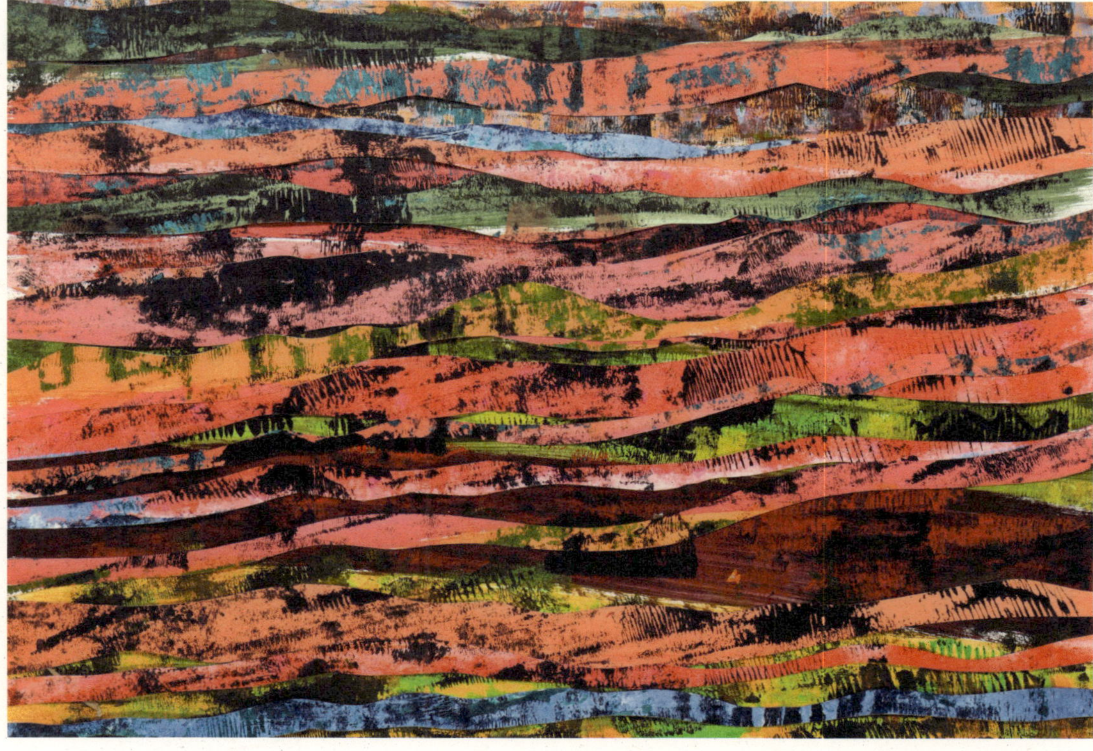

Thinking about harsher palettes, and harsher music, Cooper deliberately set
out to create works that not only conveyed the moods of jazz, but of rock and punk
songs, too. As a drummer in rock bands since his early teens, Cooper was still involved
in playing live music into his thirties. Commenting on the contemporaneous and
burgeoning cultural milieu of punk, he mentions how he found it deeply exhilarating:
"I loved the anarchic philosophy of challenging preconceptions of what constituted
a pop song." An attitude he would later carry into, and that would inform, his 'Empire'
series, 1986-1991, of wooden constructions and collages.

Cinders, 1996, is laced with strips of turquoise, orange, peaches and greens:
collectively, the shades form a melange of stark, chromatic harmonies. It is unsurprising
that during this time Cooper began to look to the aforementioned painter Ivon Hitchens,
along with the French painter Pierre Soulages (b. 1919), paying particular attention to
how their works, through experimentations in colour and space, created atmospheres
of intense emotion. Famously, Ivon Hitchens said: "My paintings are to be listened to."
The same idea could be applied to Cooper's works, where colour is used in a related
manner to simulate and stir emotion, much like how a song can radically alter, emphasize
and soothe our moods. Perhaps more than any other musical genre, classical compositions
offered the most fruitful source of emotional potential for Cooper to visually reflect.
Pieces such as the 'Second Symphony', 1911, by the British composer Edward Elgar
(1857-1934) are renowned for their animated, multidimensional tenor, containing a welter
of counterpoint accompanied by an enmeshing of counter-themes and harmonisations.
It is music that critics consider to be of extraordinary emotional exactitude – even when
it can feel emotionally ambiguous – conveyed through a kaleidoscopic selection of
orchestral colours. Elgar creates symphonies that bloom and dissipate. Listening to his
melodies is an experience not dissimilar to looking closely at the shapes and colours
that whirl, splatter and fade across Cooper's collages. Further, Elgar penned many of his
pieces, such as the 'Enigma Variations', 1898-1899, while overlooking the very range of
hills that cascaded outwards from the horizon beyond Cooper's Gloucestershire studio.

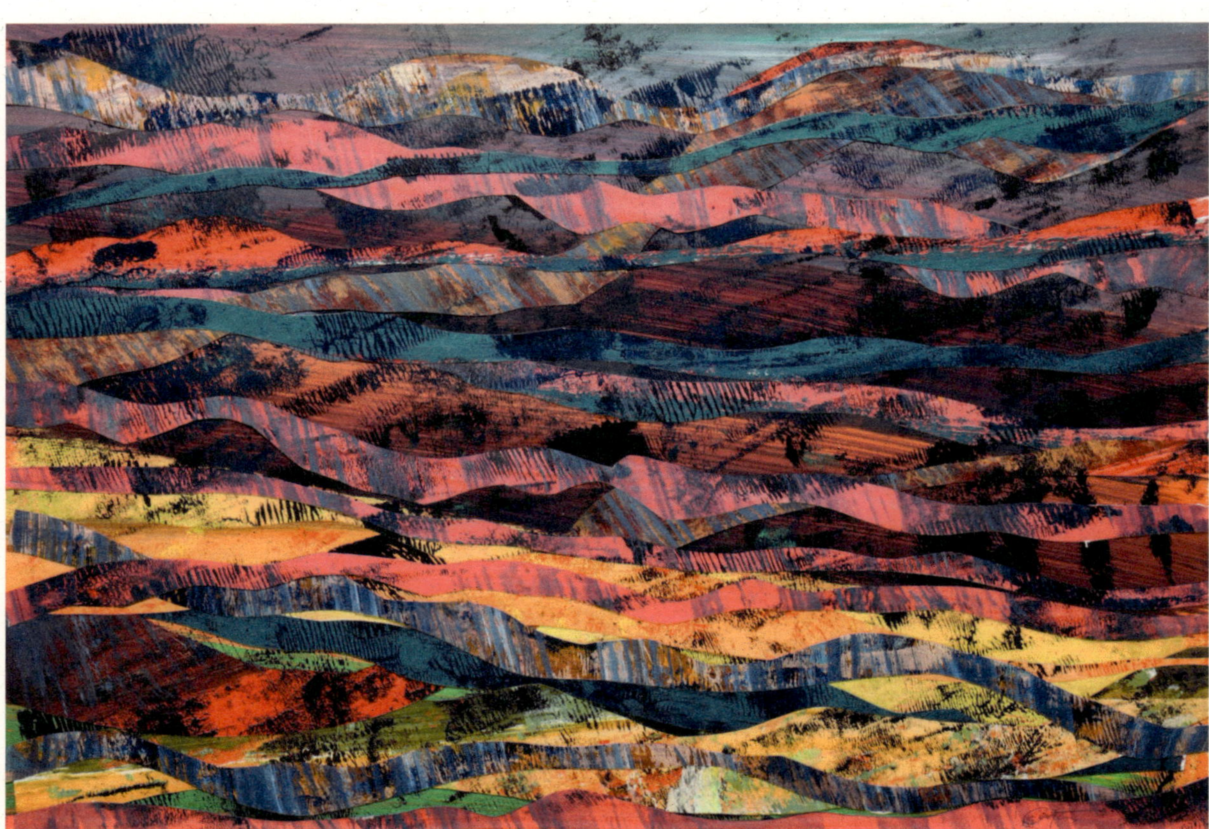

Right
Johnnie Cooper
Cinders, 1996

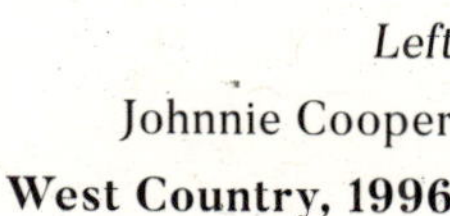

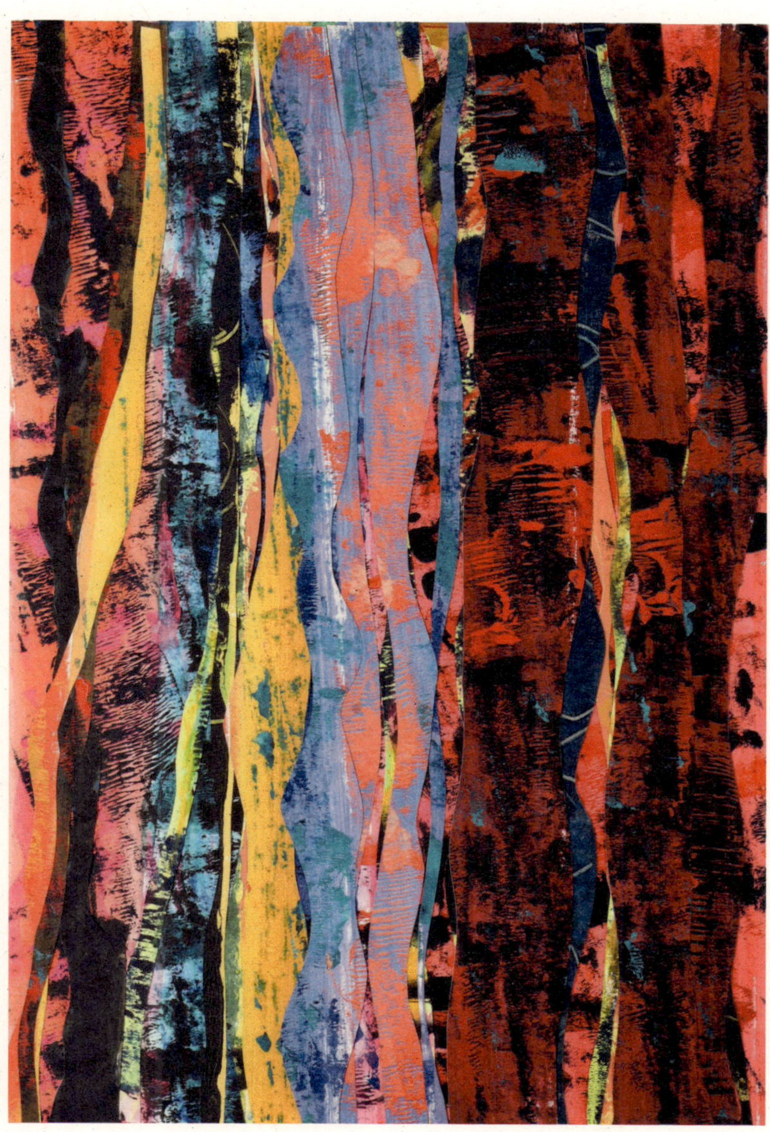

In *West Country*, 1996, scrapes of black and lilac overlie pools of pinks and reds. Looking closely, one can see areas where bottle greens meet paler tones, and cerise pinks fade into muted corals. When discussing Cooper's longstanding interest in the edges, where two or more colours meet, he has noted:

> The interaction where two colours meet is often loaded with psychological and emotional intensity. The fragmentation of one colour overlapping another can suggest movement and takes the retina on a journey that can sparkle with excitement or be suggestive of something torn. There is an ambiguity that can create a more cerebral mood of isolation; like the vagueness of a distant horizon line that pulls one into another yearned for location. And a desire for another atmosphere of contemplation to alter one's present state of mind.

From his earliest paintings in the early 1980s, Cooper was attracted to the exciting interaction of brushstroke marks that bled around the edges of a shape. These quiet collisions led him to experiment: diluting the edges of an opaque colour and allowing it to bleed. This created what Cooper has referred to as a "No Man's Land" between two shades, a technique that recurs throughout the 'Brook Farm' series. Although the edges of the collage strips were brittle, Cooper softened them by working over the finished pattern with a roller, which squeezed and spread the paint over two or three strips, blurring the edges.

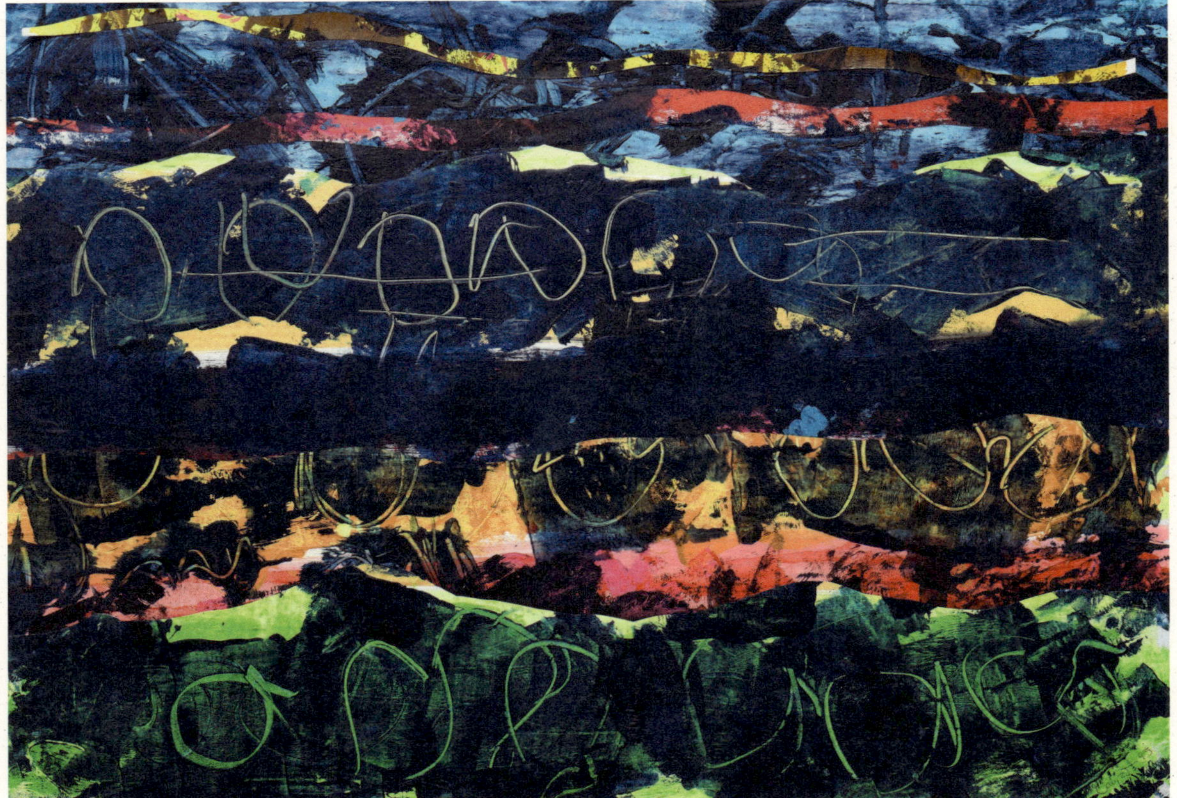

Night

Similarly, the pools of navy that comprise works such as *Thunder Sunset*, 1993, relay the importance and emotional intensity of darkness - a technique foregrounded by painters such as the aforementioned Pierre Soulages, and also the American painter Mark Rothko (1903-1970). Rothko famously discussed seeking to create paintings that brought people to tears. "I'm interested only in expressing basic human emotions - tragedy, ecstasy, doom and so on," he declared. "If you are moved only by their colour relationships then you miss the point." Cooper notes how both Rothko's and Soulages' sombre canvasses "relate deeply to the fragile and beautiful quiet moods of the [Malvern Hills] woodland, draped in early-morning mist, or the beckoning of inky shadows of a summer's evening, calling one into the mystical world beyond".

In *Storm Sky*, 1995, blotches of yellow burn across a gloomy backdrop like dripping embers. Cooper has availed himself of a tumultuous weather's wicked palette: crimsons unfurl like looming clouds, smudges of ochre and burgundy smoulder in the darkness. Along with visual and aural references, many of the paintings in the 'Brook Farm' series are imbued with literary flourishes. As a painter and writer, Cooper blends poetic imagery with the formal qualities of abstraction. For example, citing the Italian modernist poet Cesare Pavese (1908-1950) as an inspiration, many of the evening works rhyme with the haunting imagery of Pavese's prose. In *Toward Evening*, 1996, terrestrial daubs of black, auburn and bottle-green run like muddied water across the page. In the first verse of Pavese's poem 'Smokers of Paper' he describes a "hellish racket" with "flashes of lightning, wind gusts and rain whips, knocking the lights out every five minutes". This imagery invokes the flurries of ashy colours that rush over the pages of the series at night. Similarly, Cooper recounts the poetic sequence

Crow: From the Life and Songs of the Crow, 1970, by British poet Ted Hughes (1930-1998), renowned for his bleak images, as another influence. Hughes' disposition metamorphoses into paint here: the infernal reds and prelapsarian twilight settings of Cooper's evening works echo Hughes' world: "nailing heaven and earth together".

References to fiction, along with poetry, abound. In the appendix to the American writer Henry Miller's (1891-1980) impressionistic travelogue *The Colossus of Maroussi*, 1941, for instance, there is an epistolary note. It describes a group of writers including Miller's protagonist ('colossus') George Katsimbalis. They travel up to the ancient Acropolis in Athens - "exalted by wine and poetry" and "blood roaring with cognac" - where Katsimbalis experiences a strange seizure. He runs to the edge of the precipice, "like a faery queen, a black faery queen, in his black clothes" and releases a blood-curdling clarion. It echoes all over the city like "a sort of dark bowl dotted with lights like cherries". In Cooper's *Bonfire Night*, 1994, the central paper panel contains slashes of maraschino red against a charred backdrop. *Strobe Dancer*, 1997, meanwhile, features an infernal membrane materialising from khol paints. These works contain layers of literary inspirations that morph into non-representational motifs.

The other element in Cooper's choice of expression, pure abstraction, was to introduce a mood of escapism: "Of somehow being pulled into another realm beyond the reality of the world as we know it." The many dark vortexes of the night series eddy with an otherworldly essence, while the flecks of light float over the paper like dust motes in a roiling field. Cooper notes how he intends to reflect sunbeams in his collages, evoking a desire to let the viewer's mind drift. Recalling the work of English romantic poet John Keats (1795-1821), he highlights the line "and fade with thee into the forest dim", alluding to a desire to pull those whose faces float over his works into the blackened woodland of the Malvern Hills.

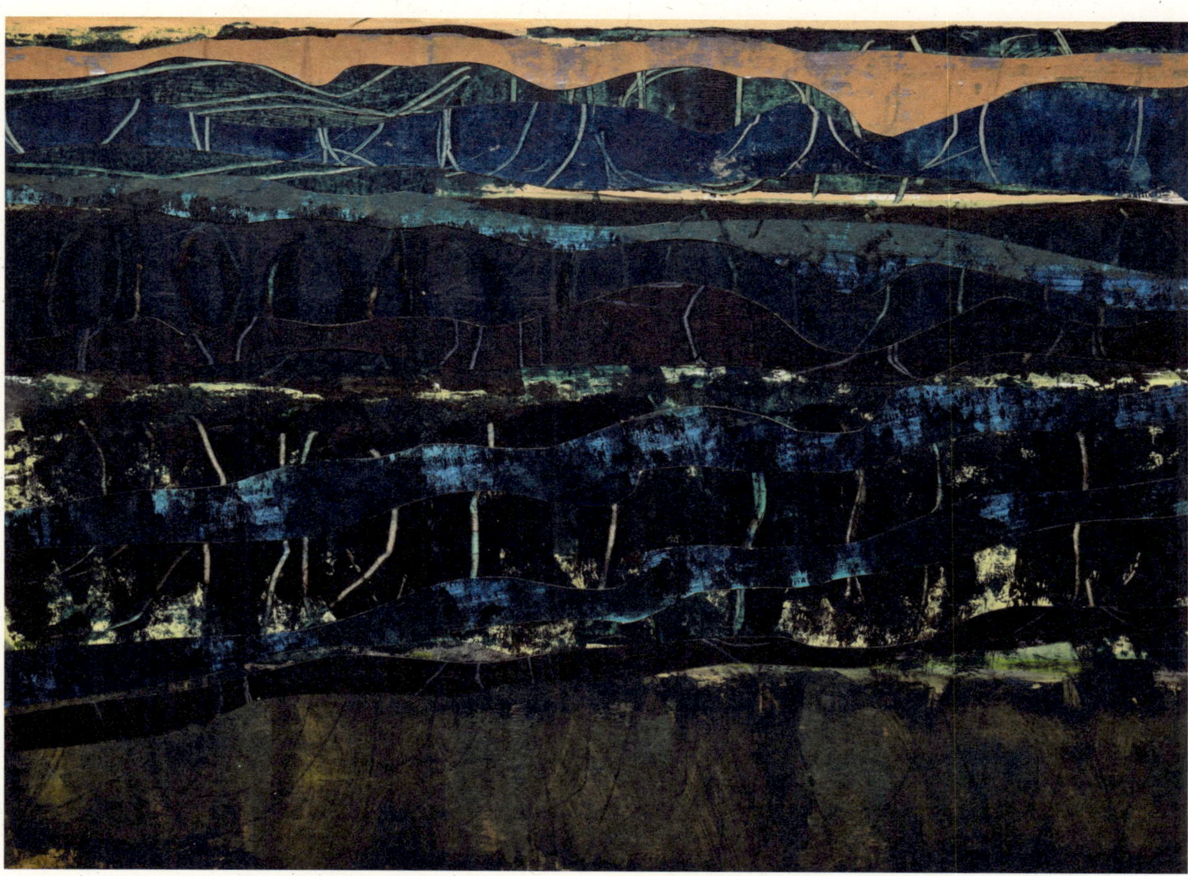

Right
Johnnie Cooper
Toward Evening, 1996

Morning

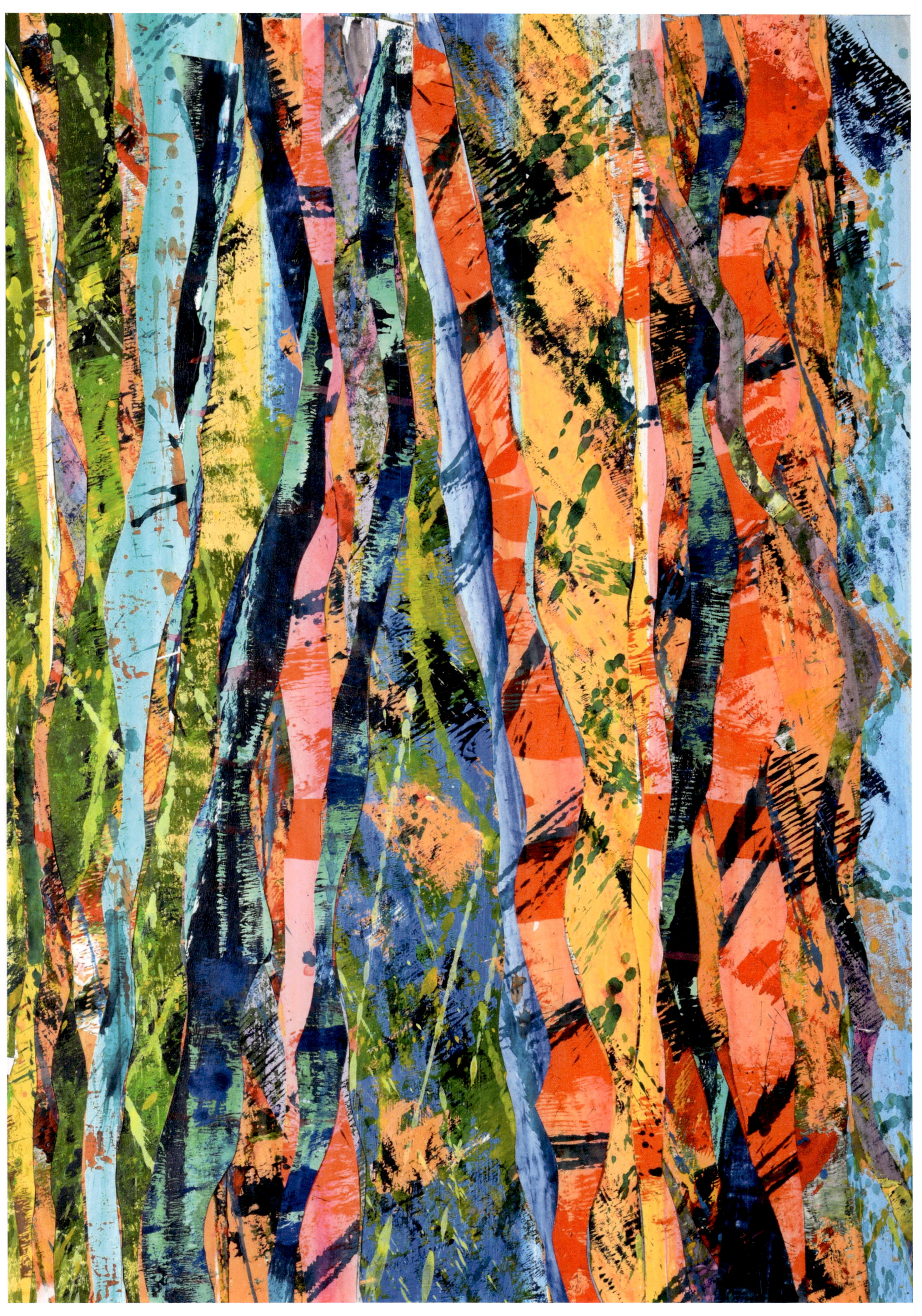

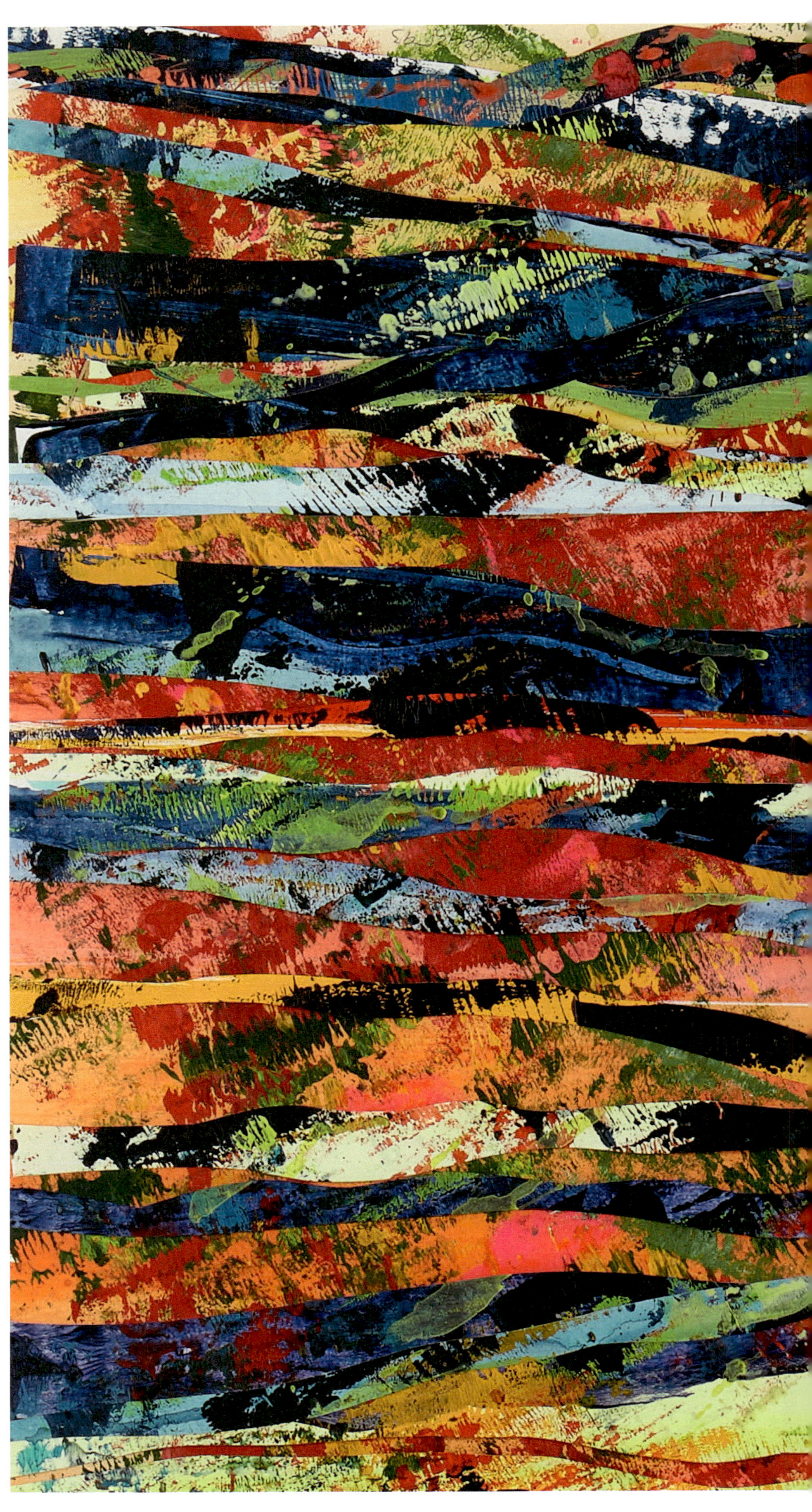

Gradations of Sunlight, 1996

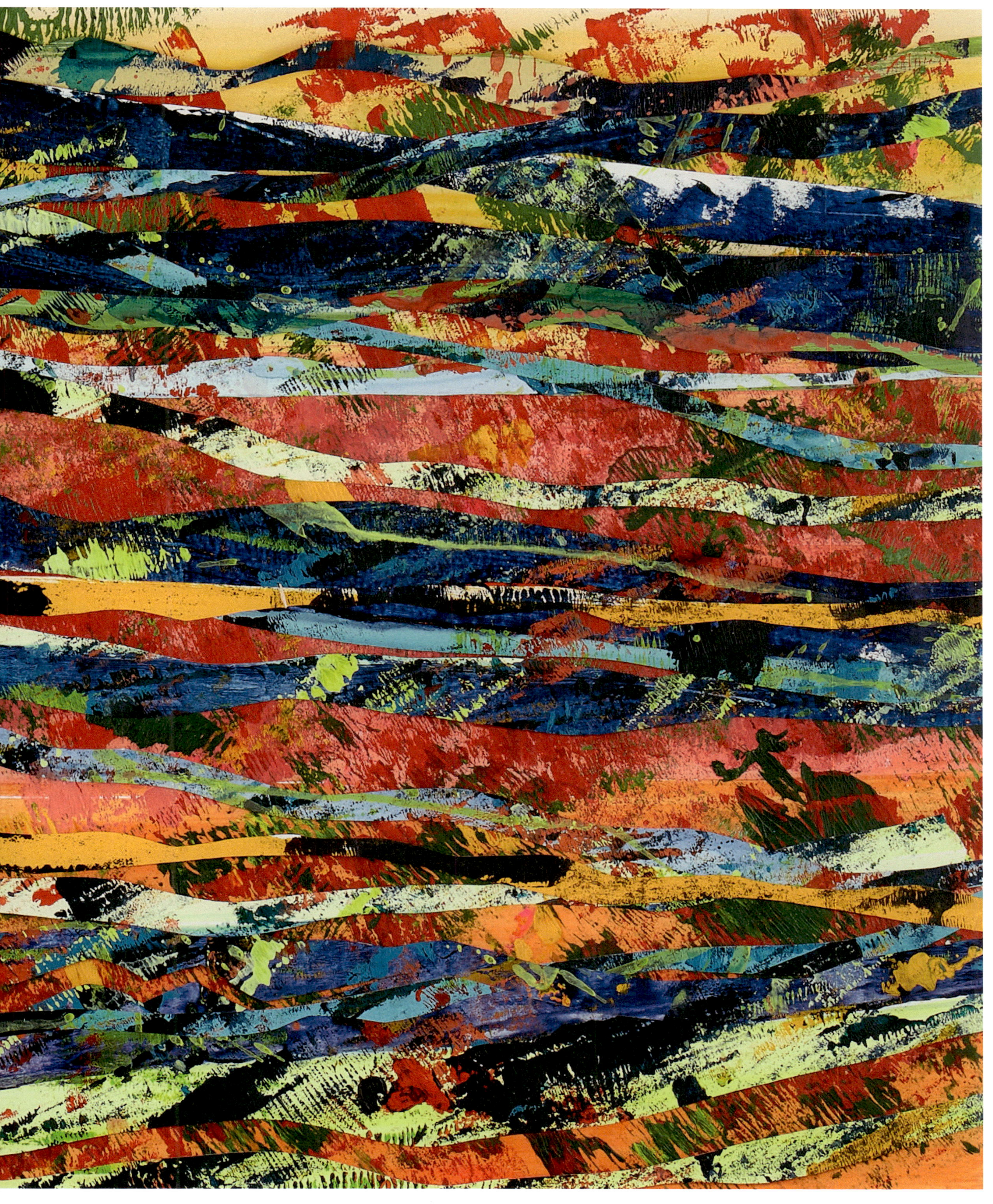

A Misty Day, 1994

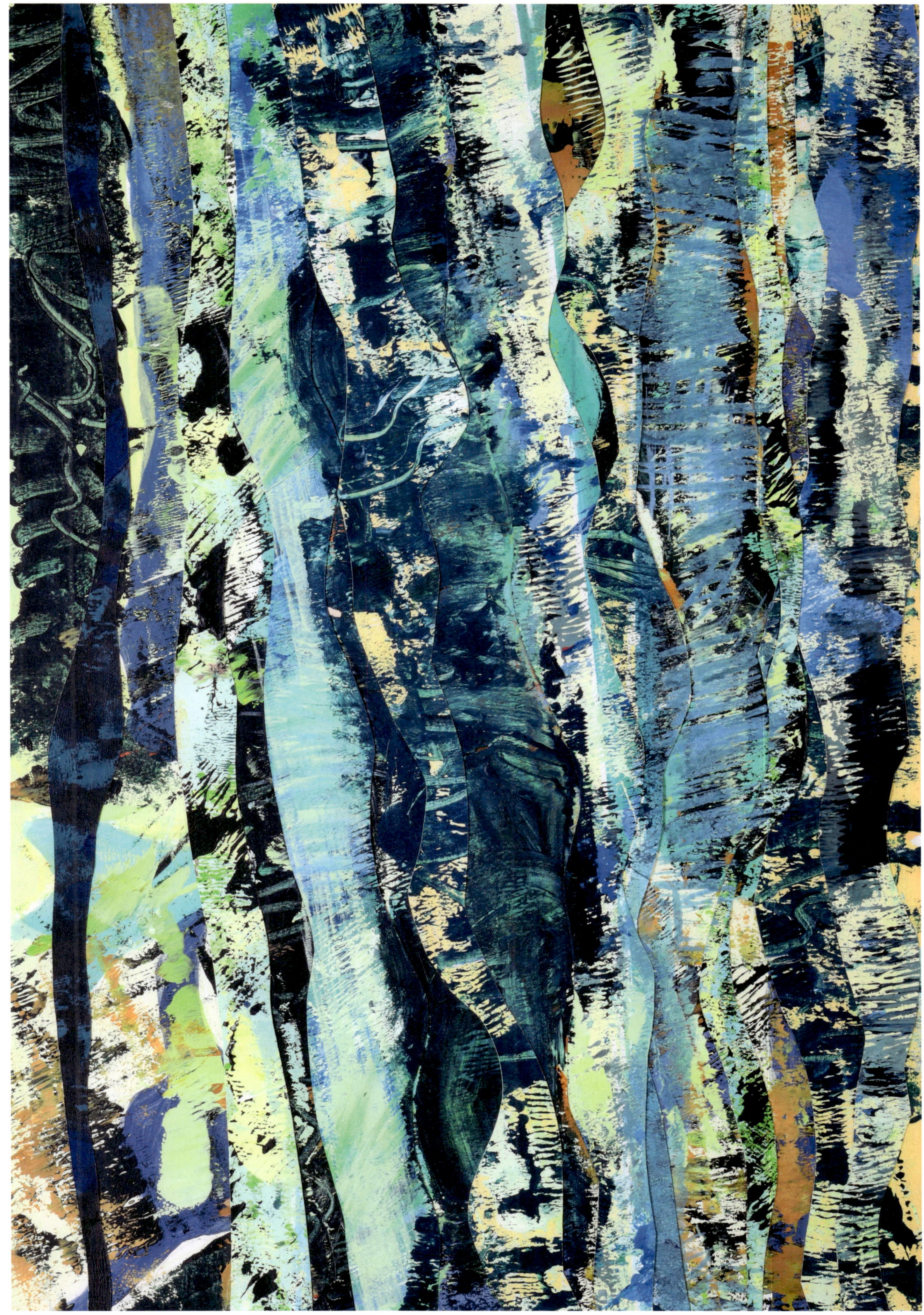

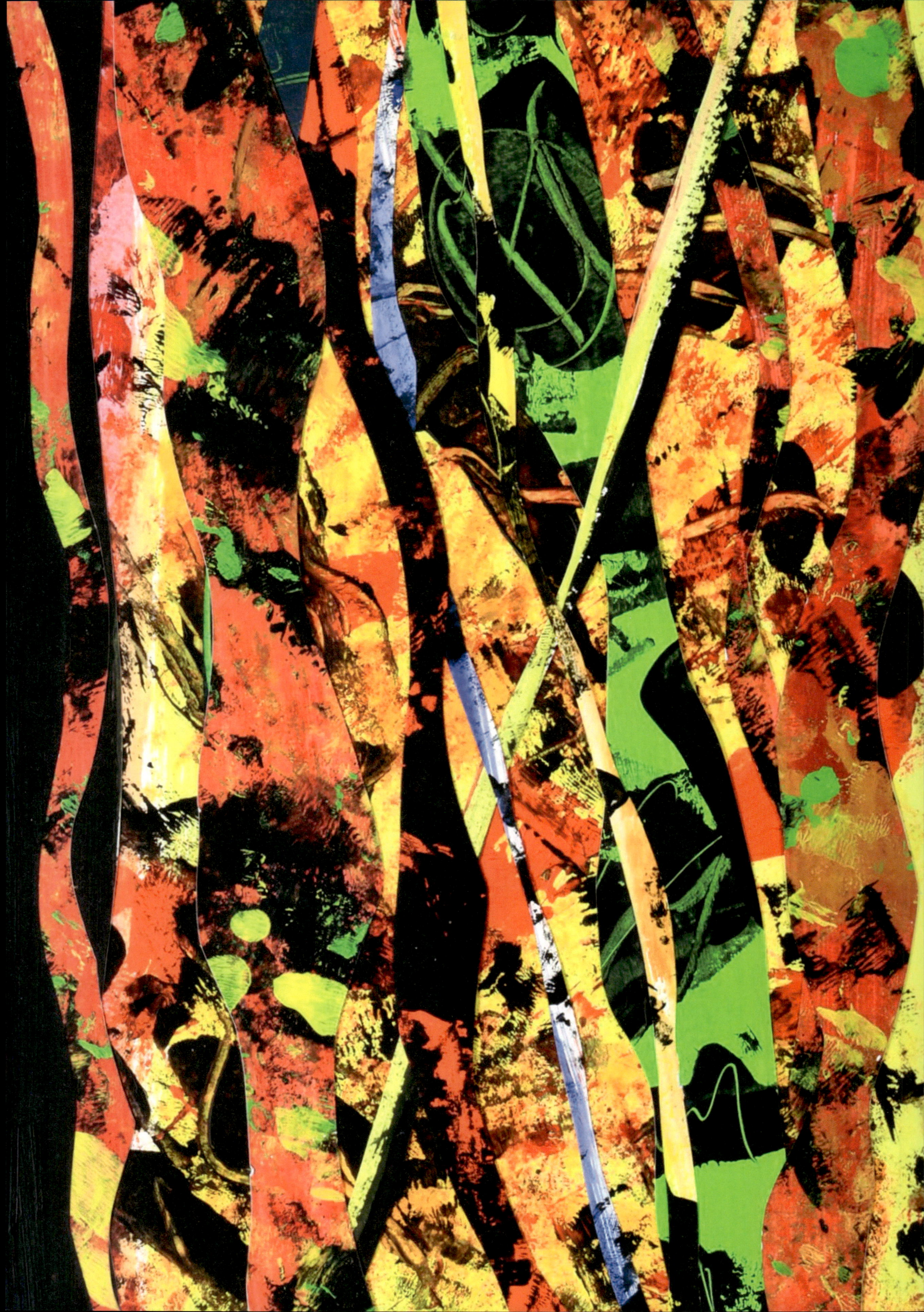

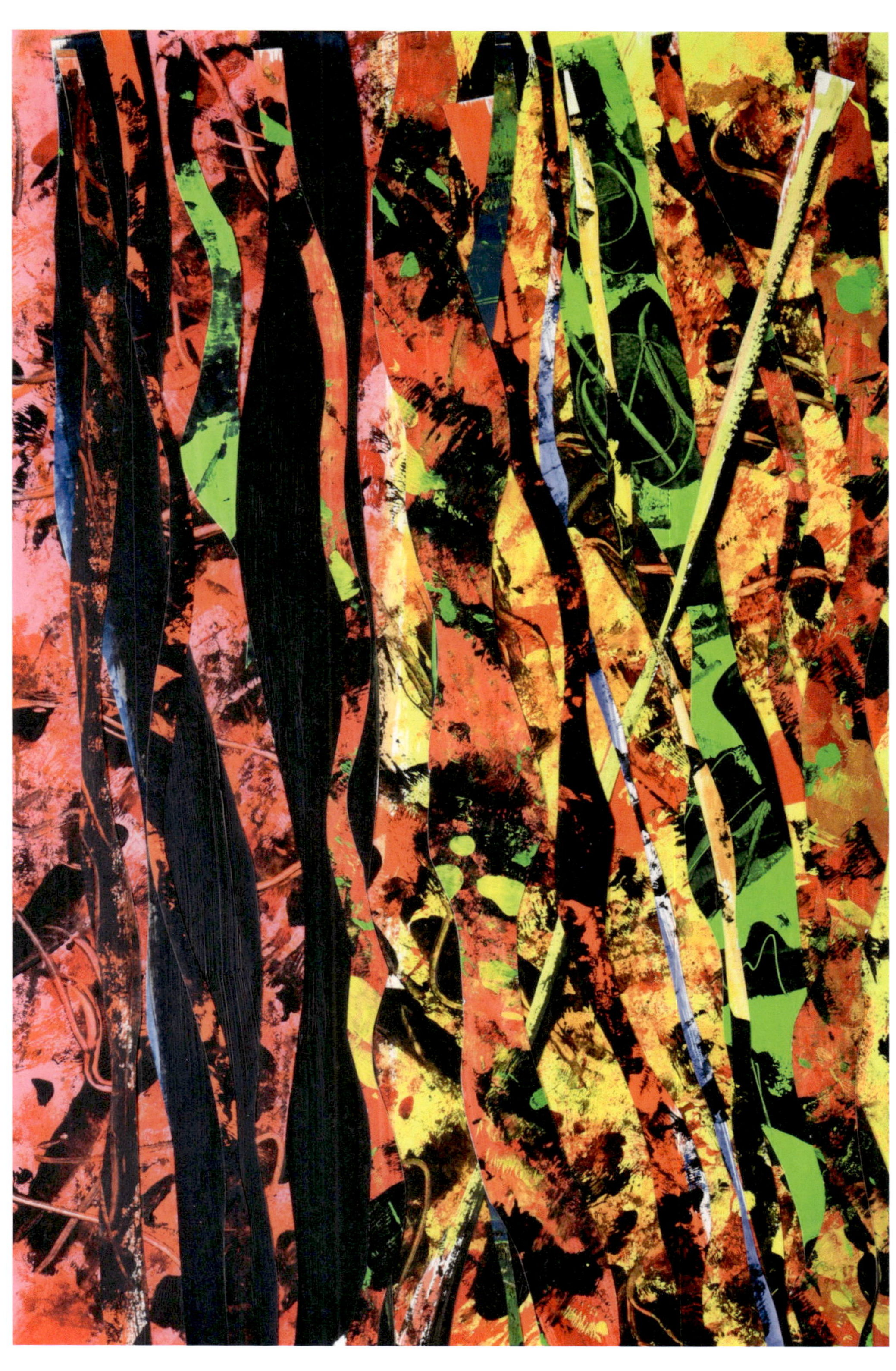

Afternoon Heat, 1992

Splintered Light, 1995

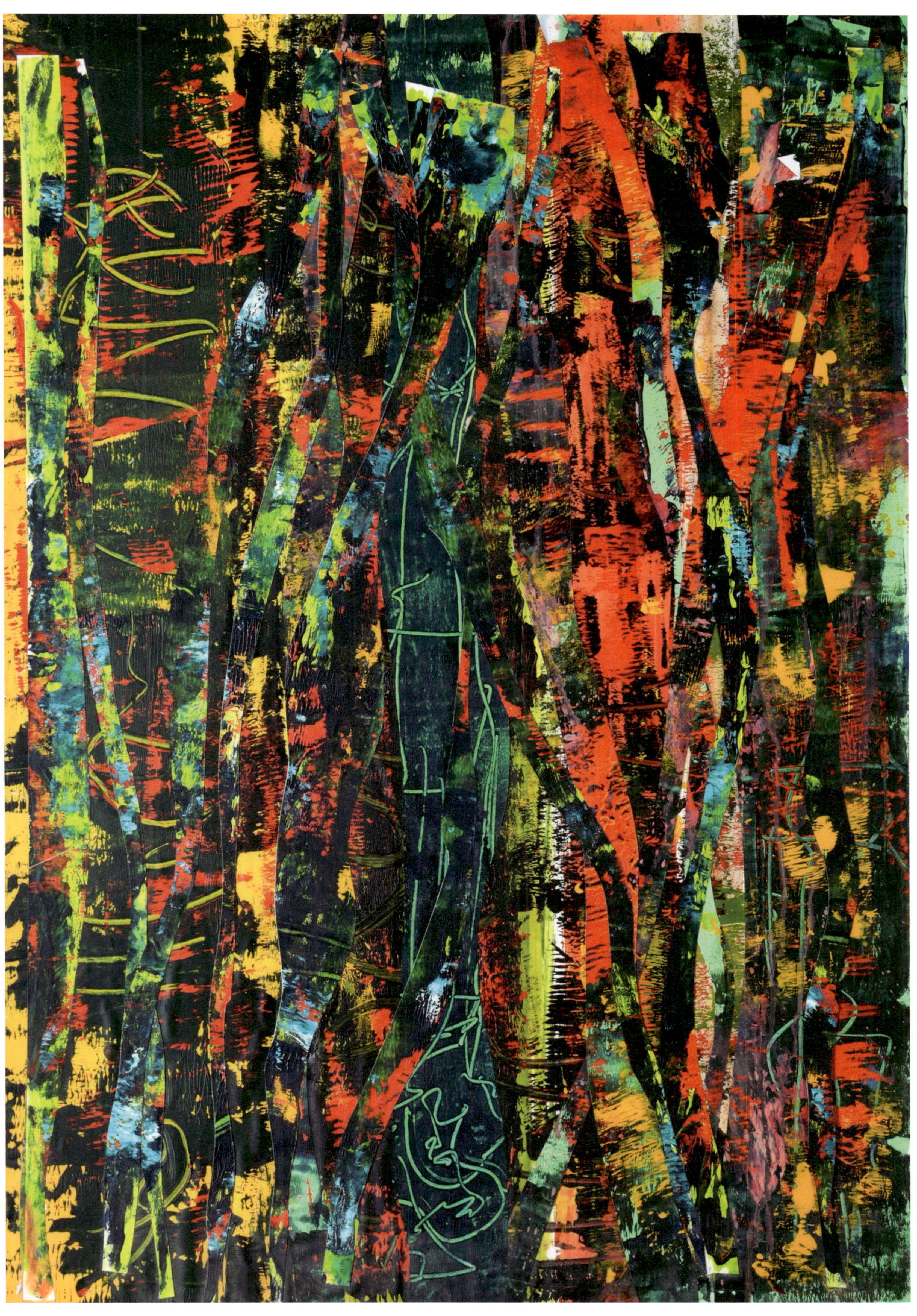

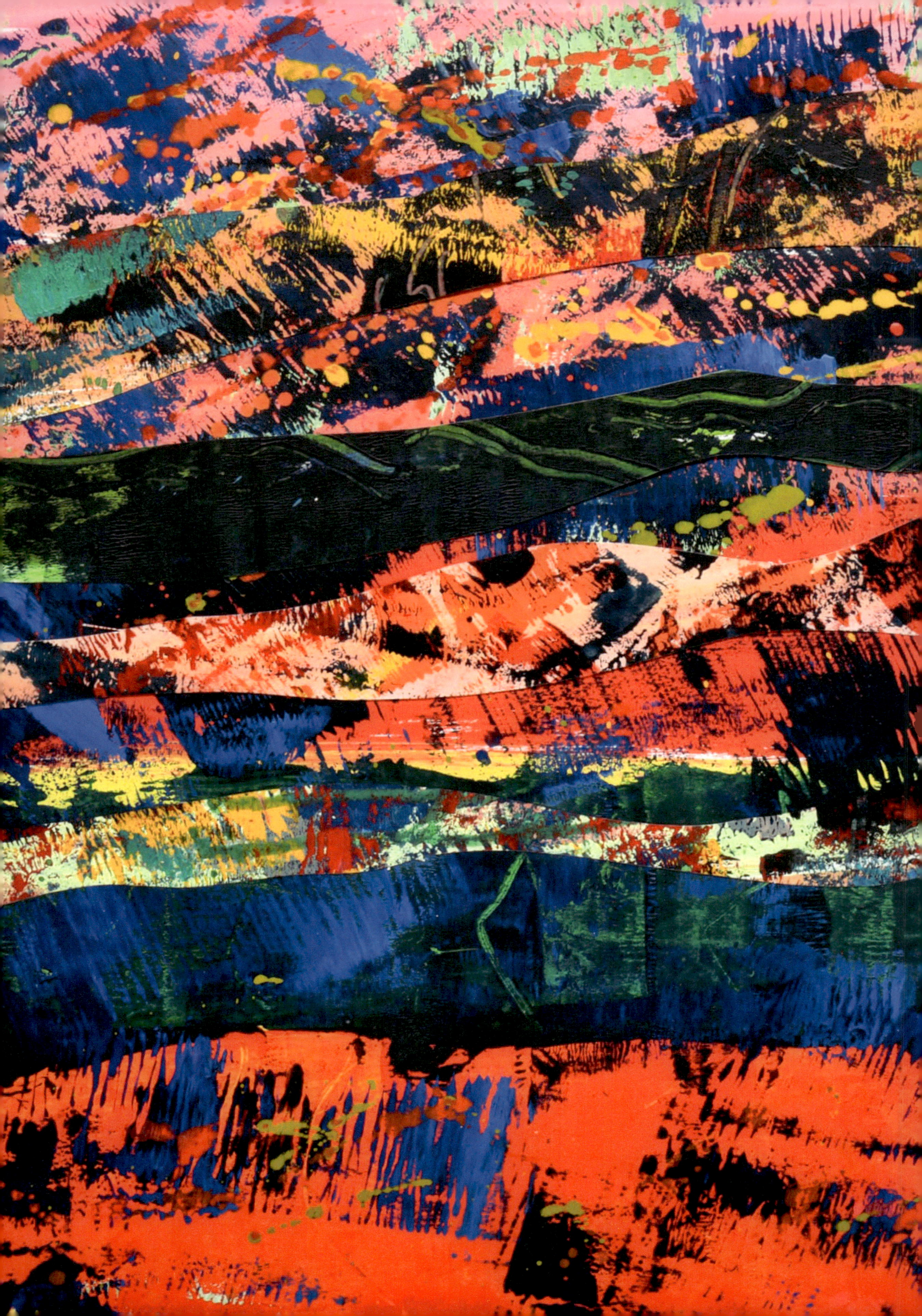

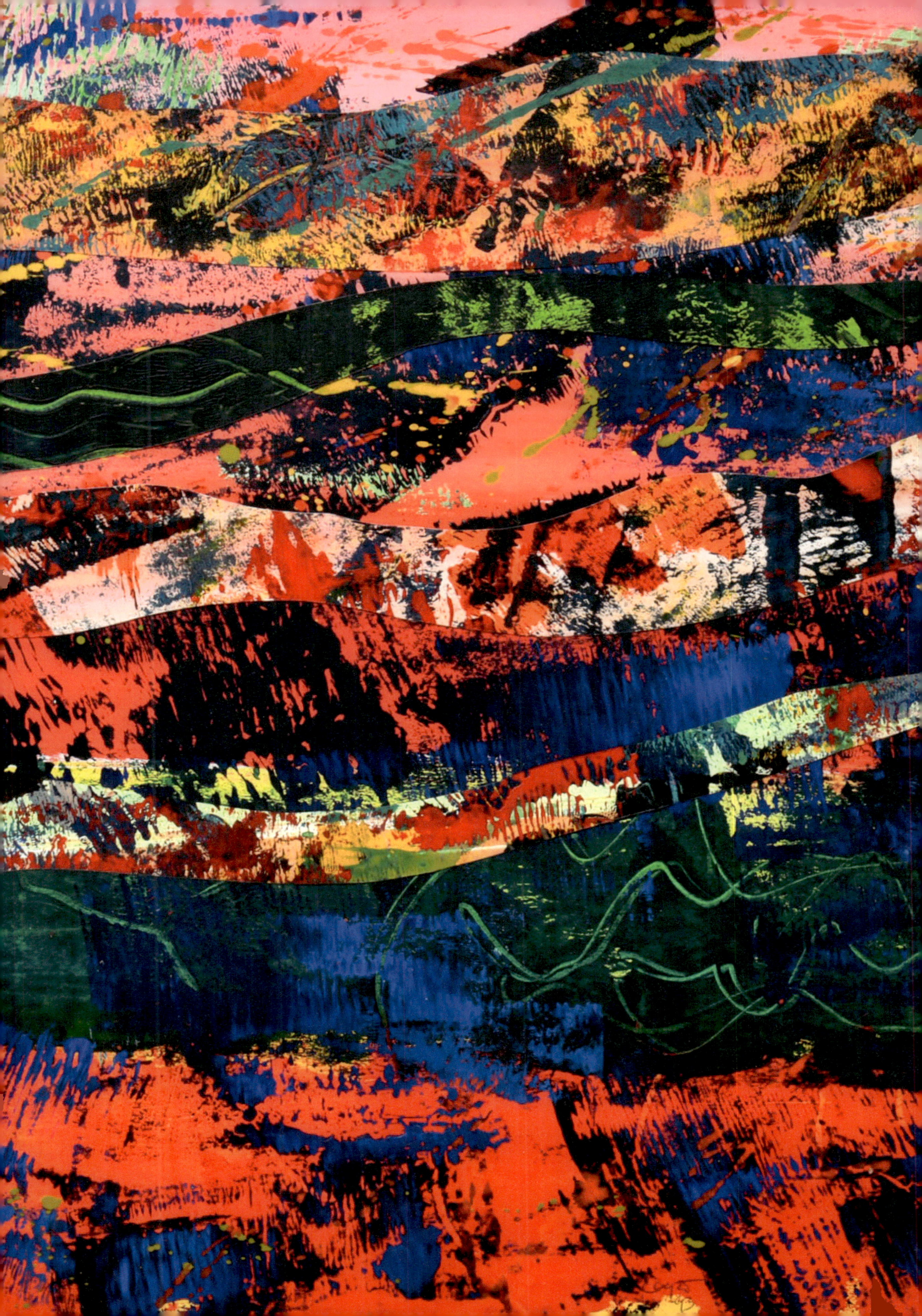

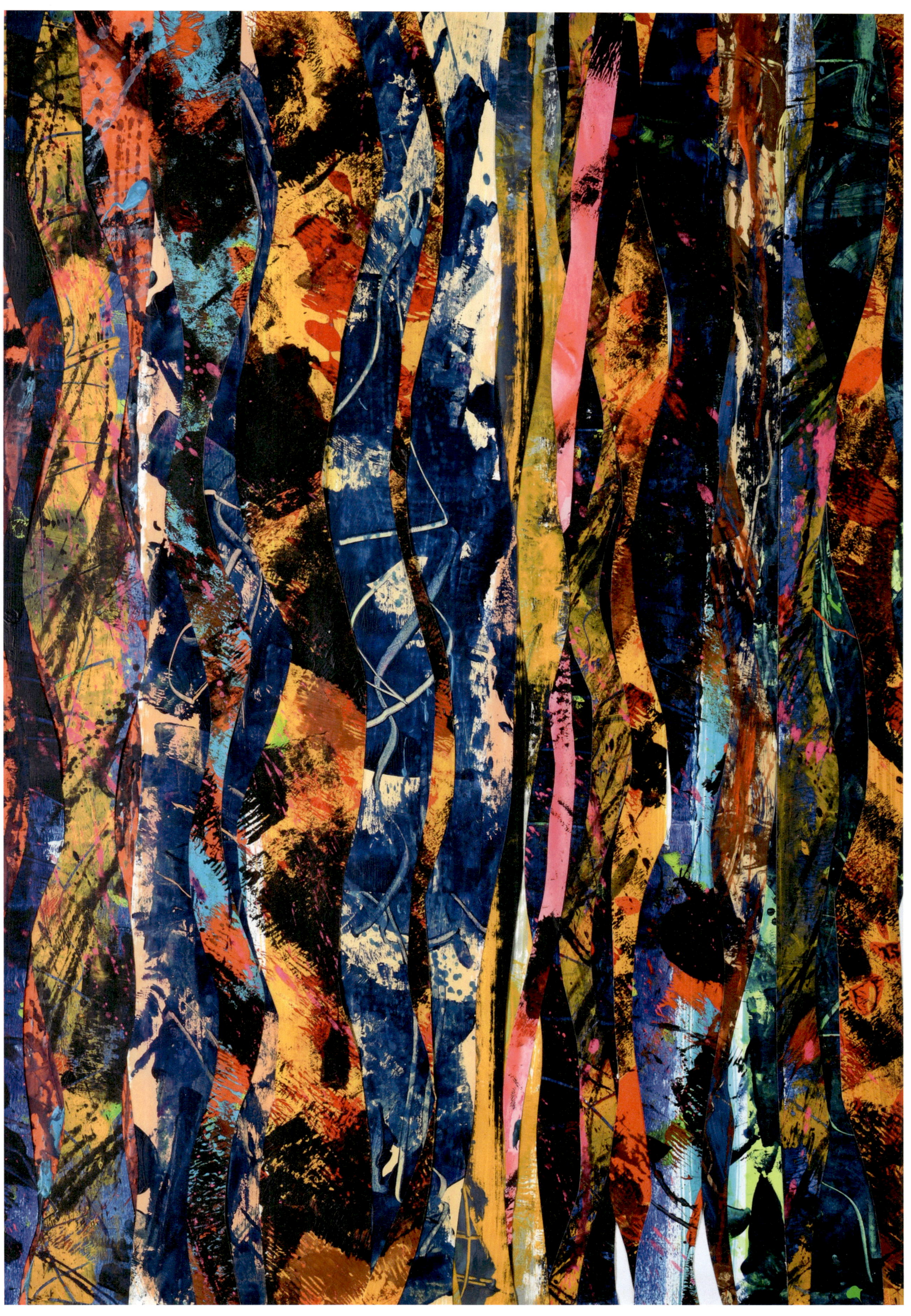

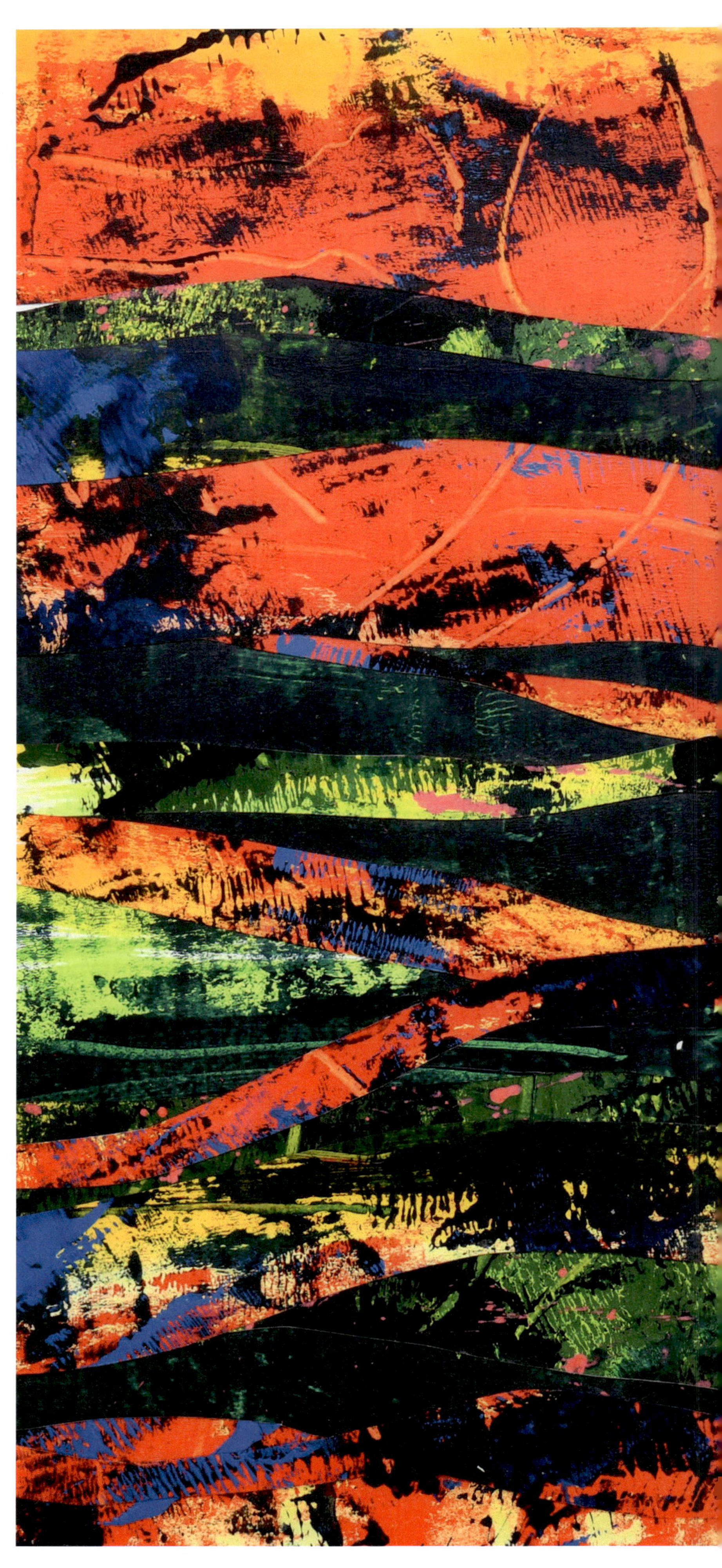

Parched Earth, 1996

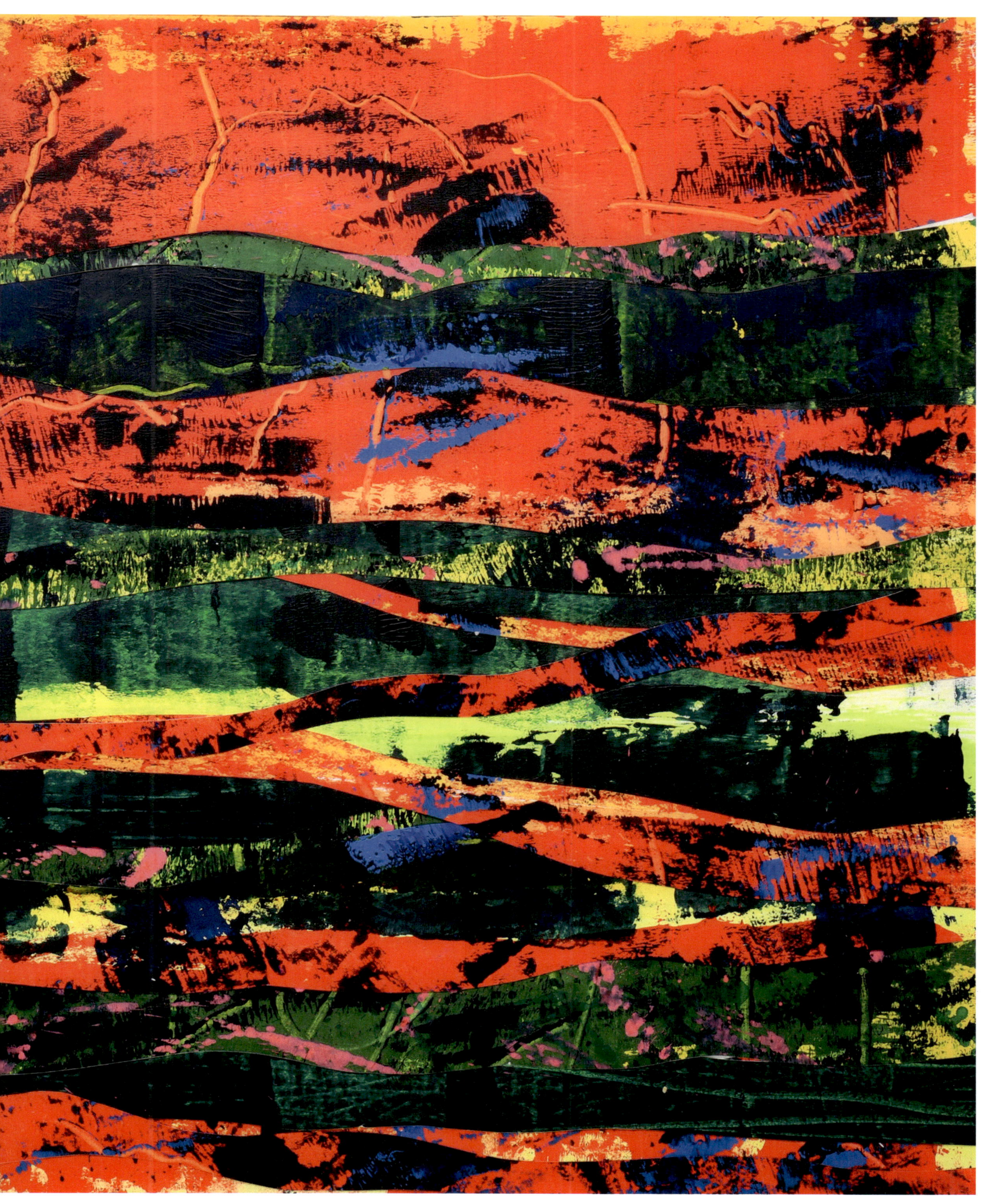

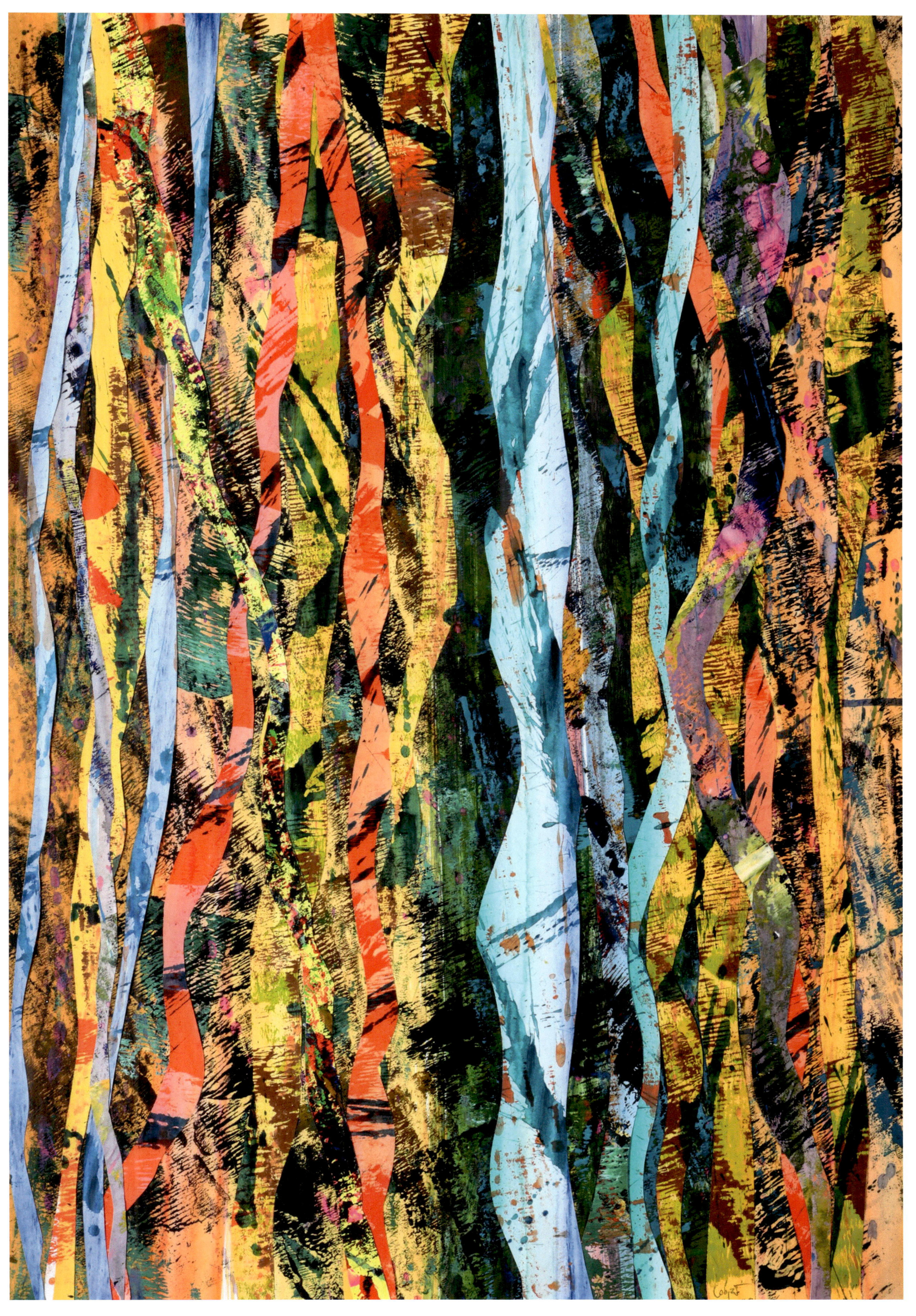

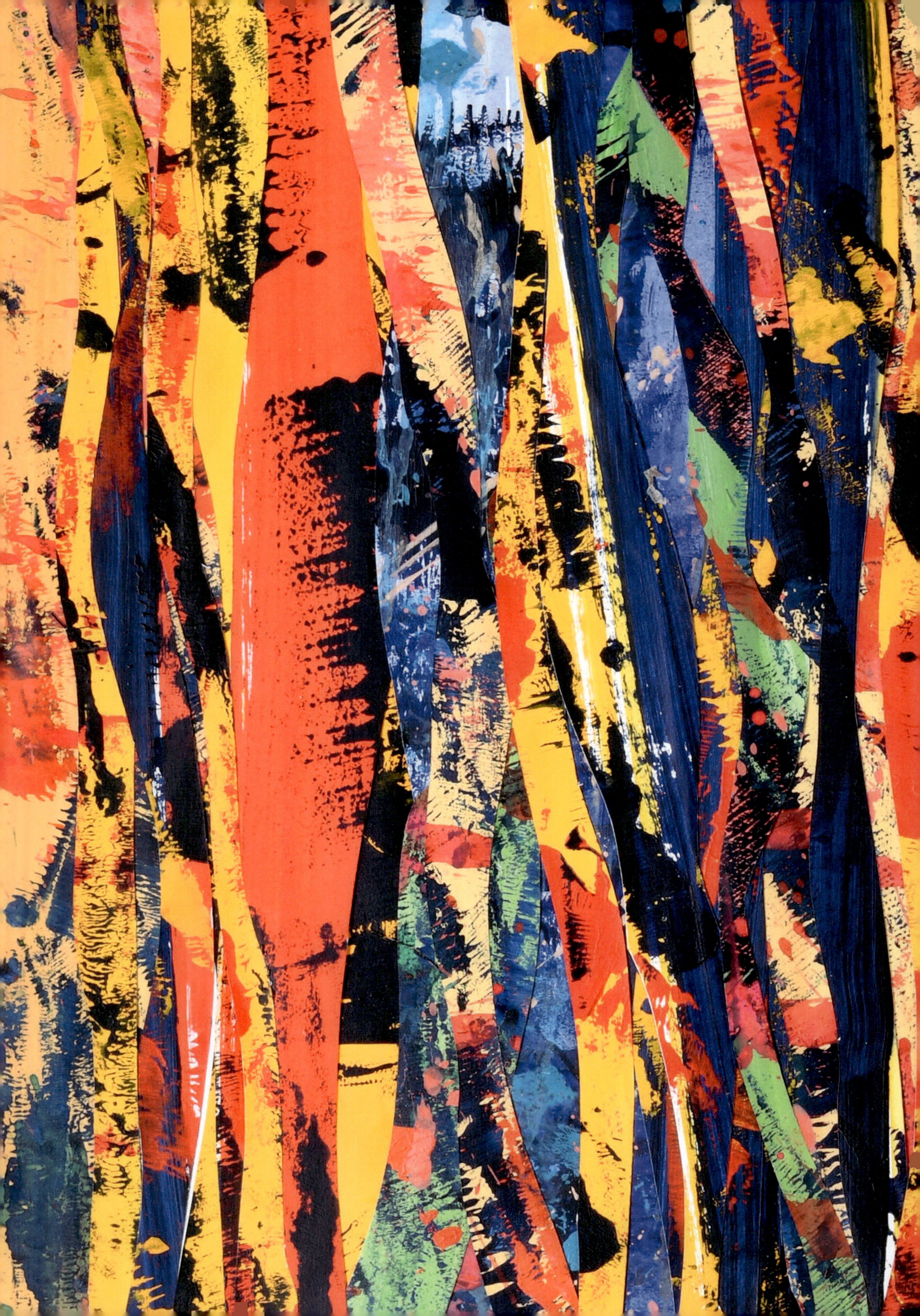

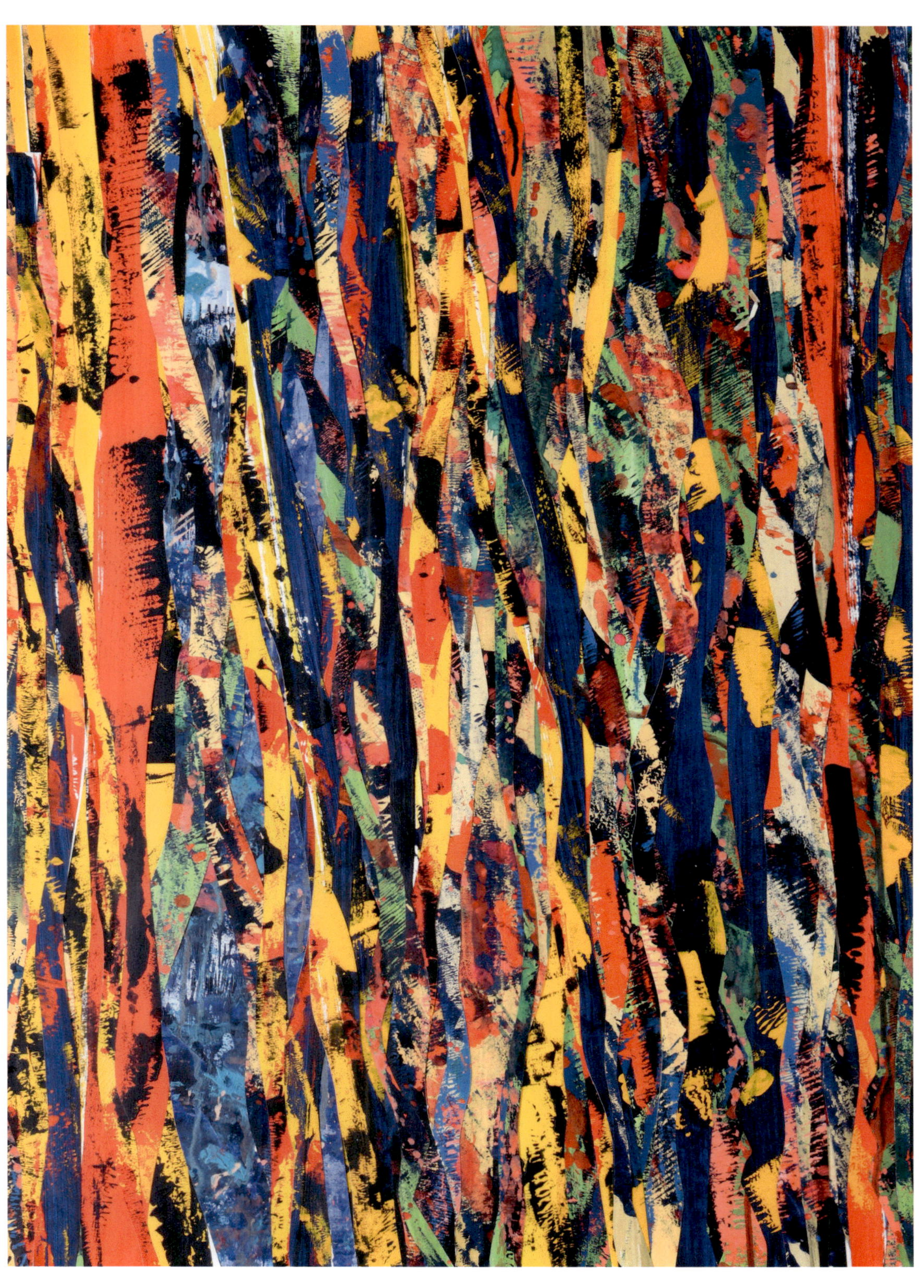

Dazzling Light, 1993

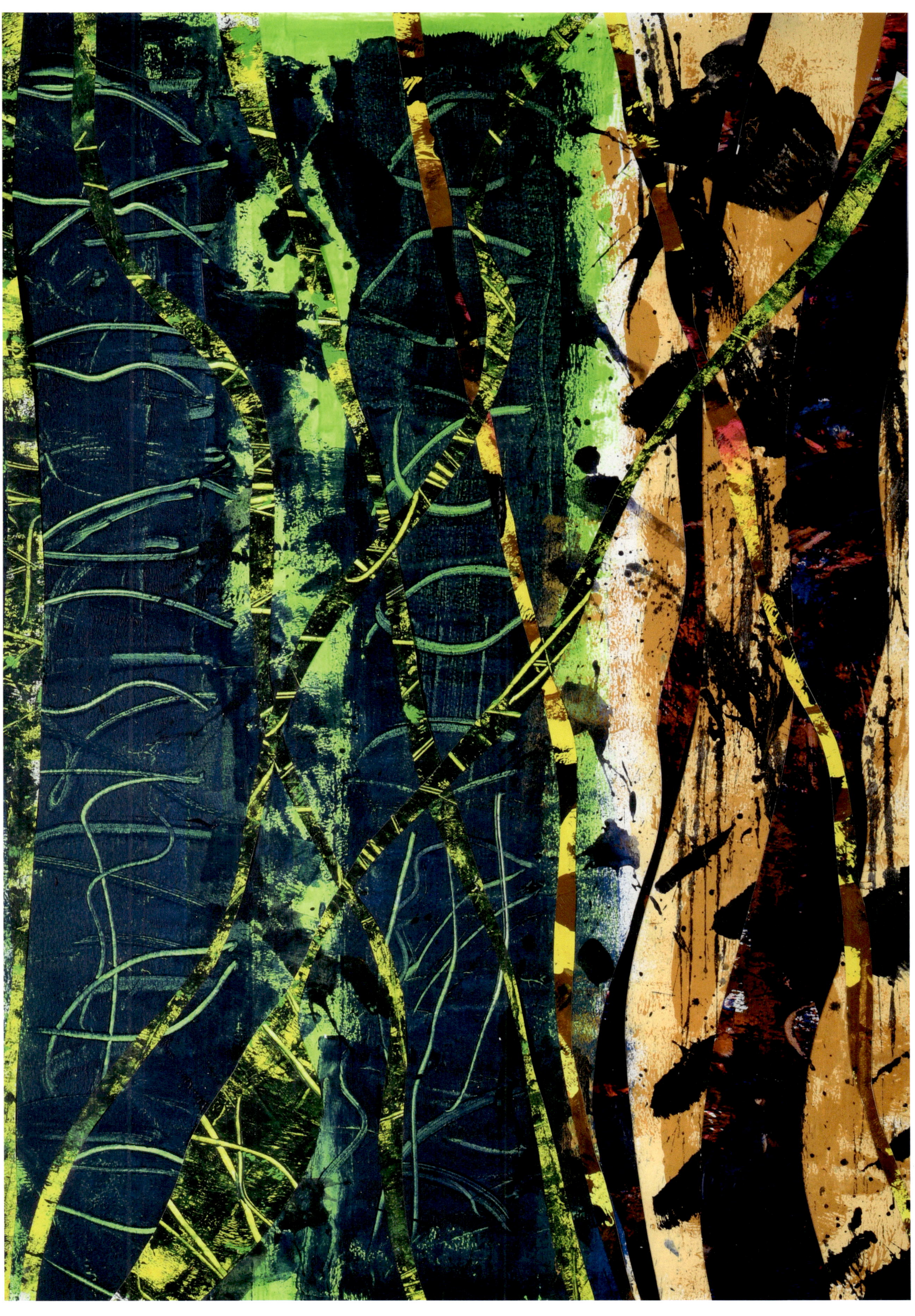

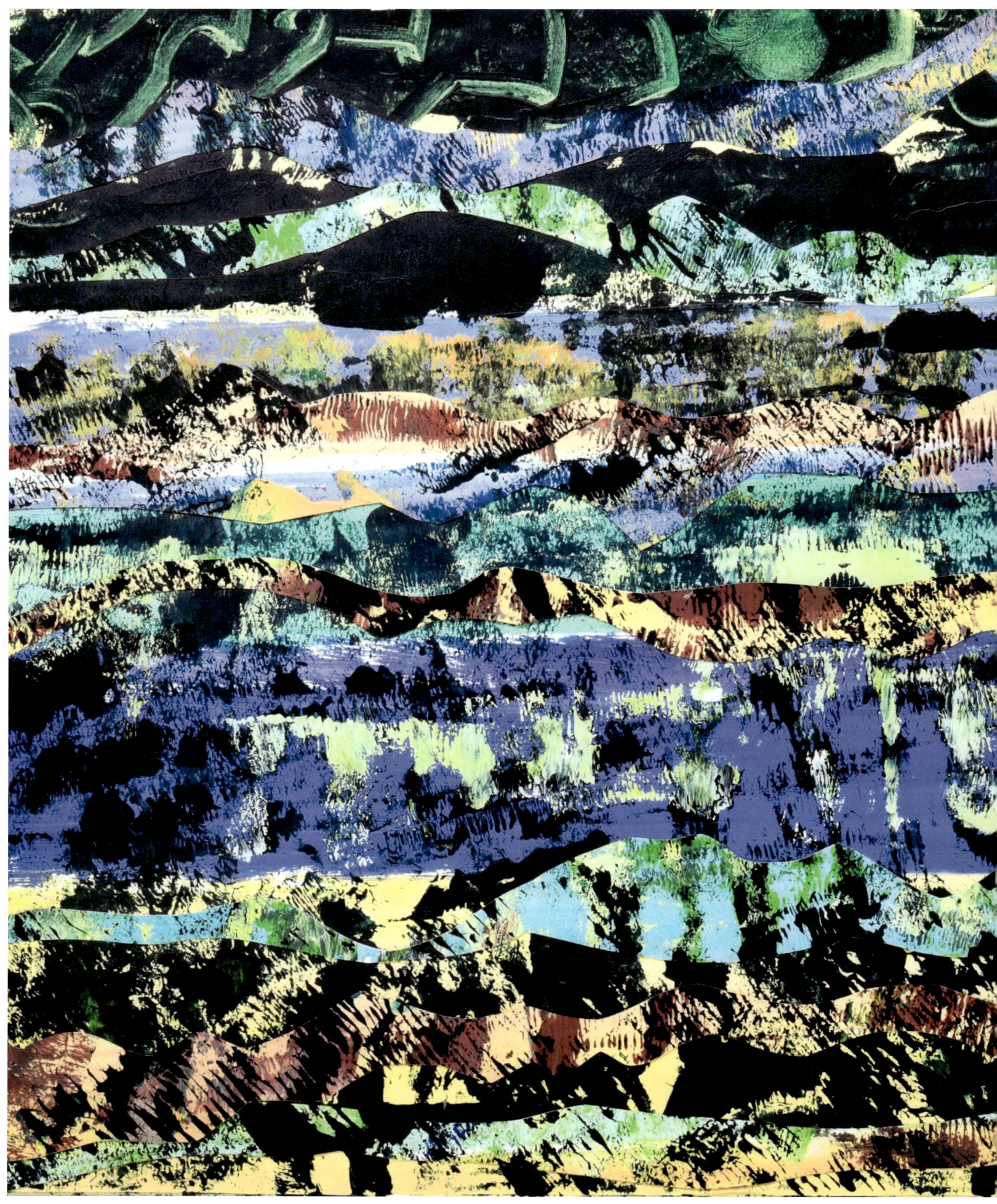

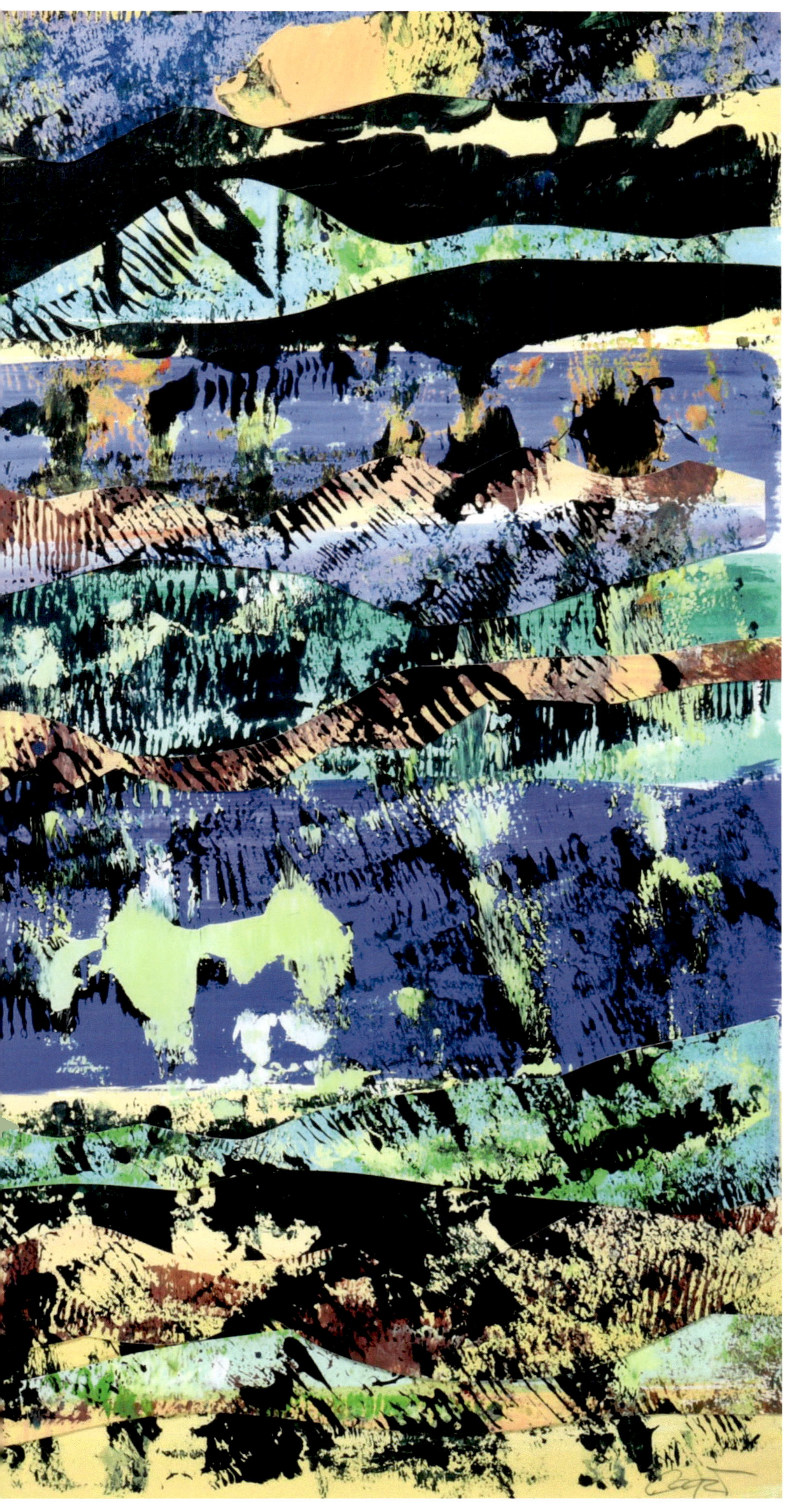

Leaves on the Path, 1995

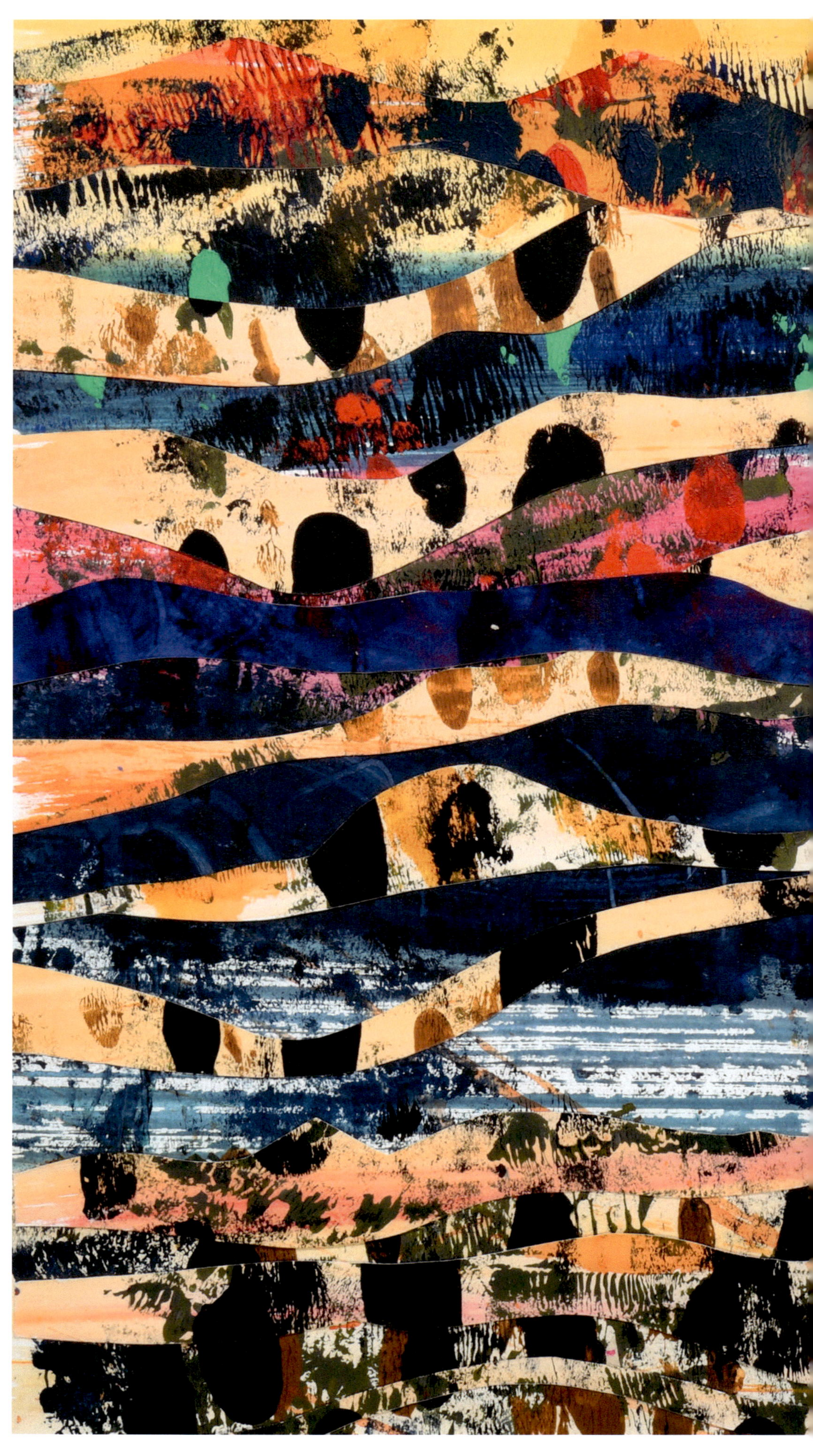

Stoney Beach, 1994

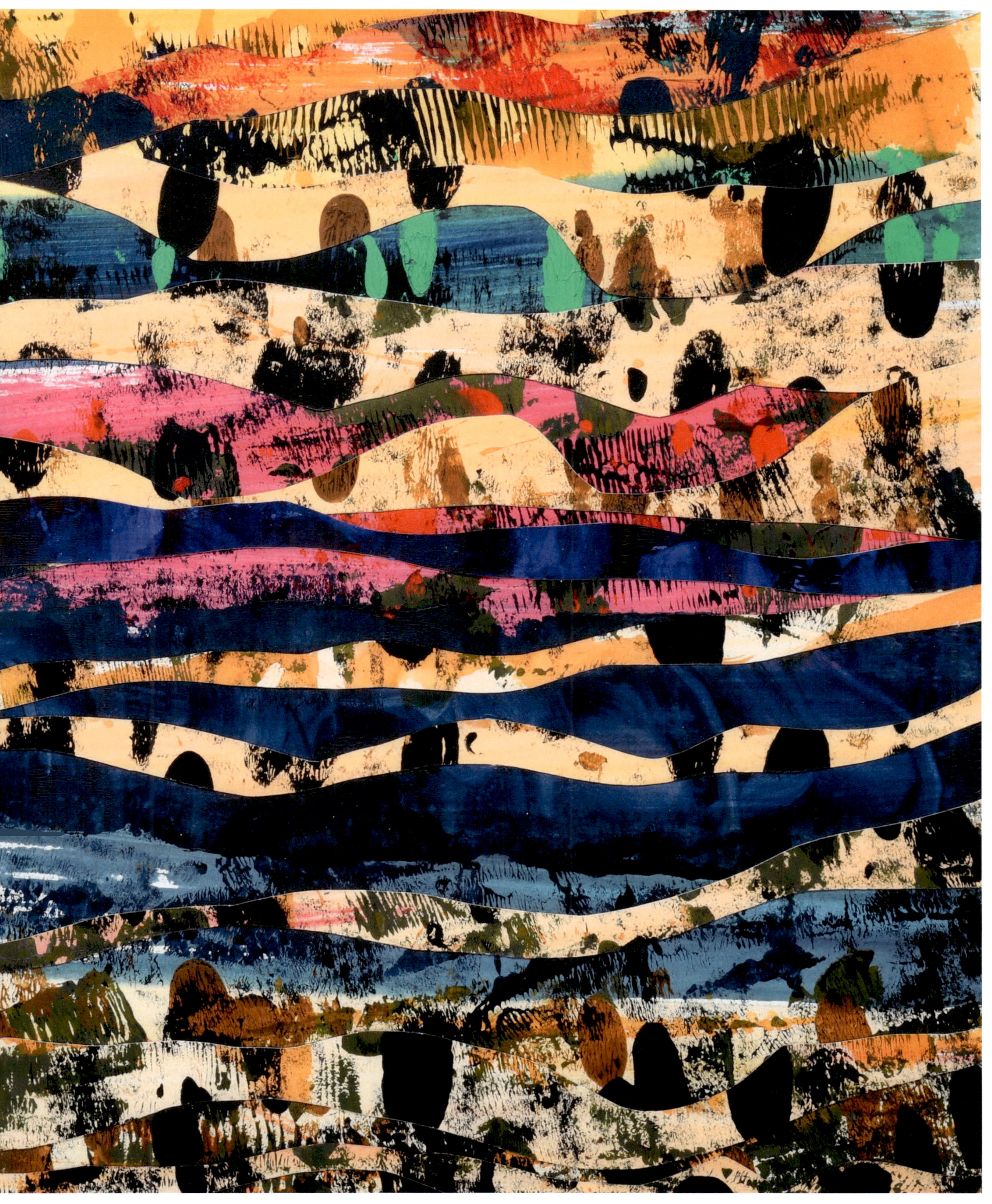

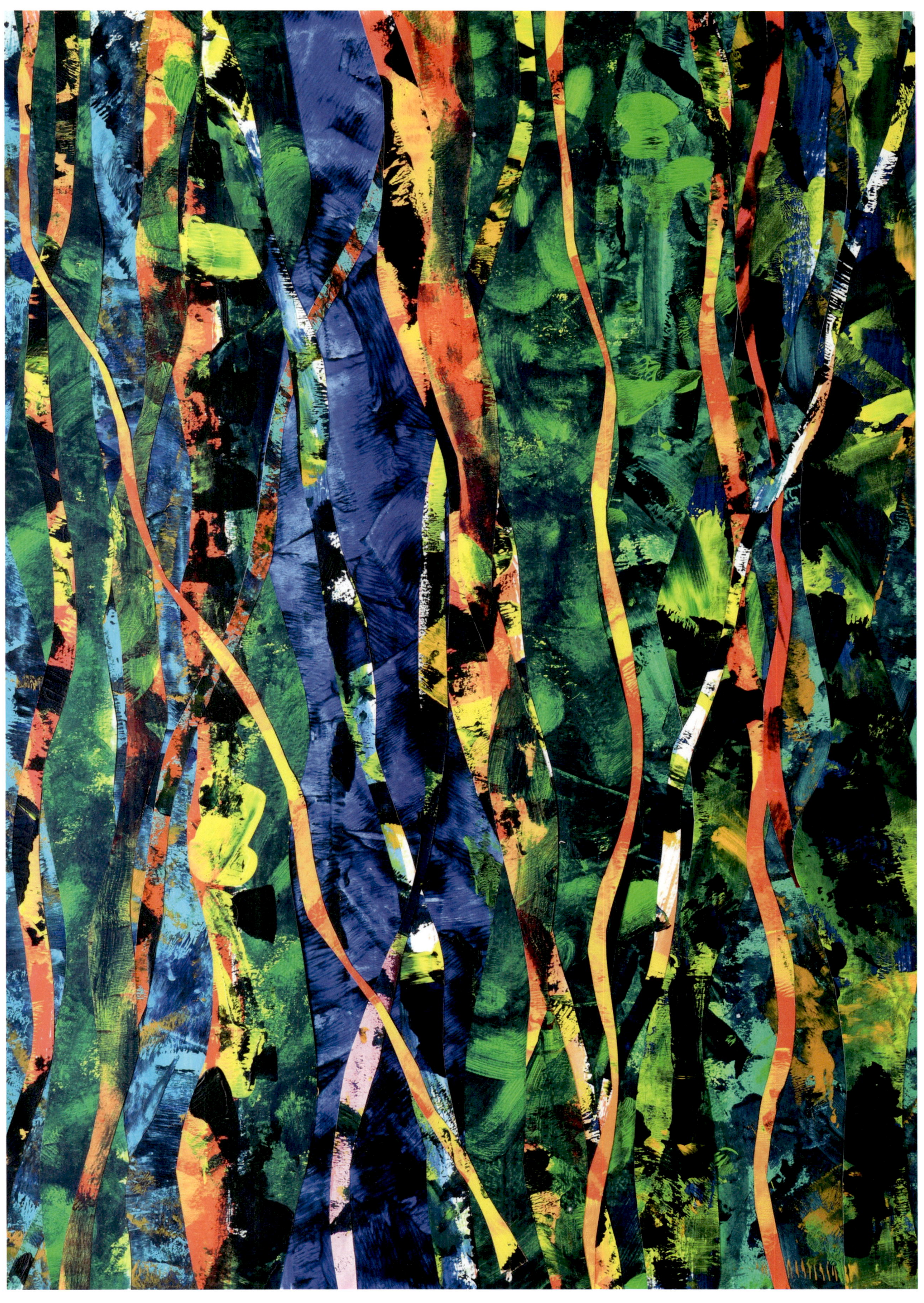

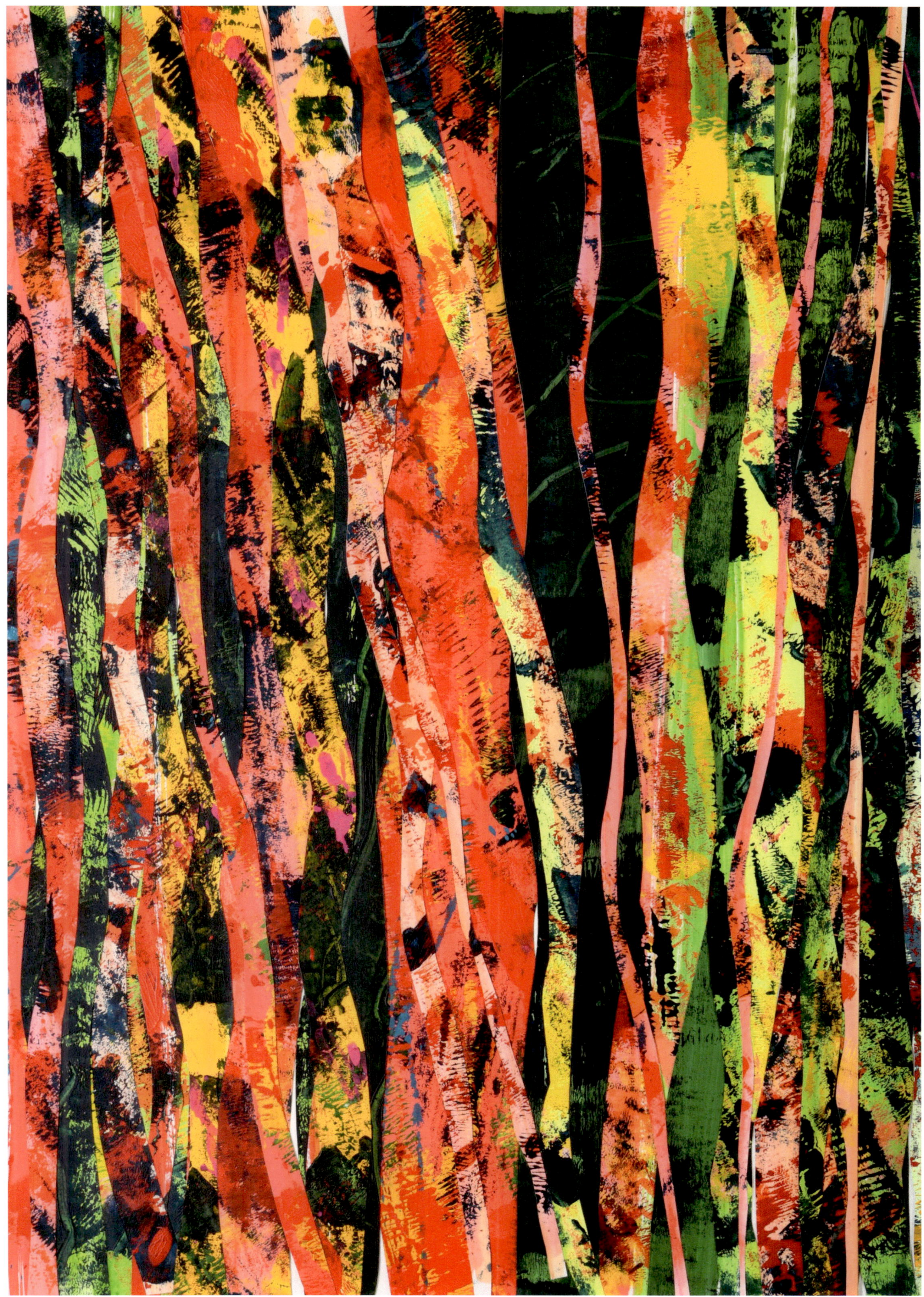

The Green Man, 1992

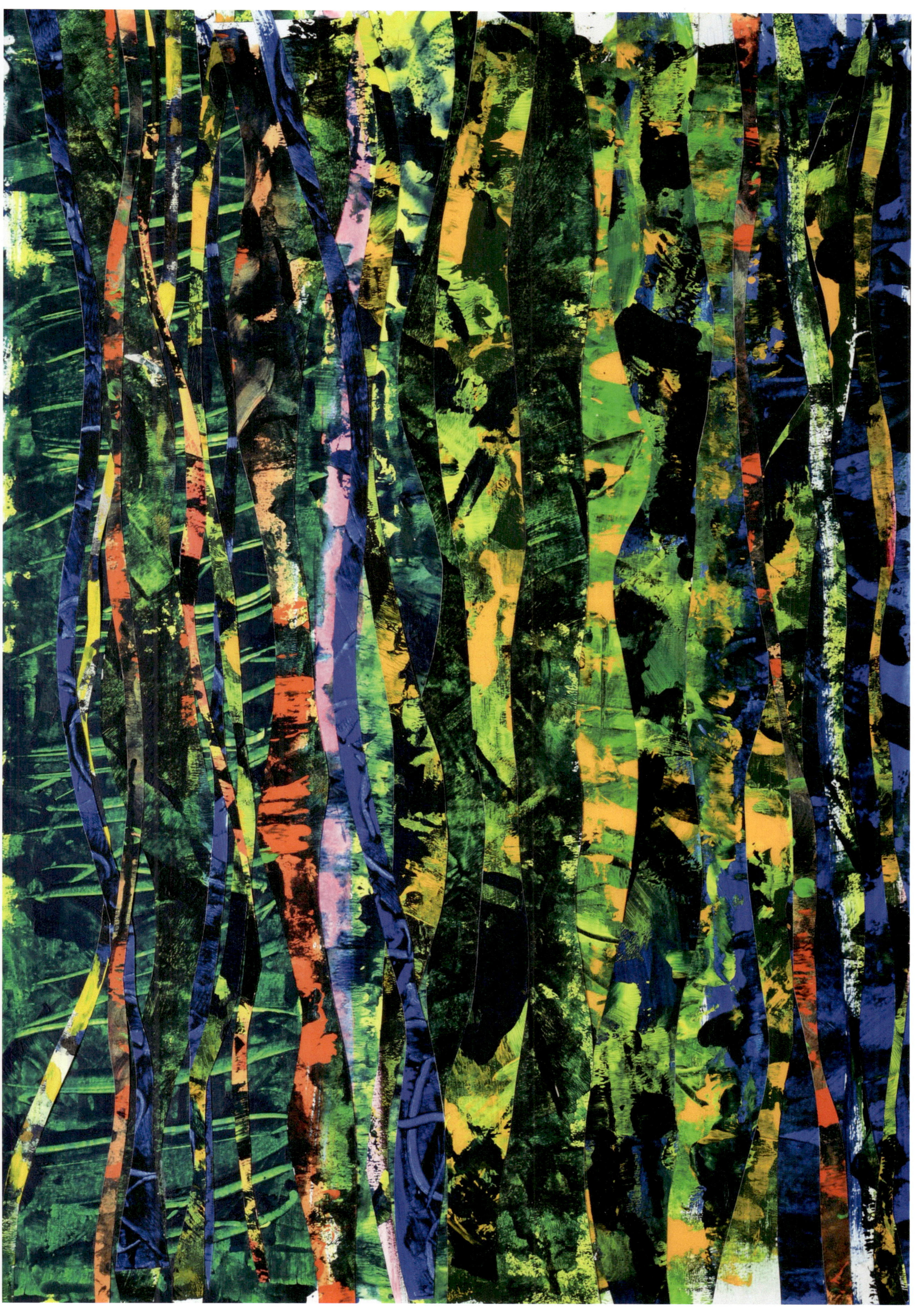

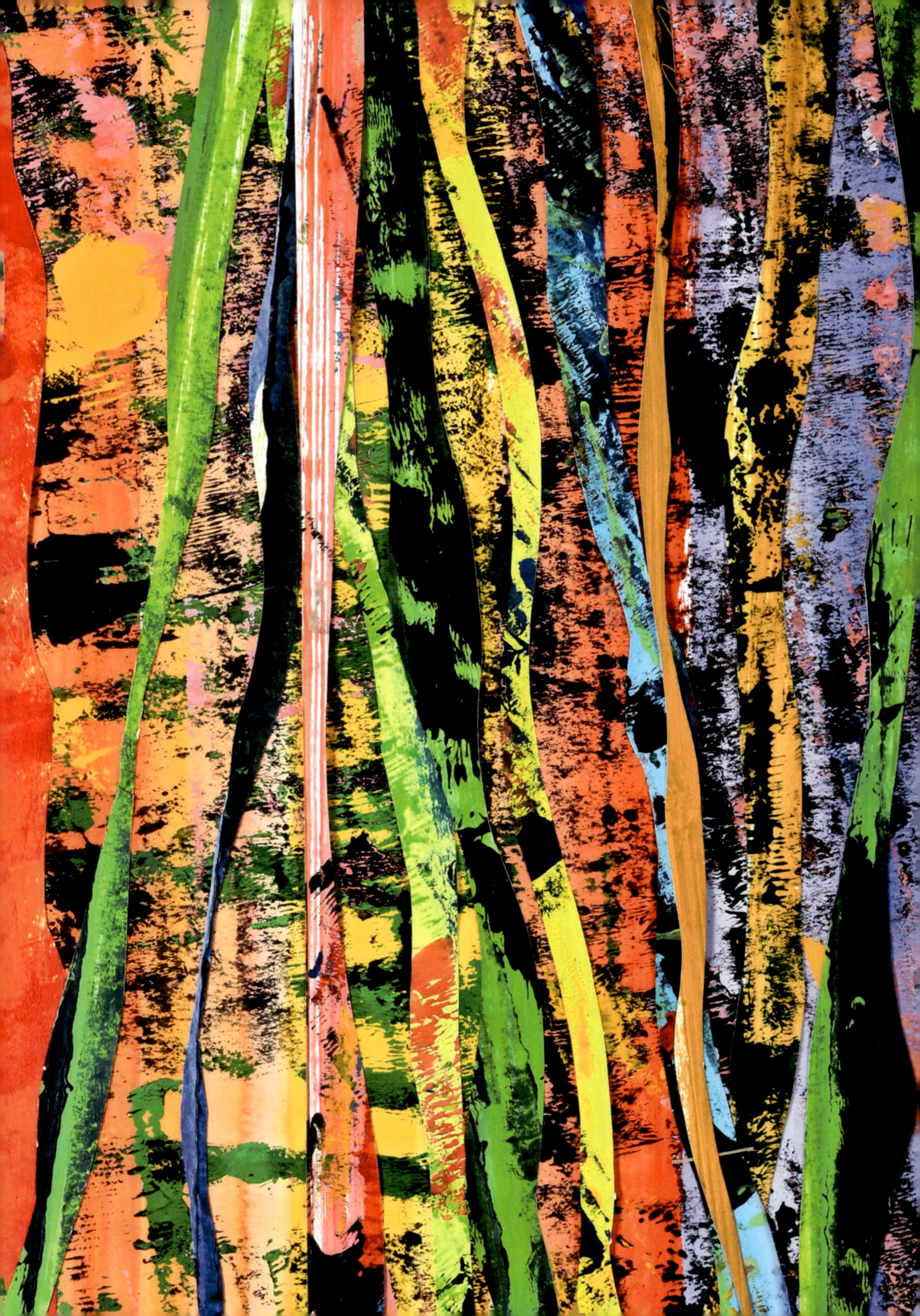

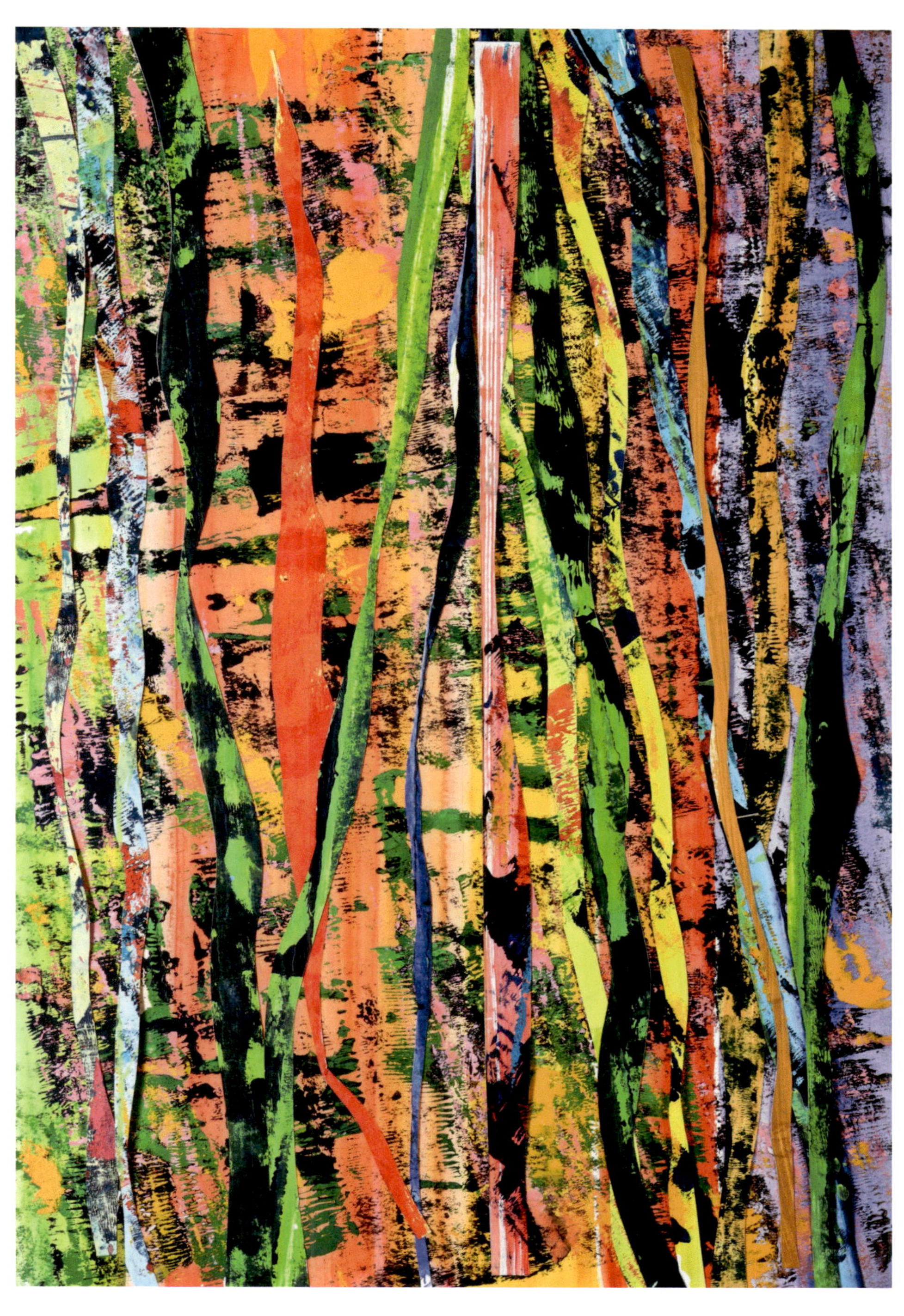

Rainbow, 1994

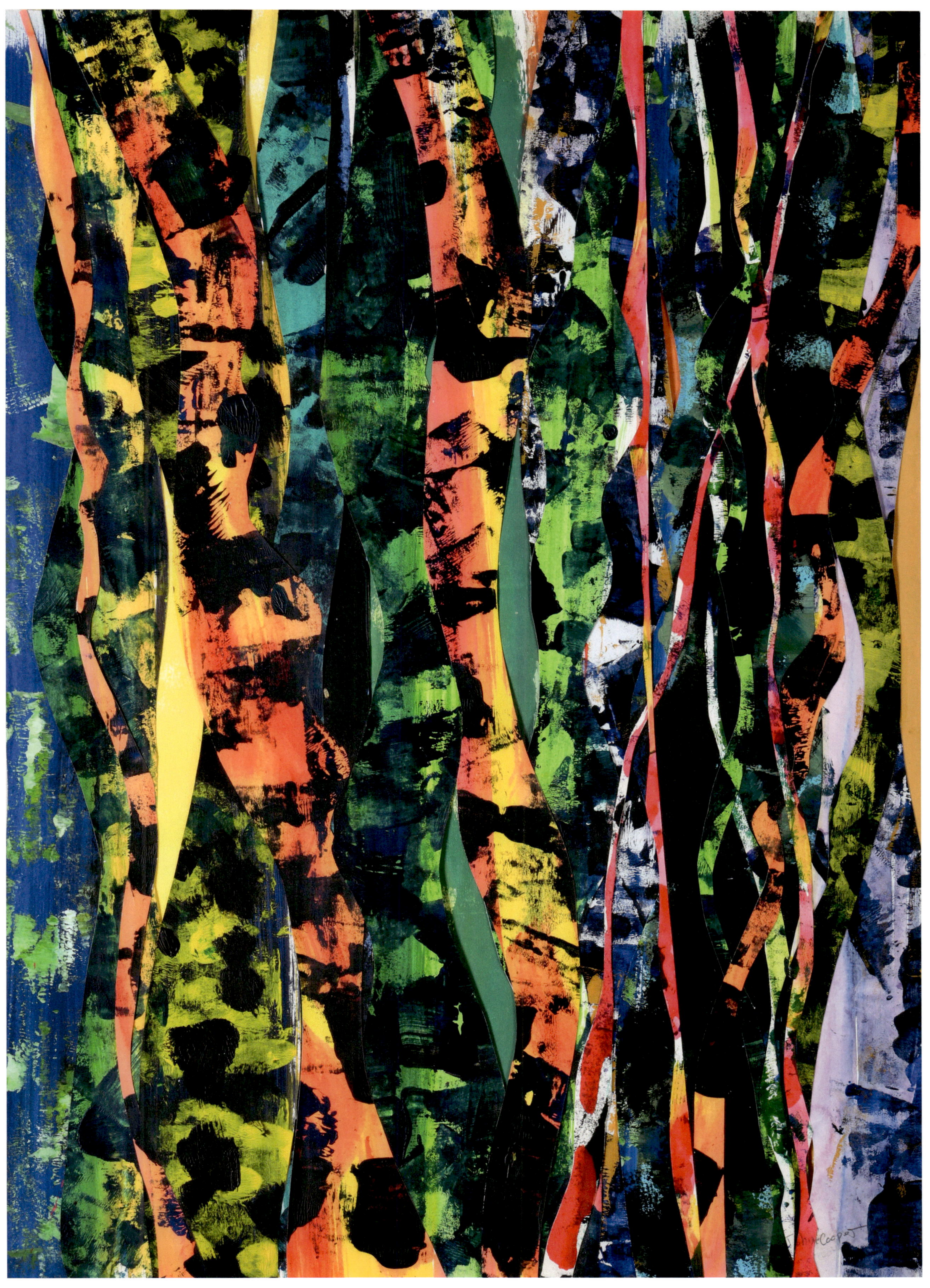

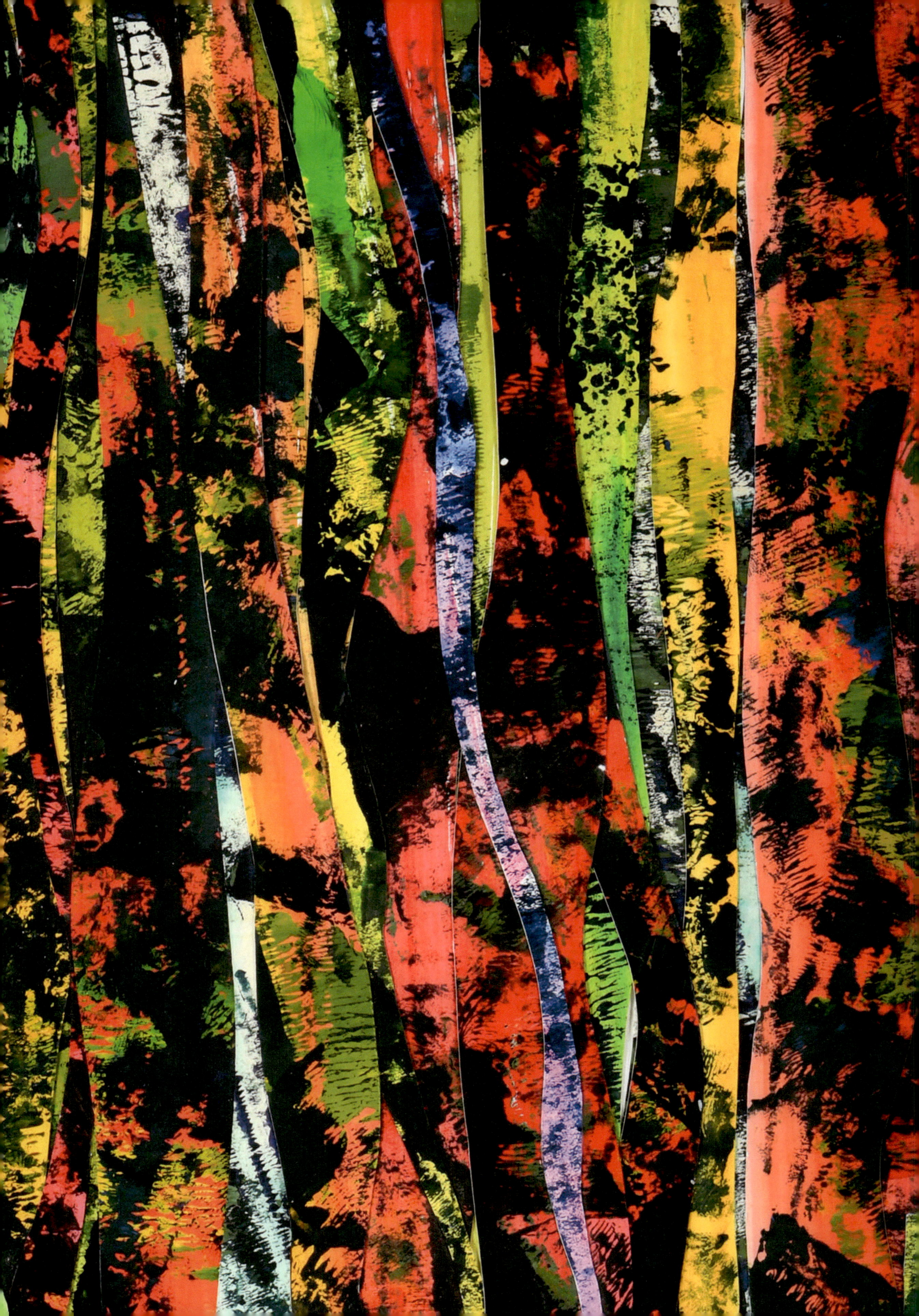

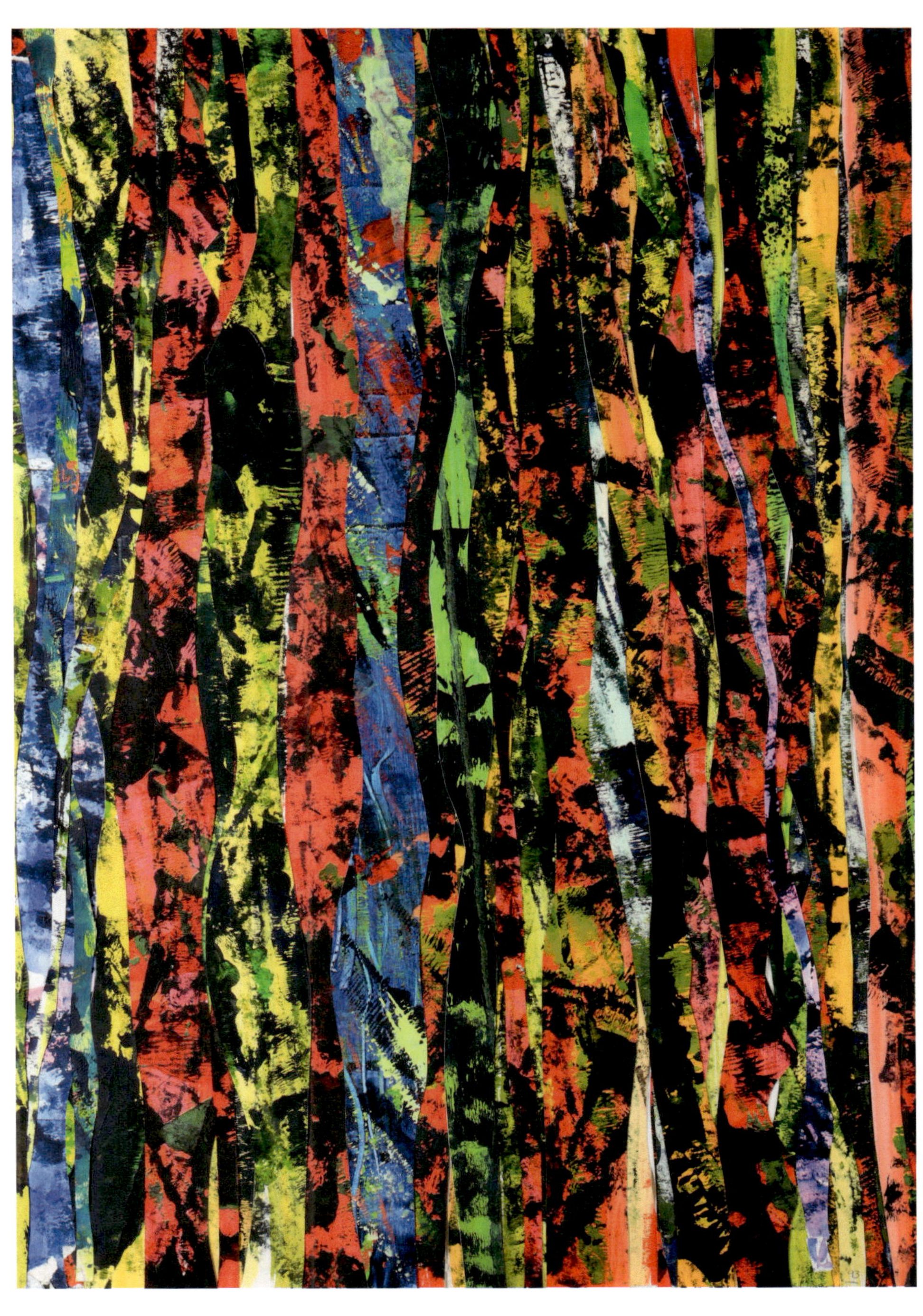

Fractured Light, 1993

Noon

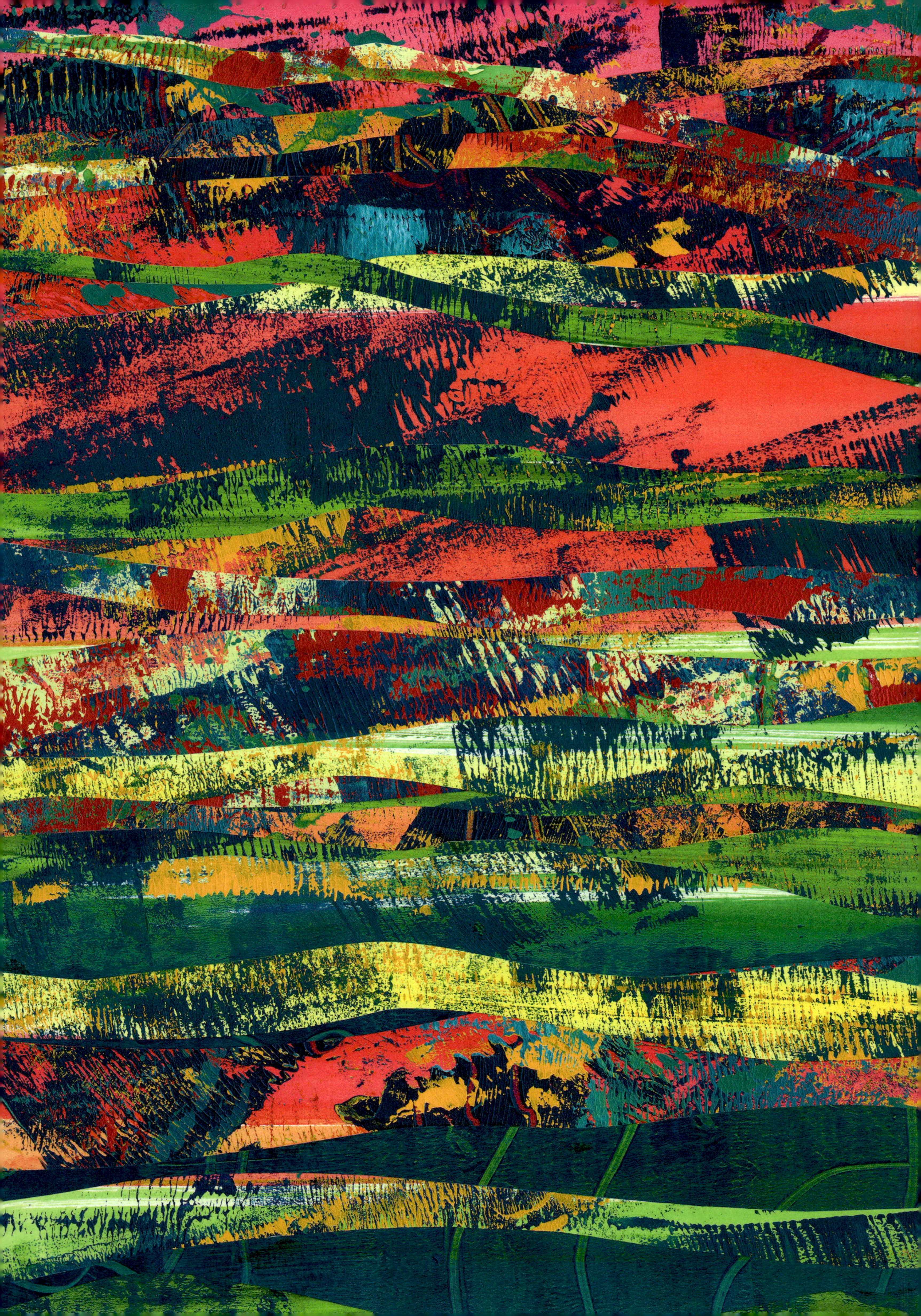

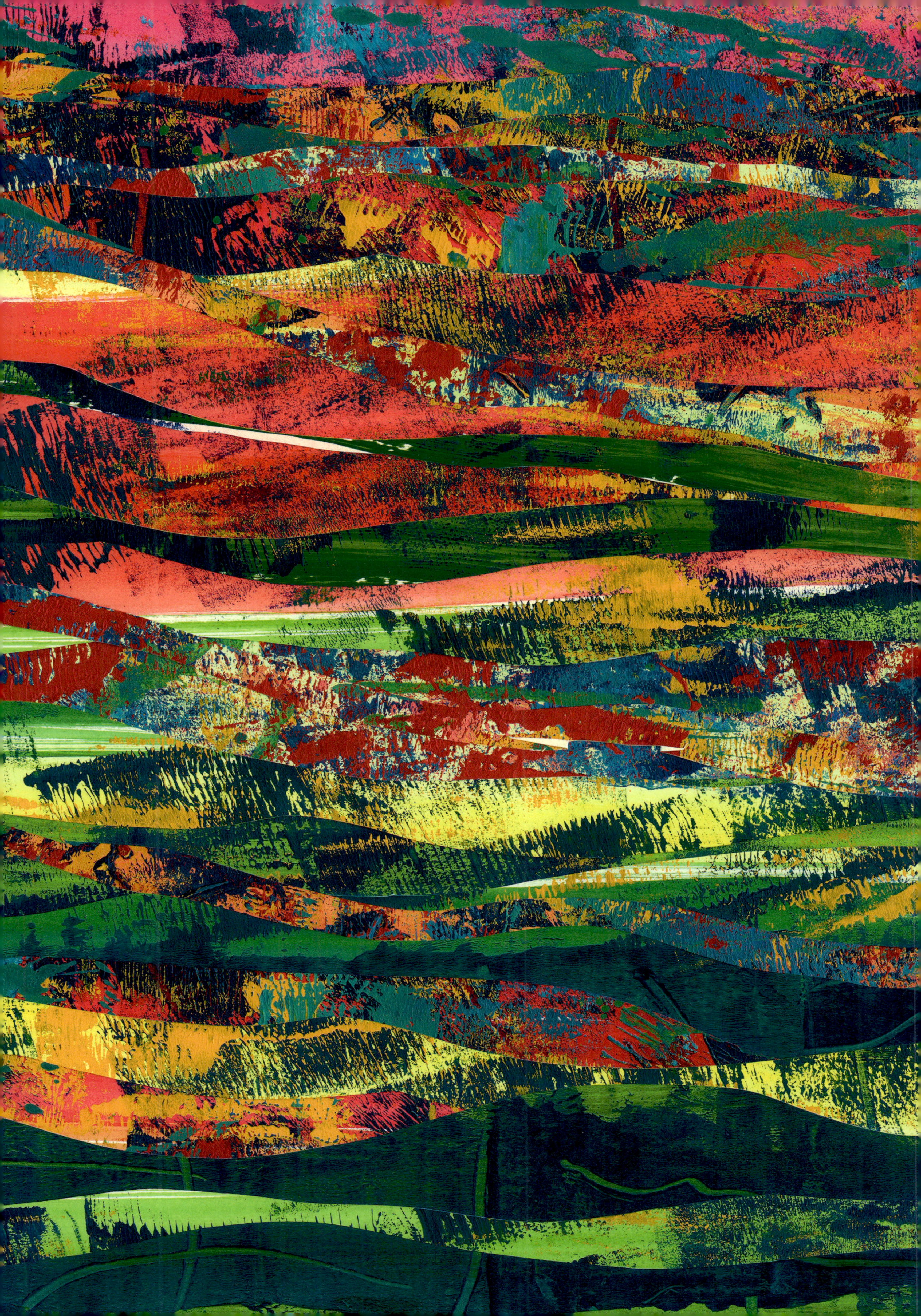

Previous pages **Sky Lark, 1994**   *Opposite* **The Paddock, 1994**

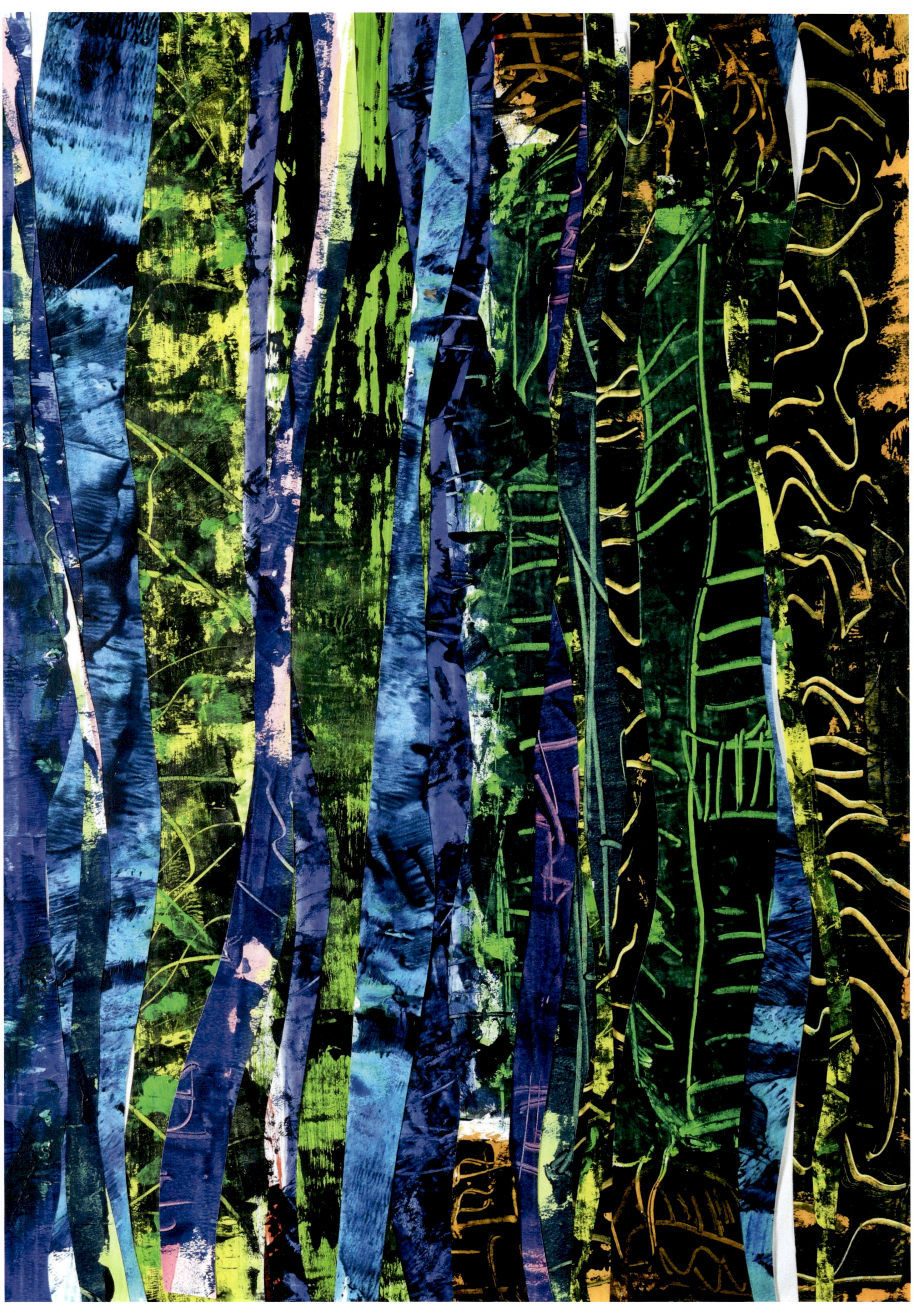

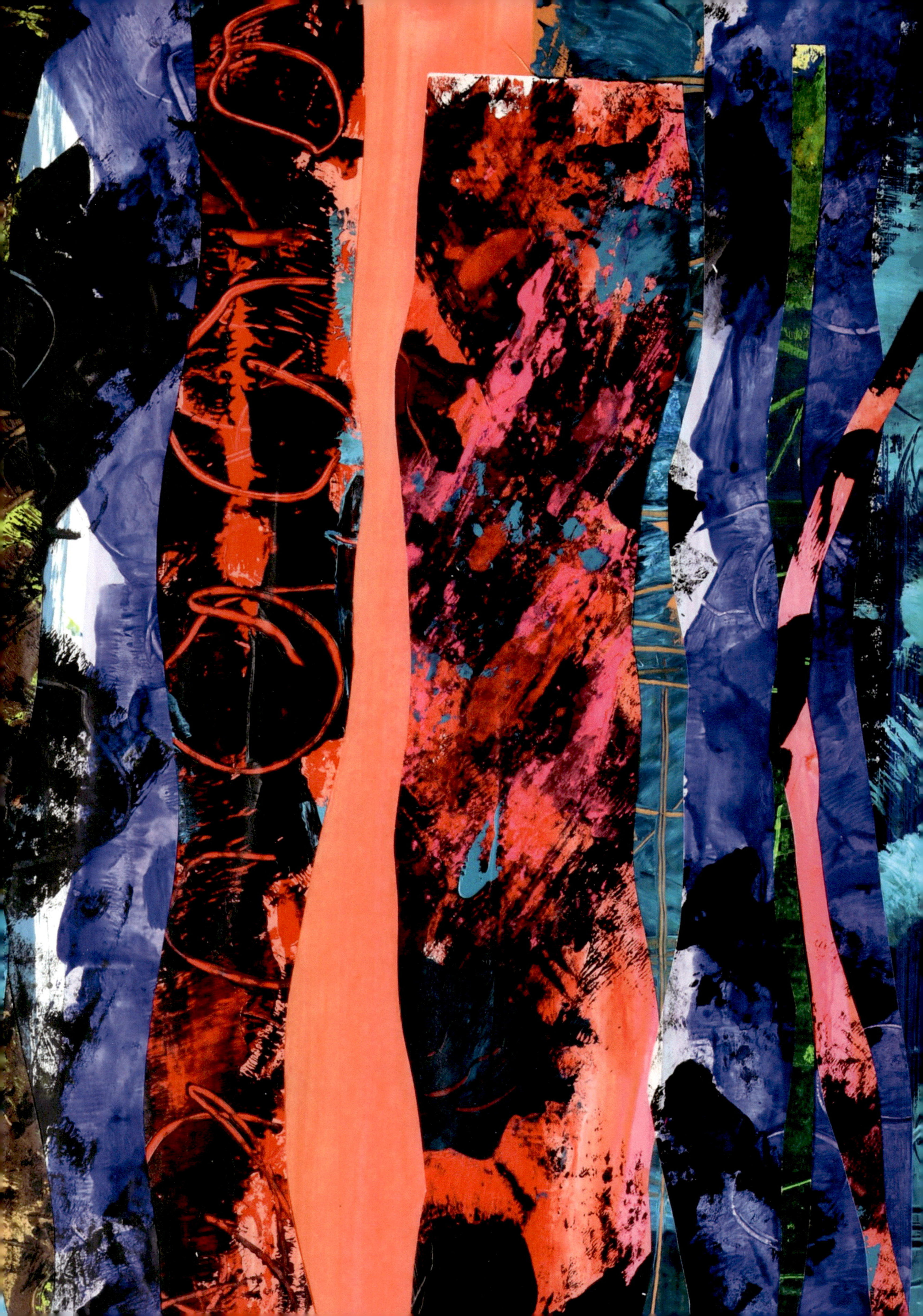

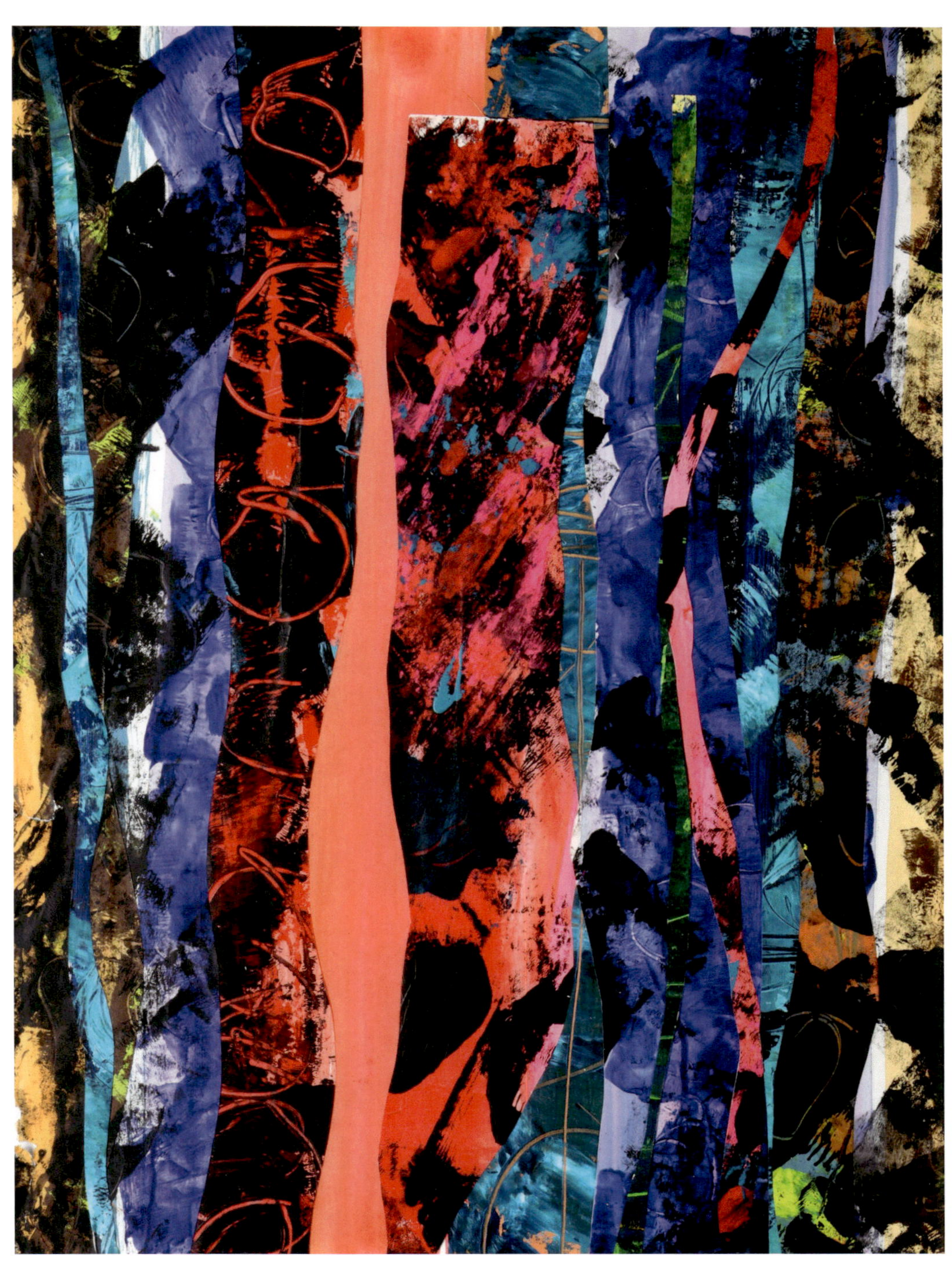

Lightening, 1994

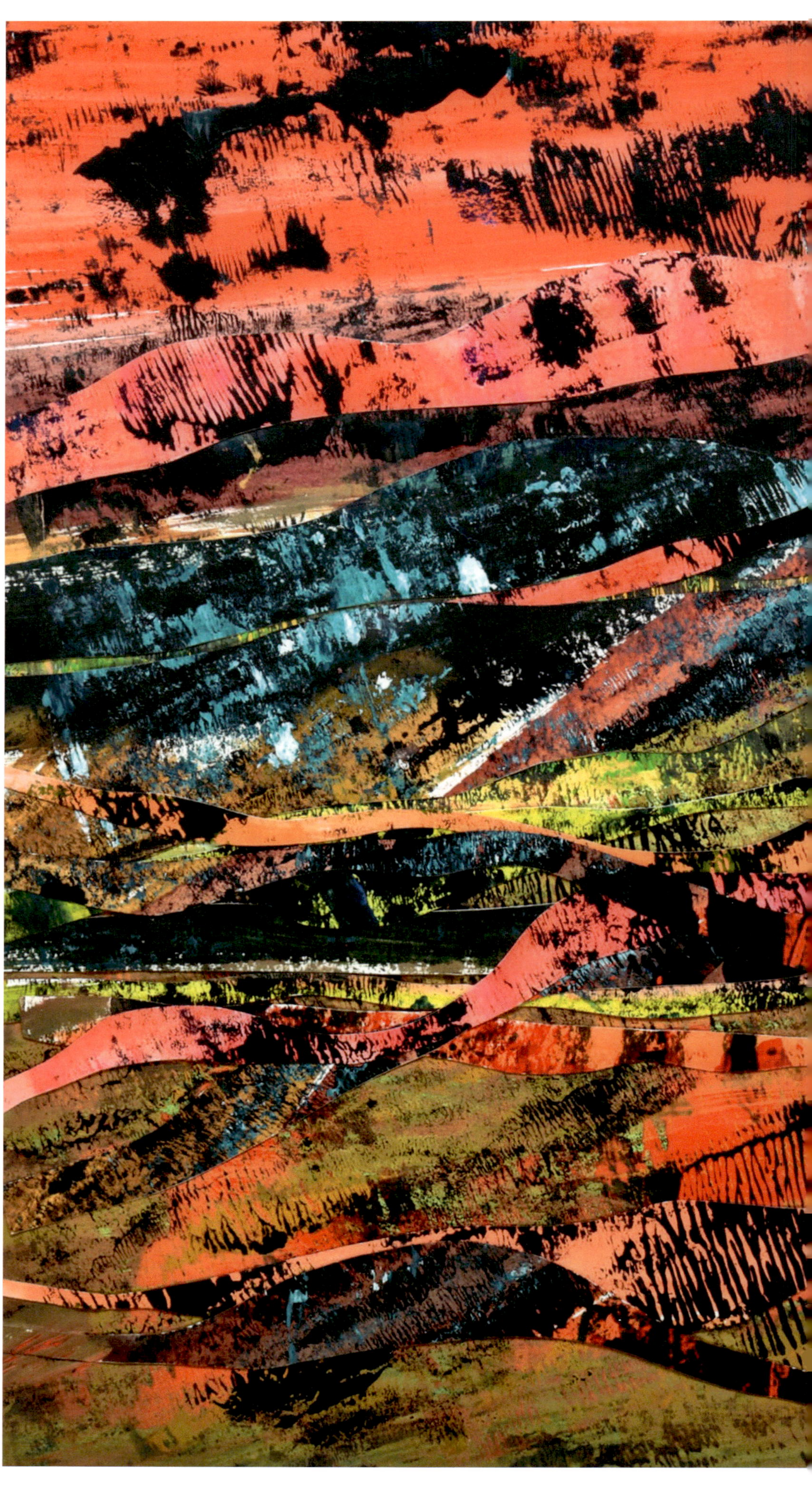

Cloud Strata, 1995

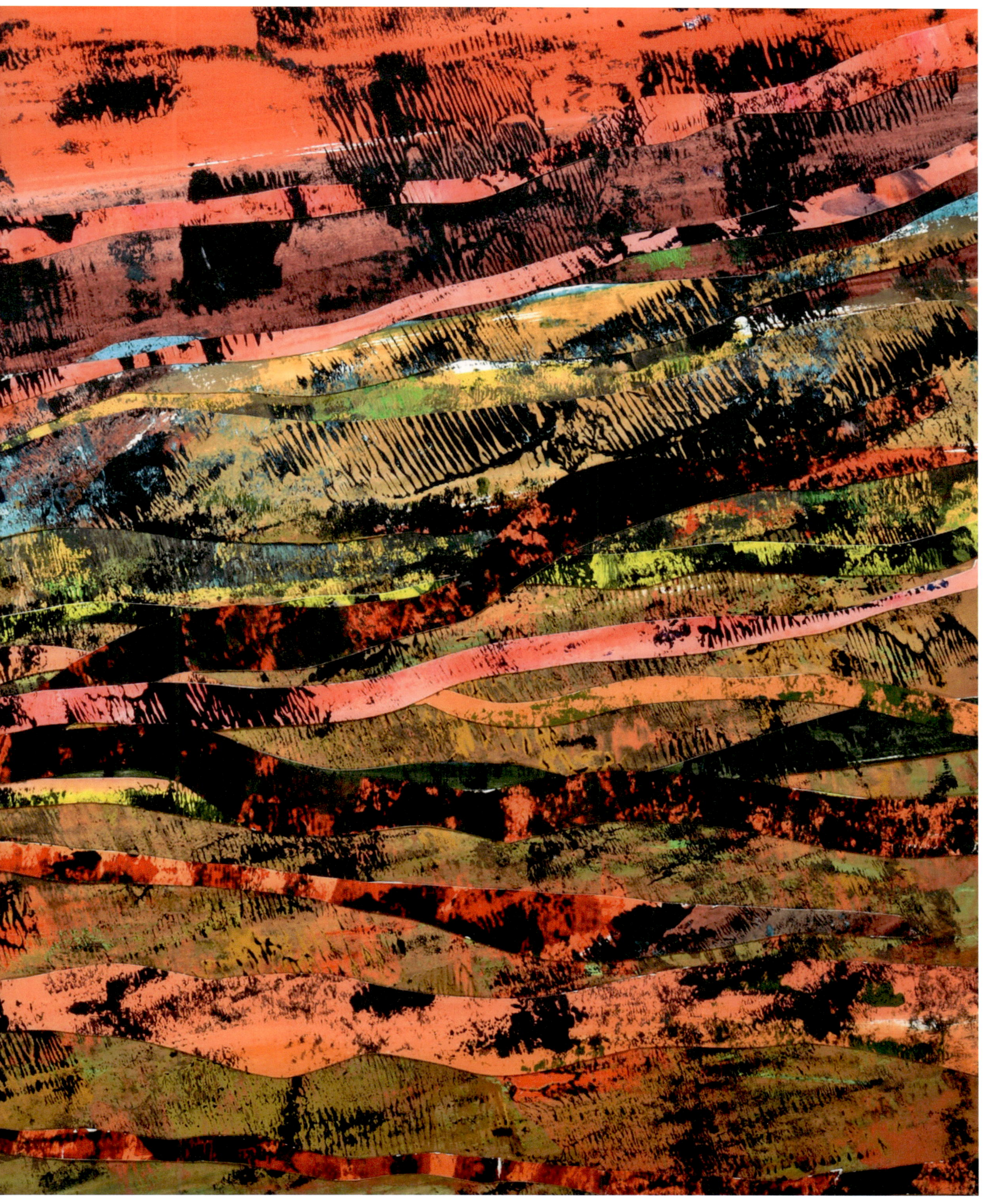

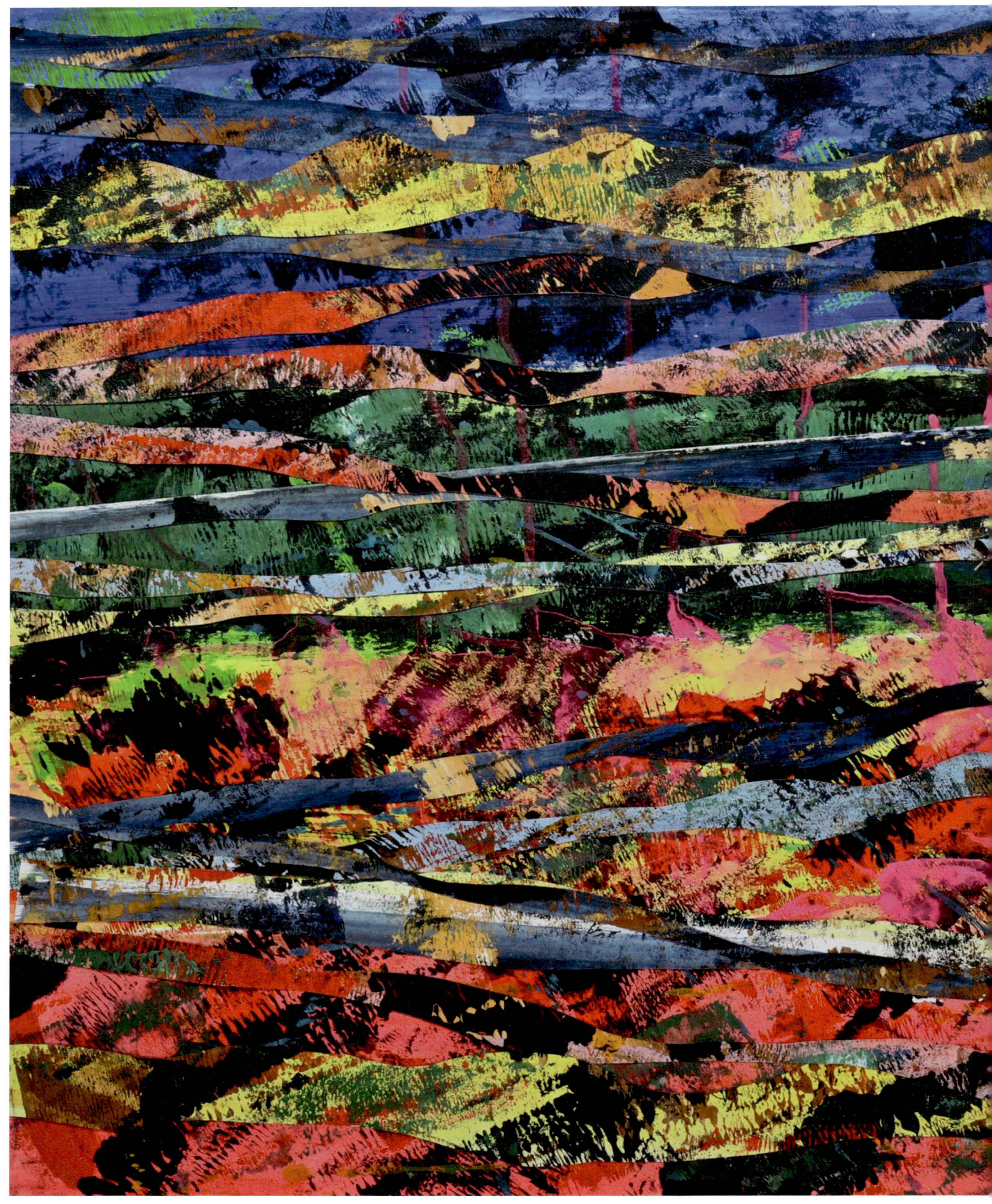

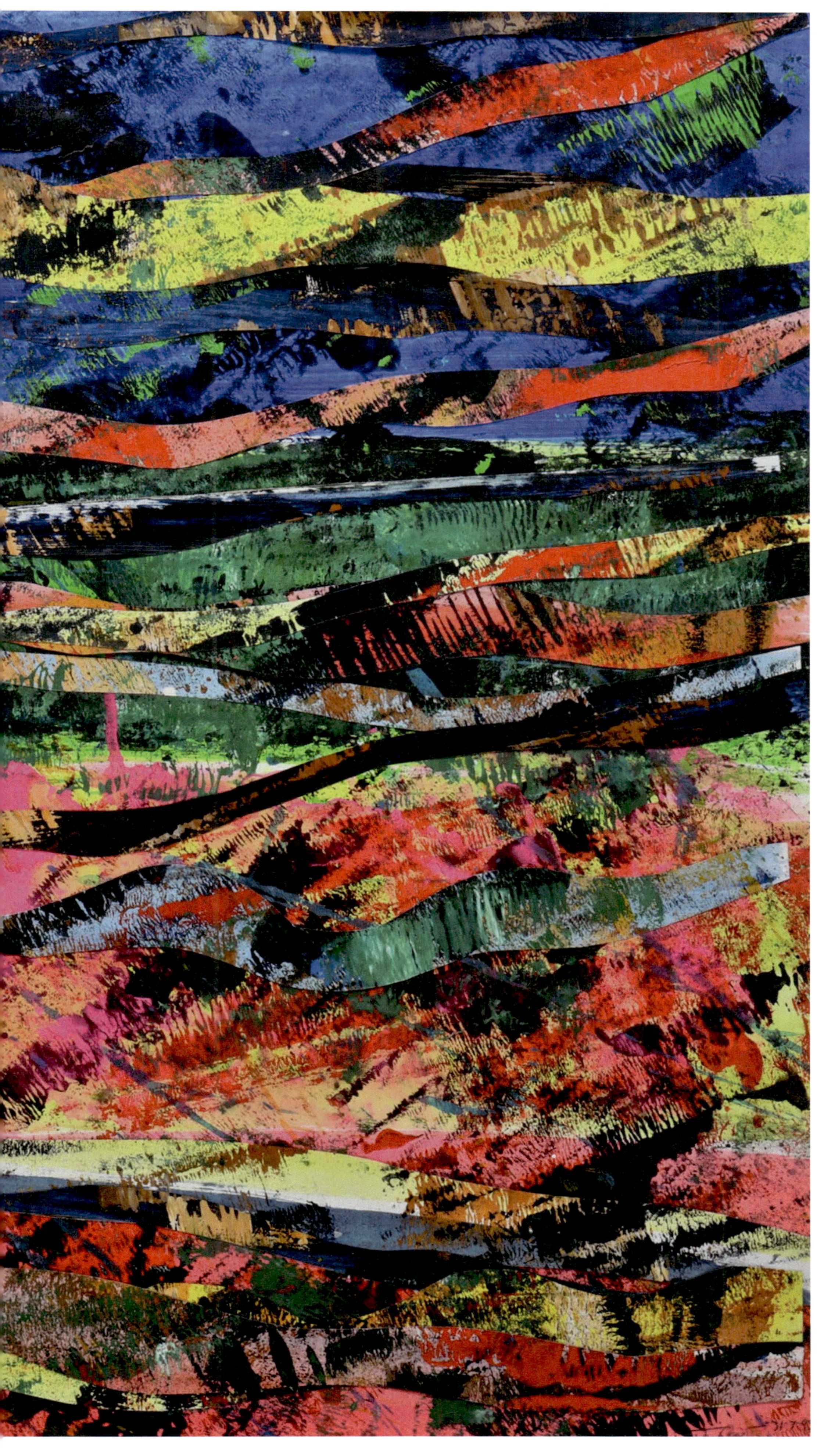

A Good Month, 1993

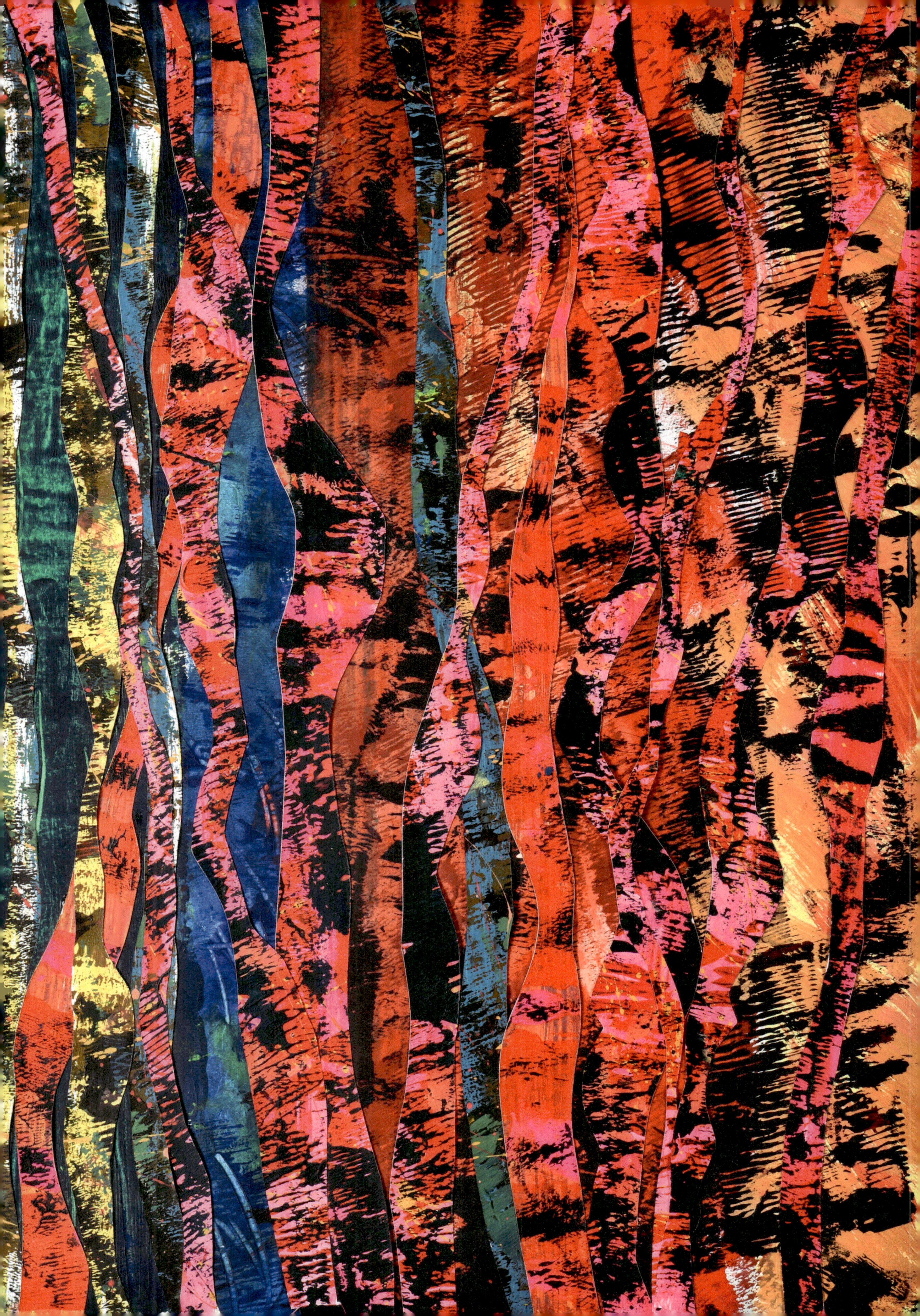

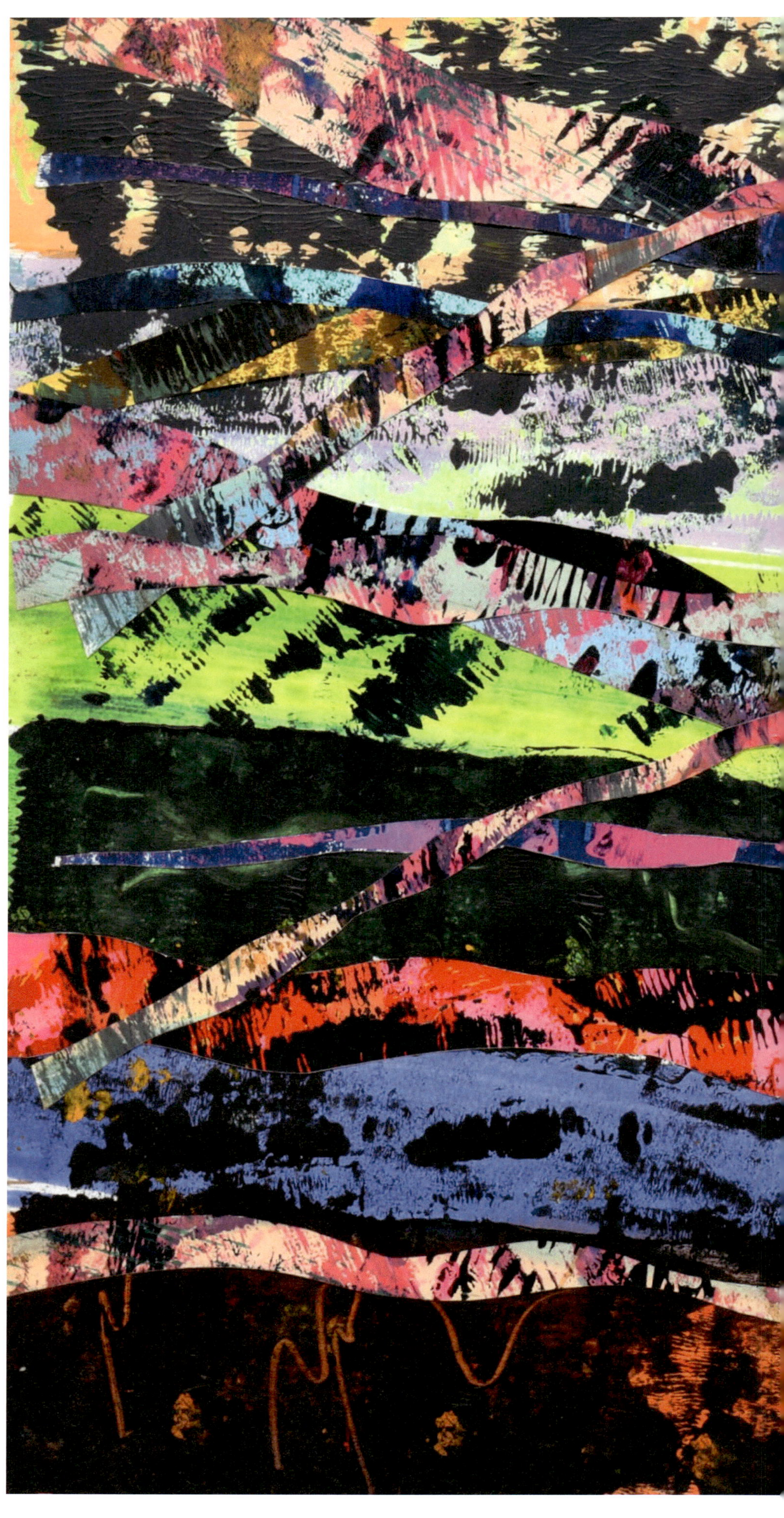

Plough Sky, 1994

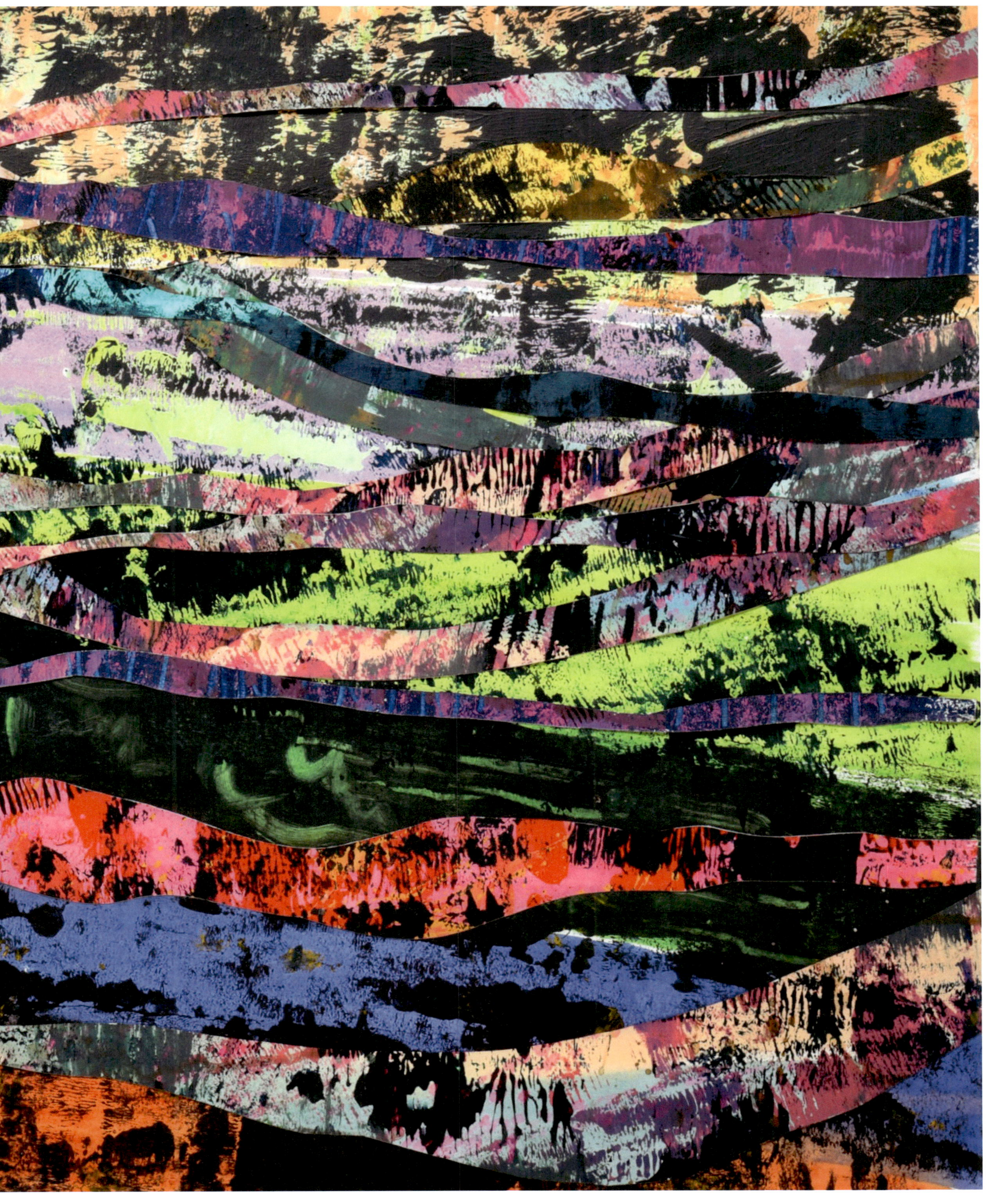

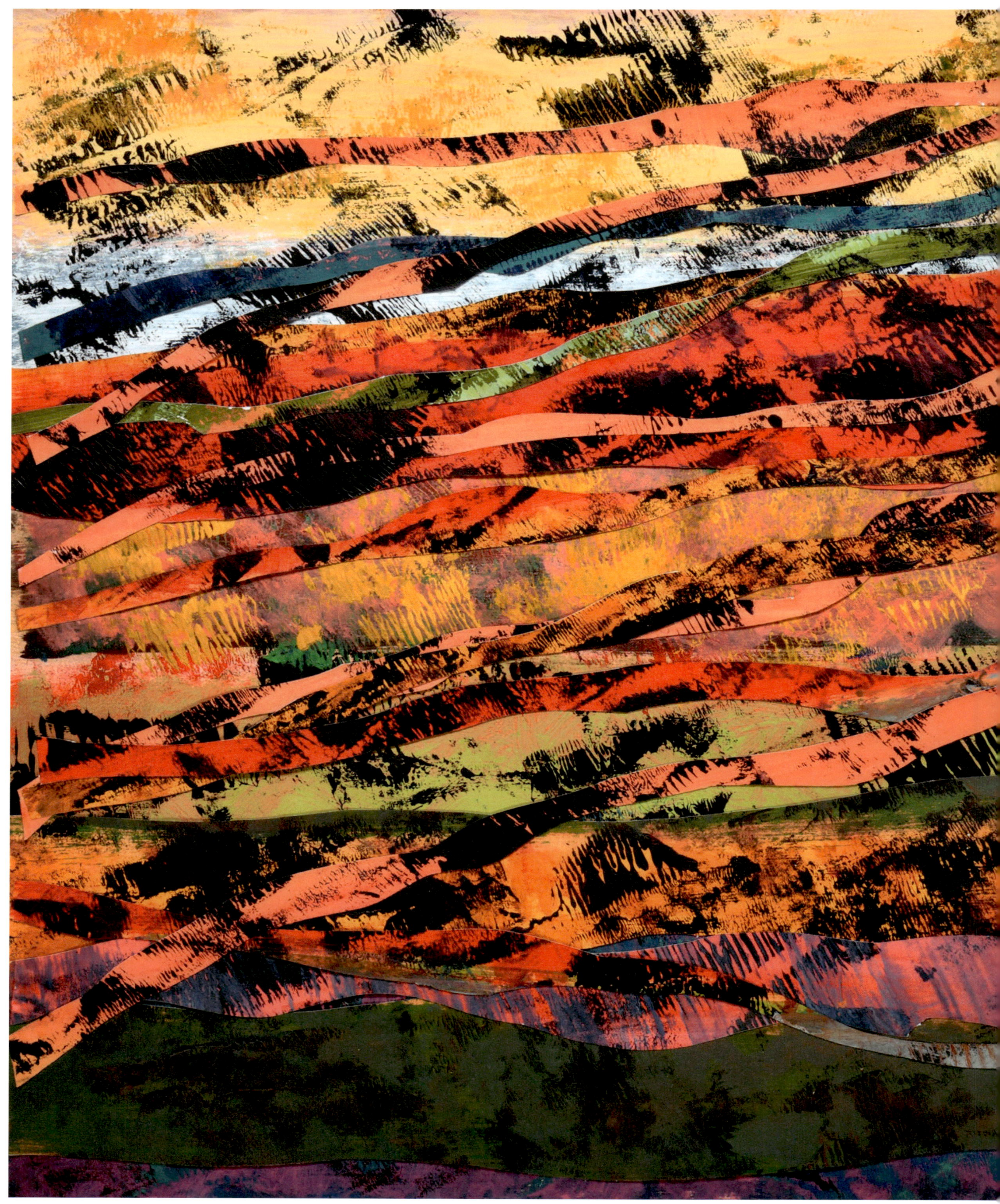

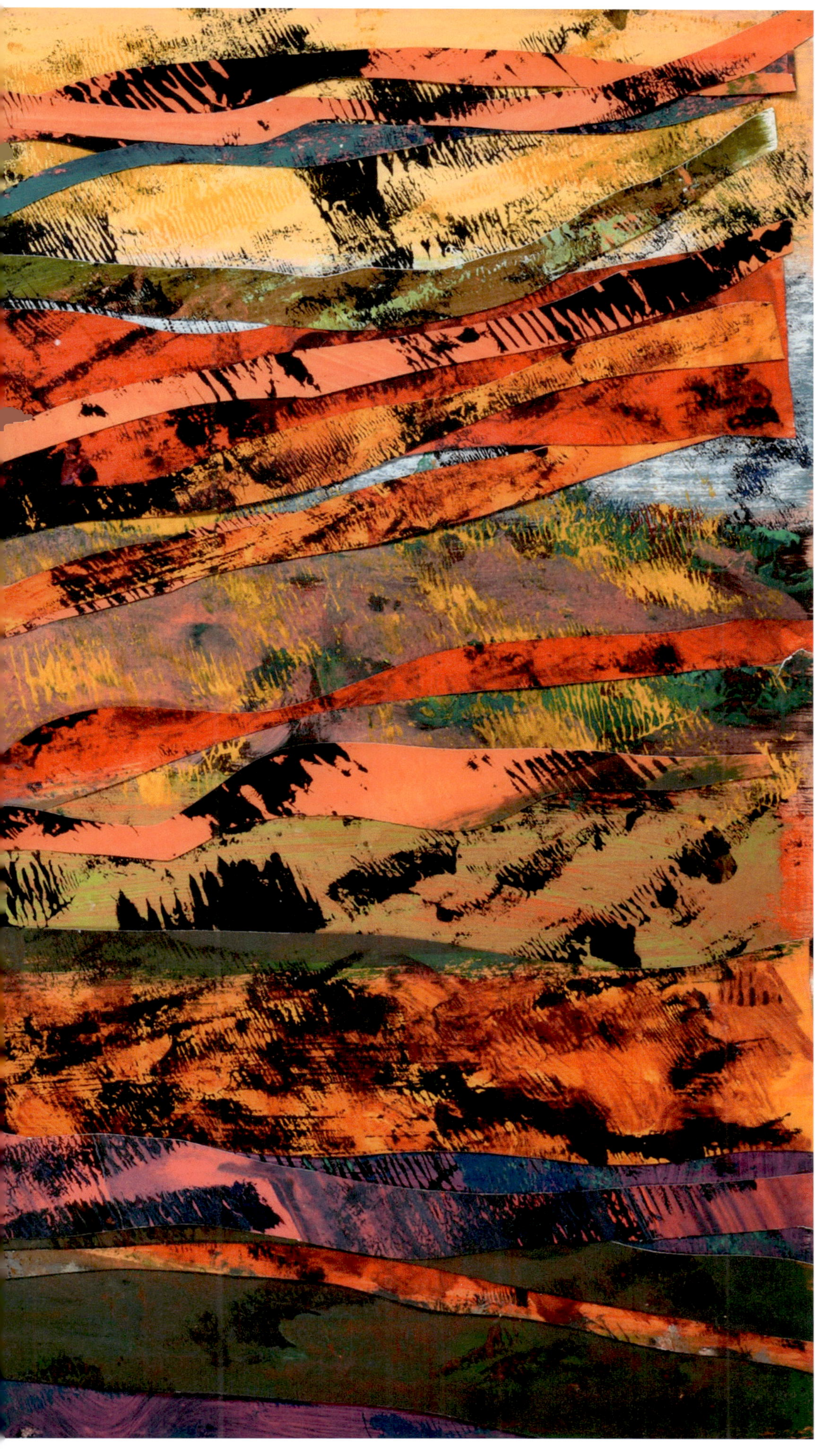

Cameo Sunset, 1994

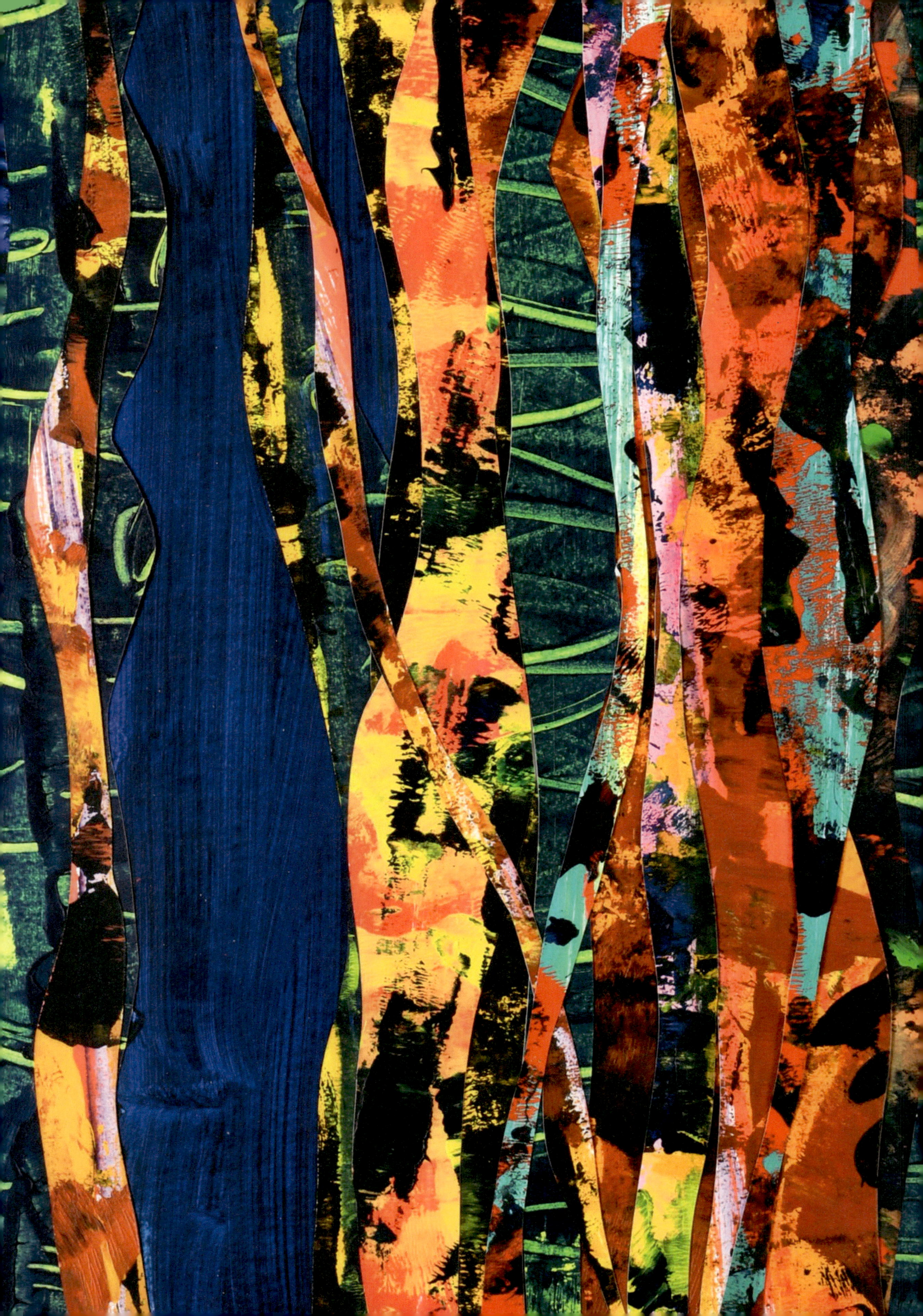

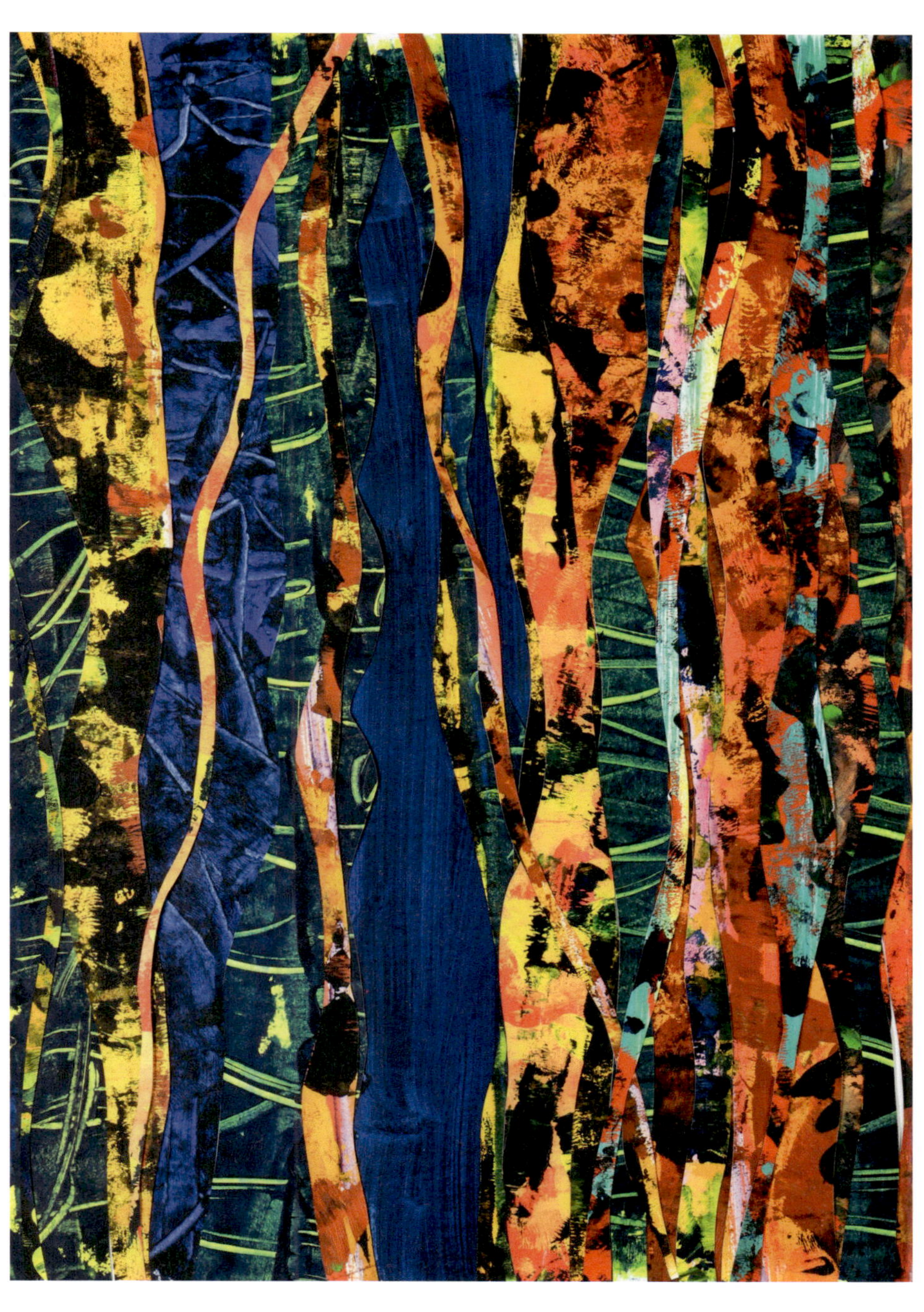

August Afternoon, 1995

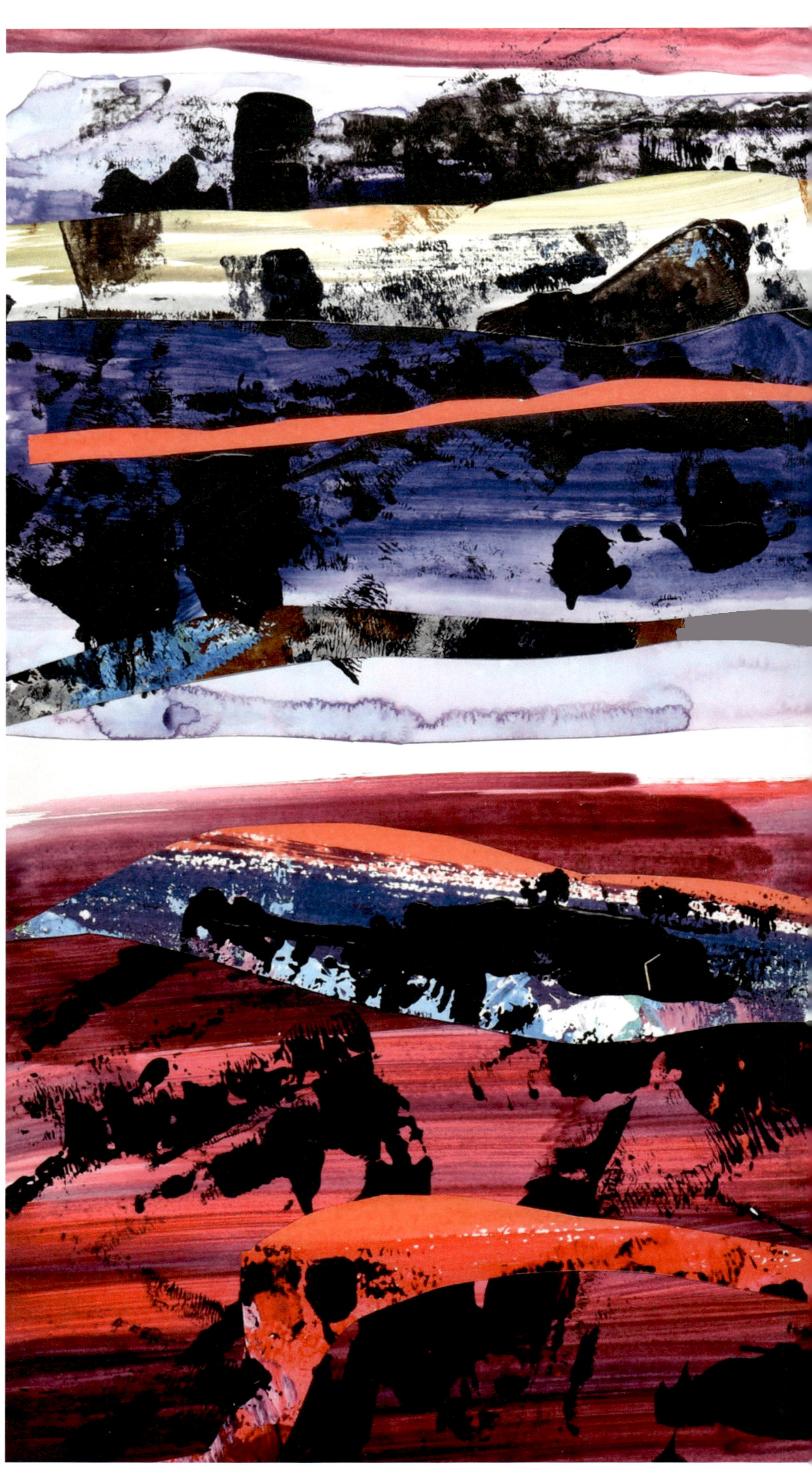

Silver Birch Shadow, 1995

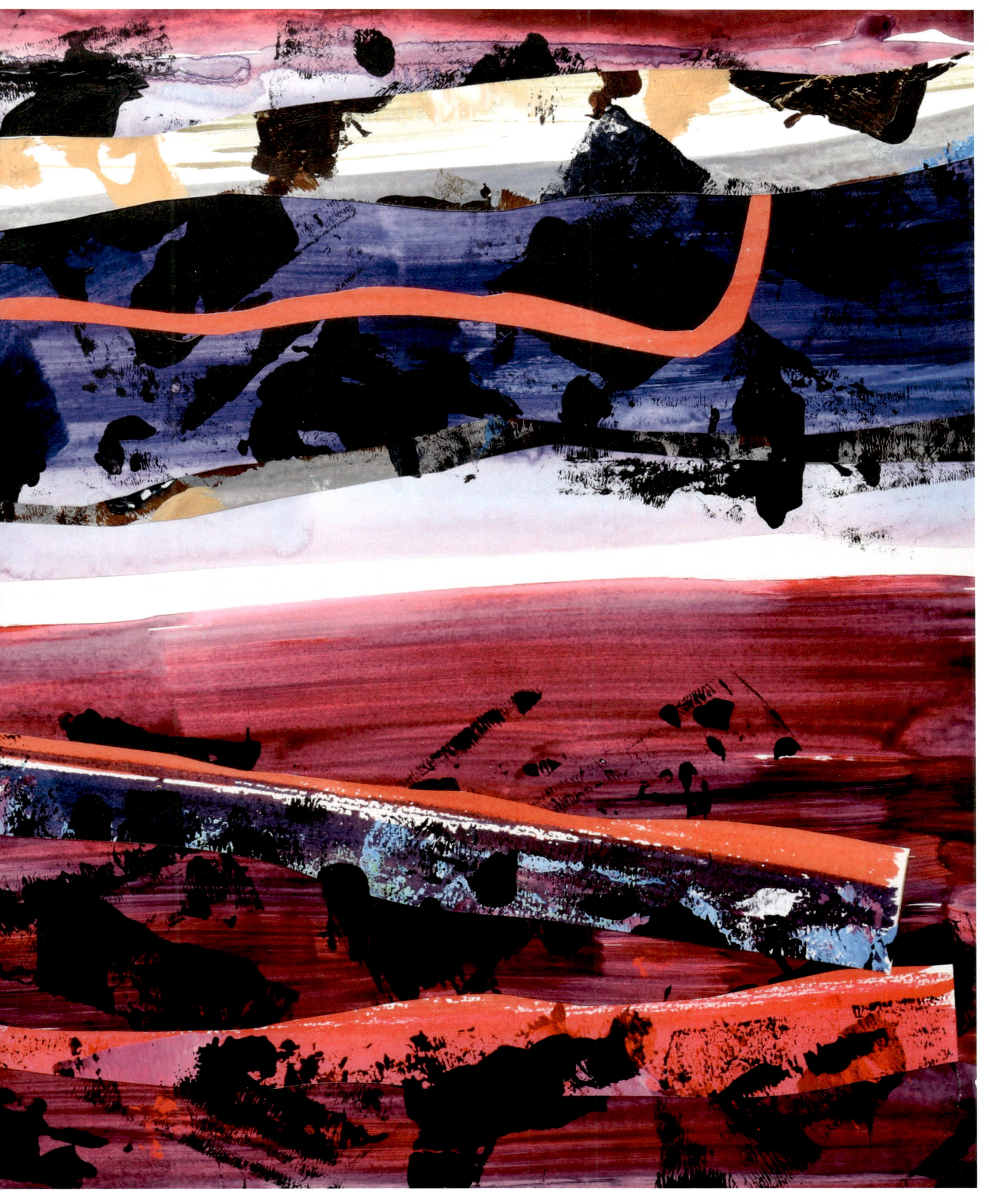

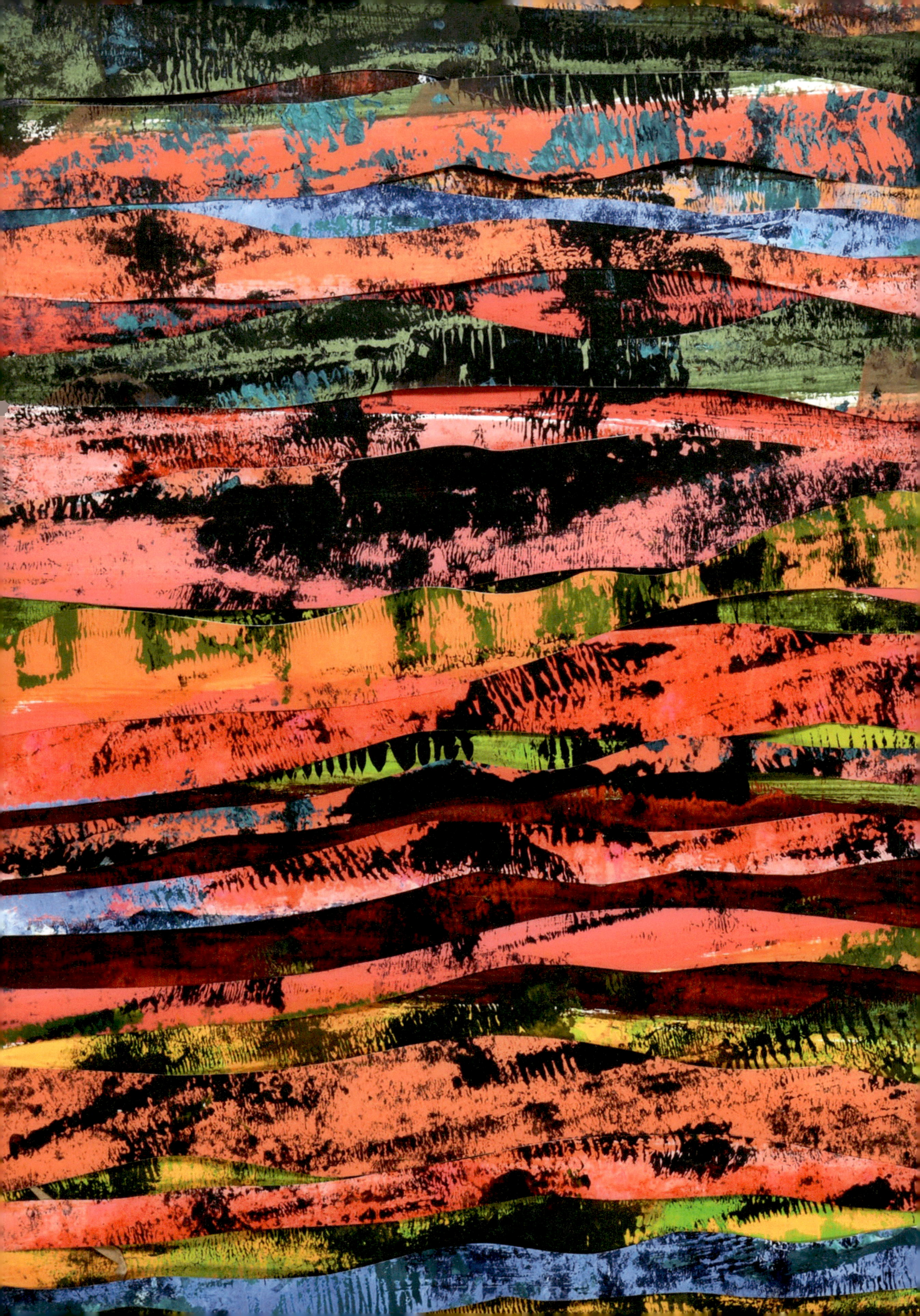

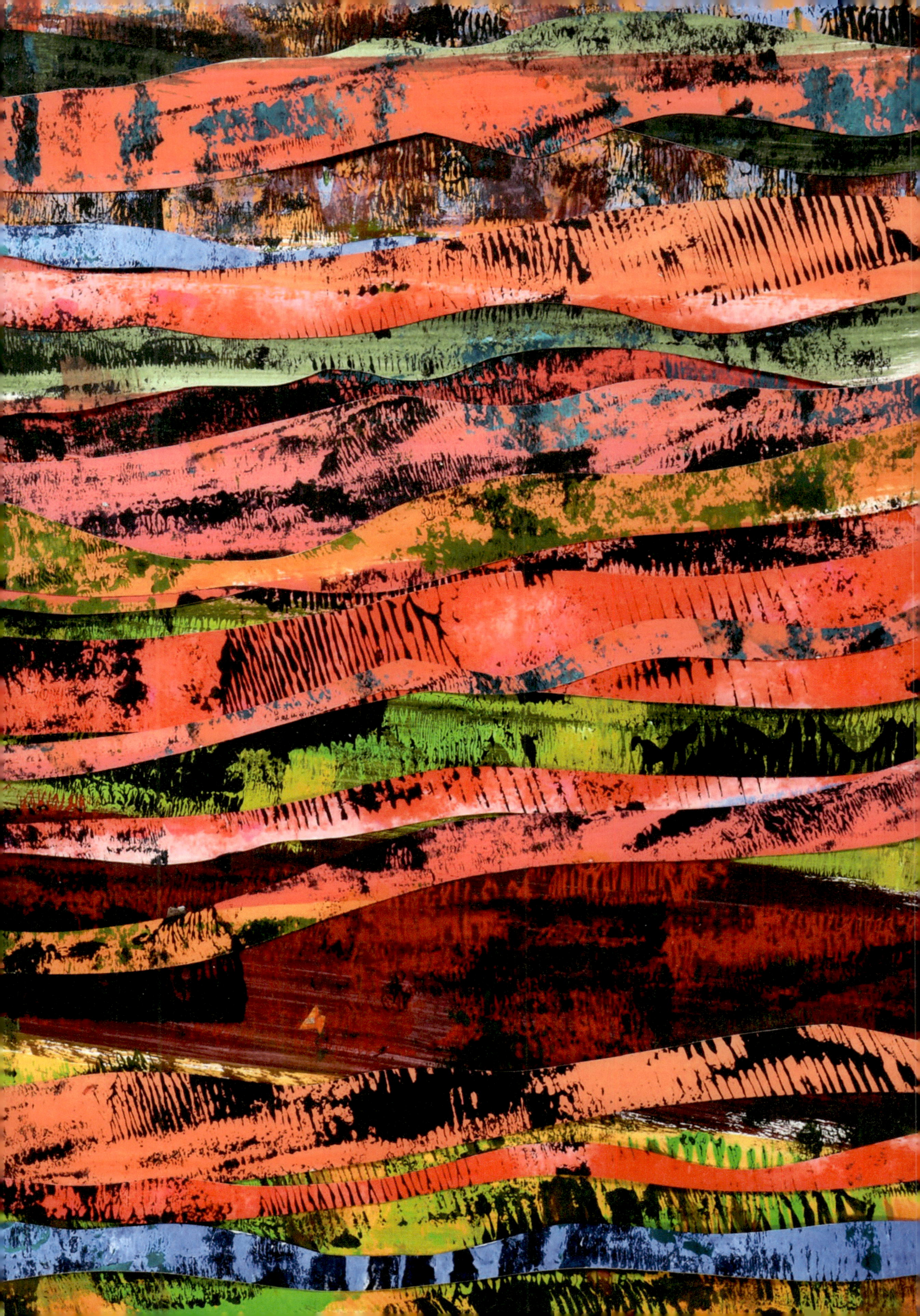

Previous pages **Solar Stream, 1996**   *Opposite* **Bull Rush Pond, 1993**

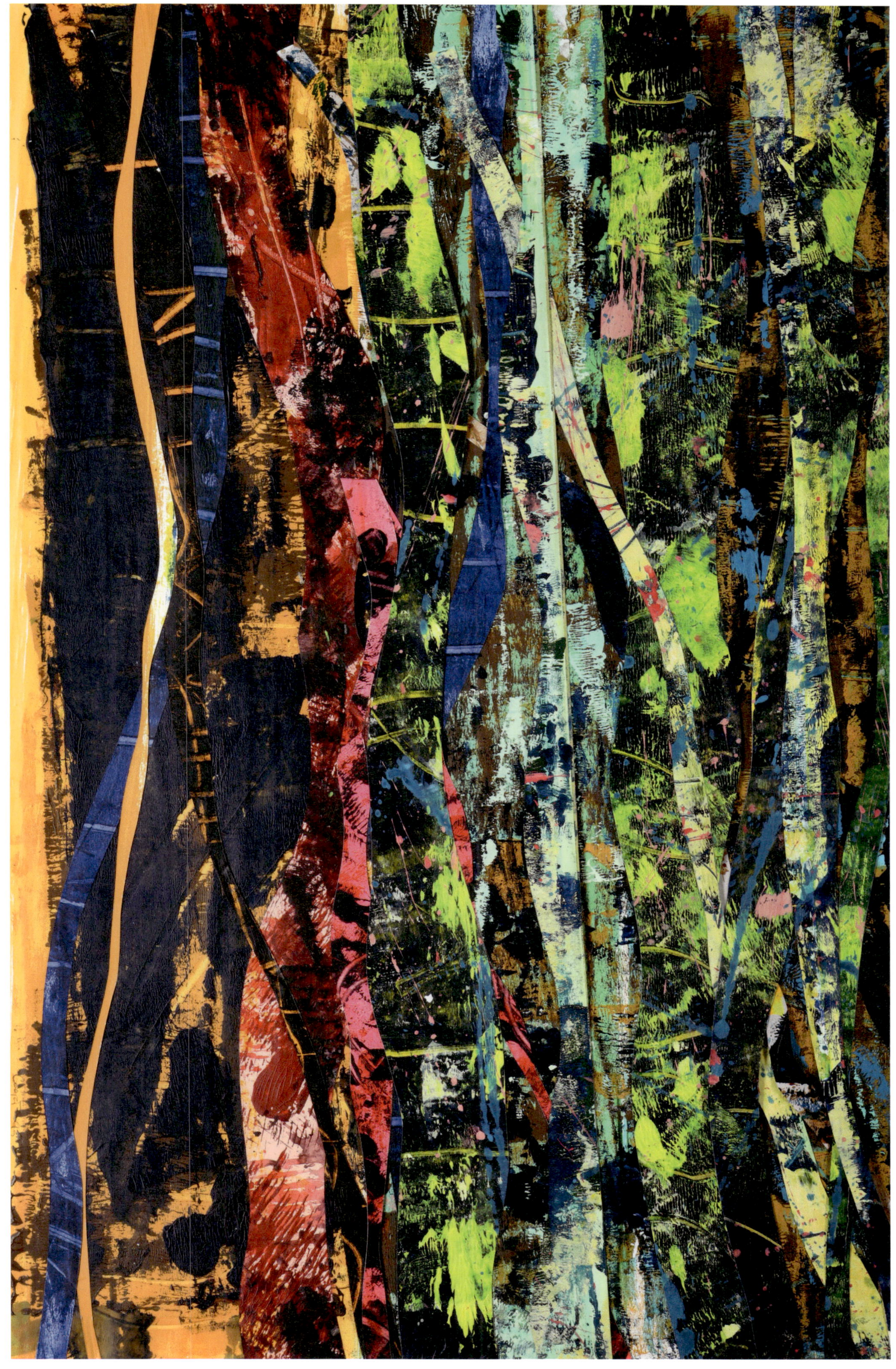

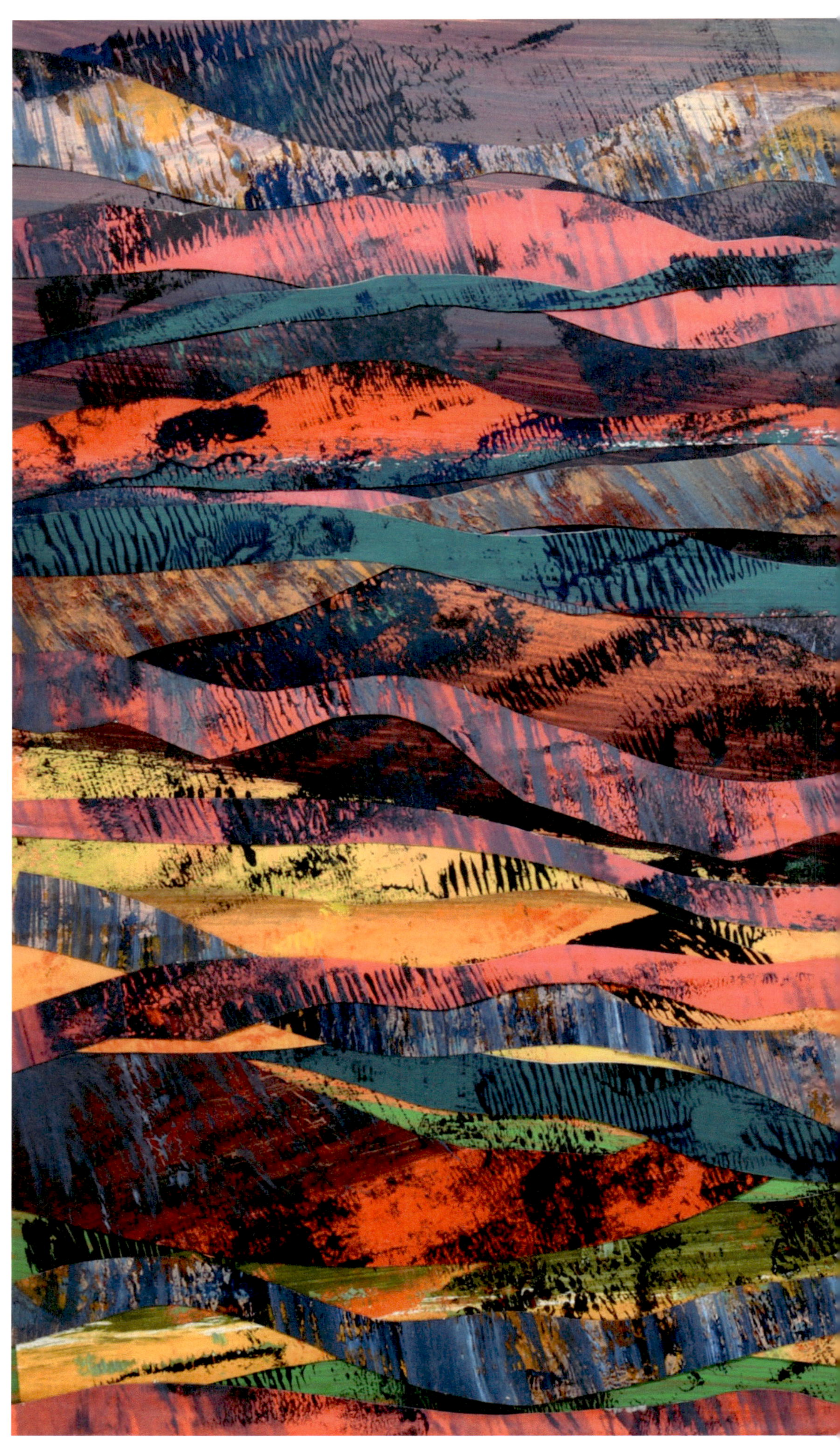

Cinders, 1996

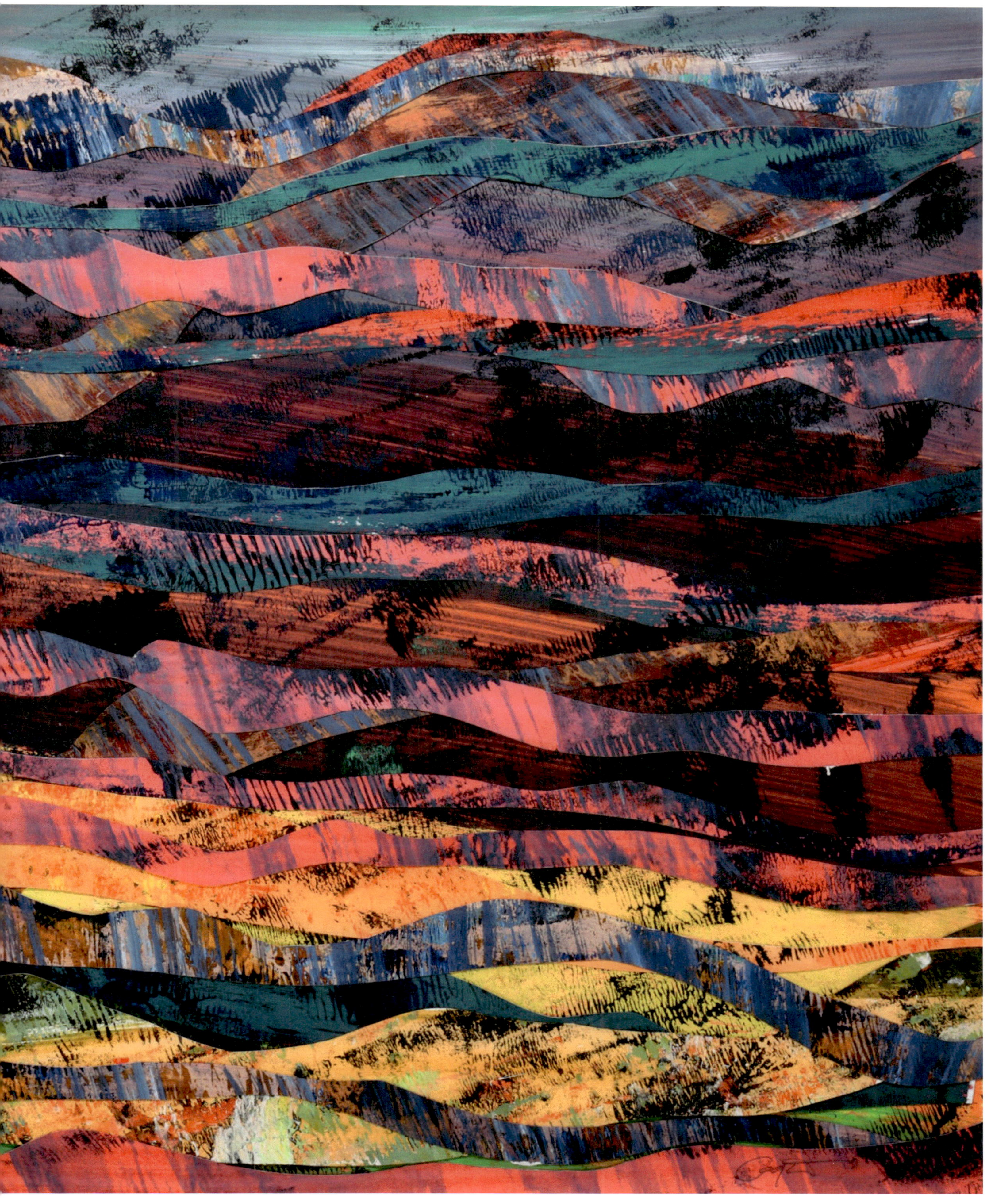

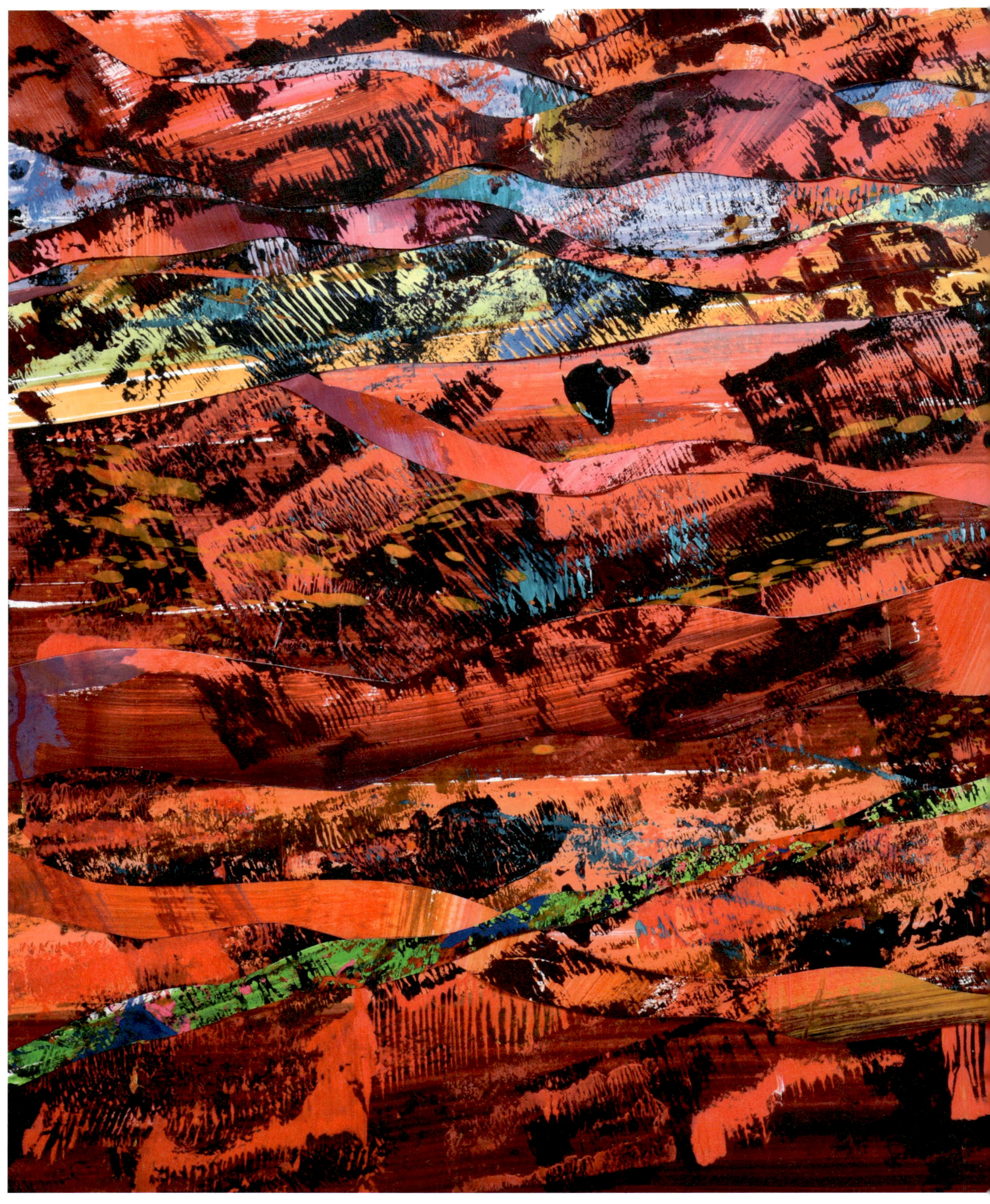

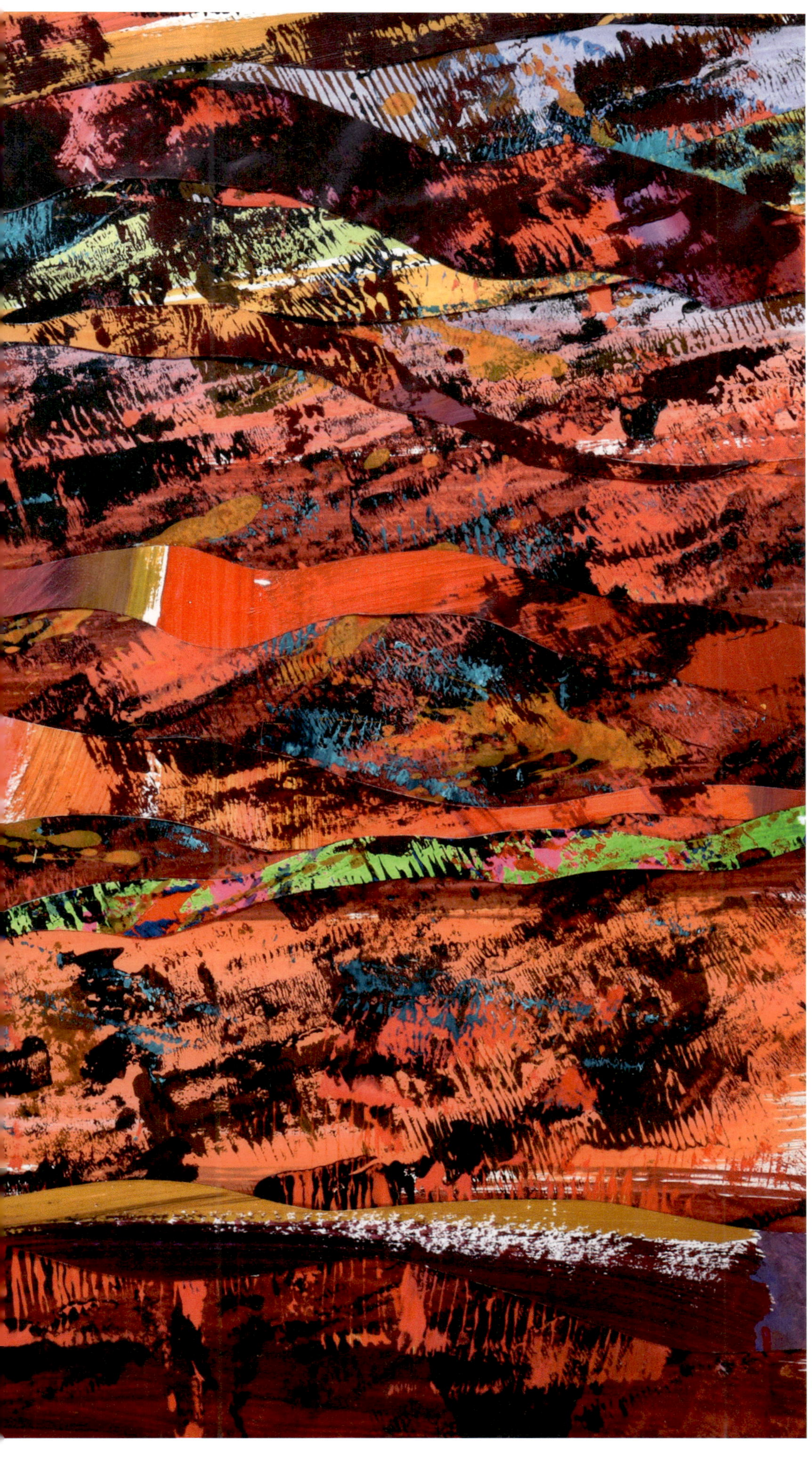

Burnished Woodland, 1994

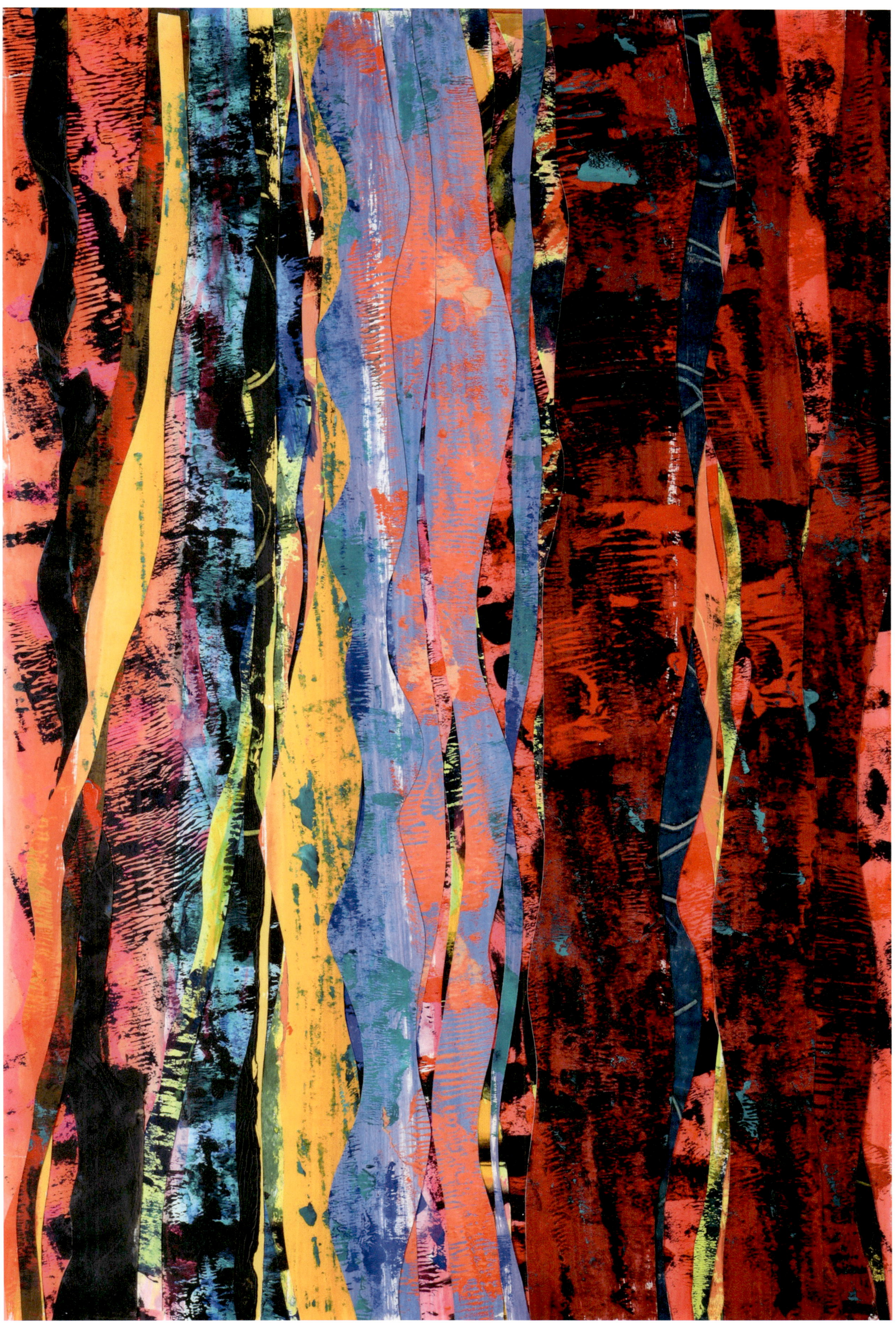

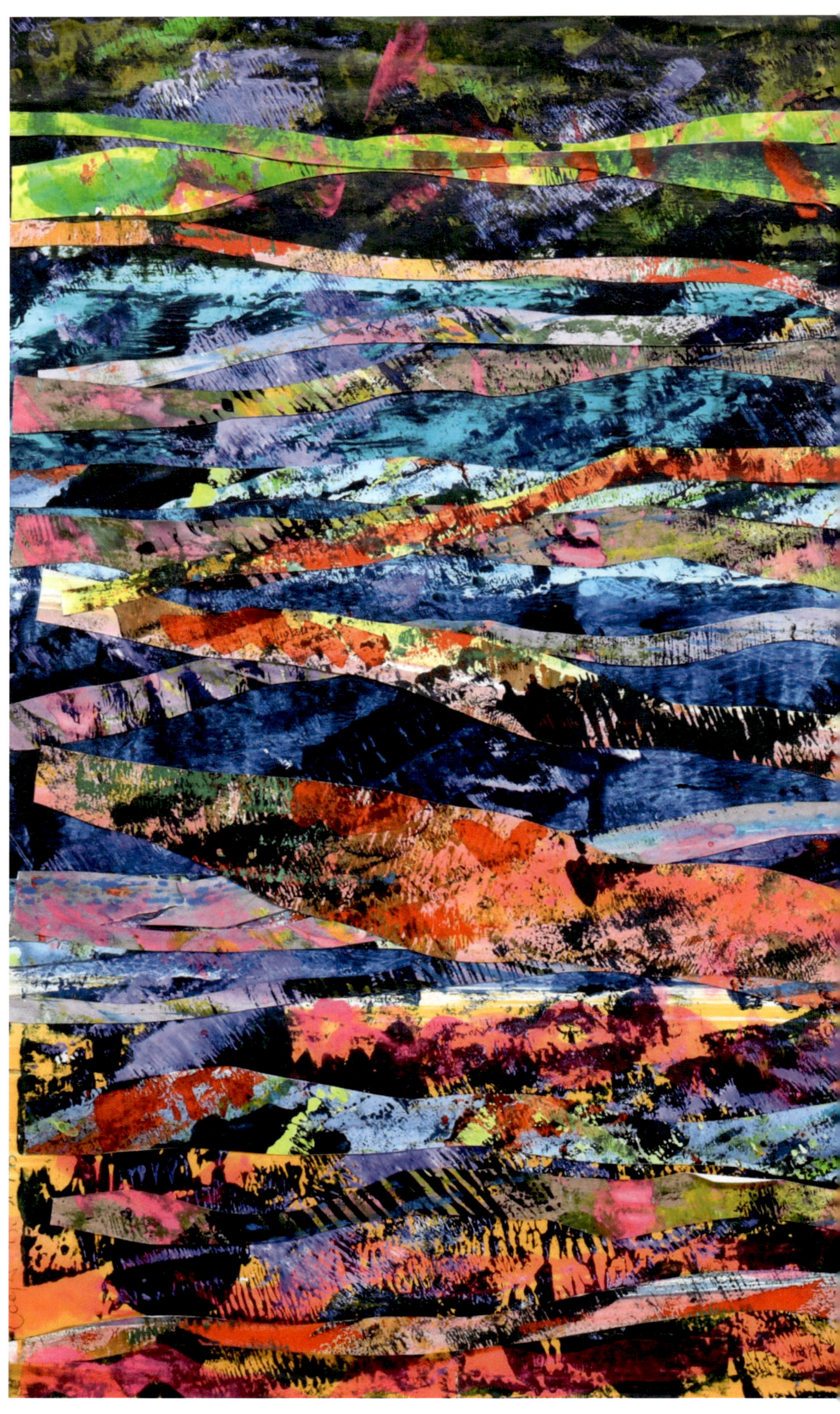

Ribbon Cloud, 1993

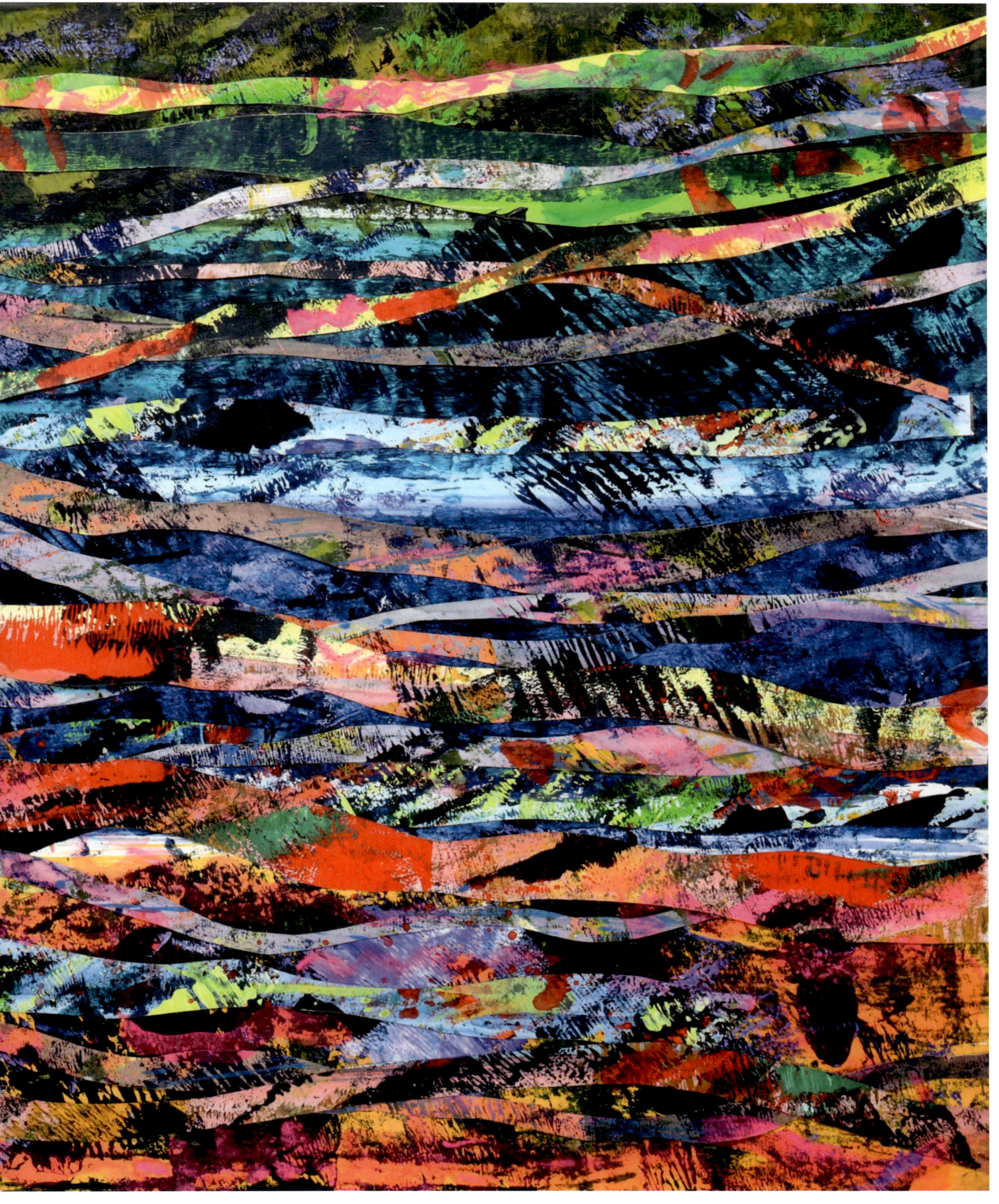

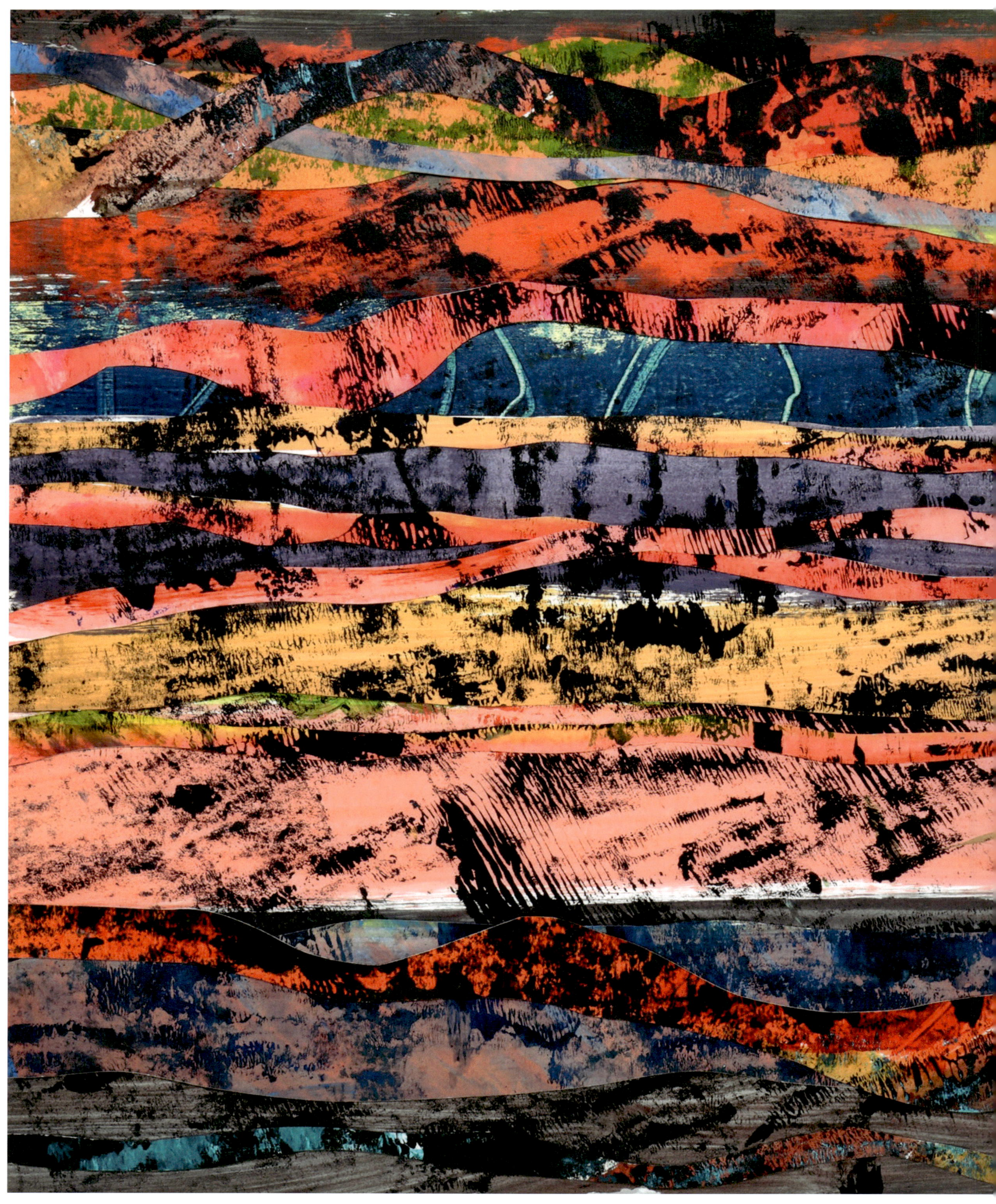

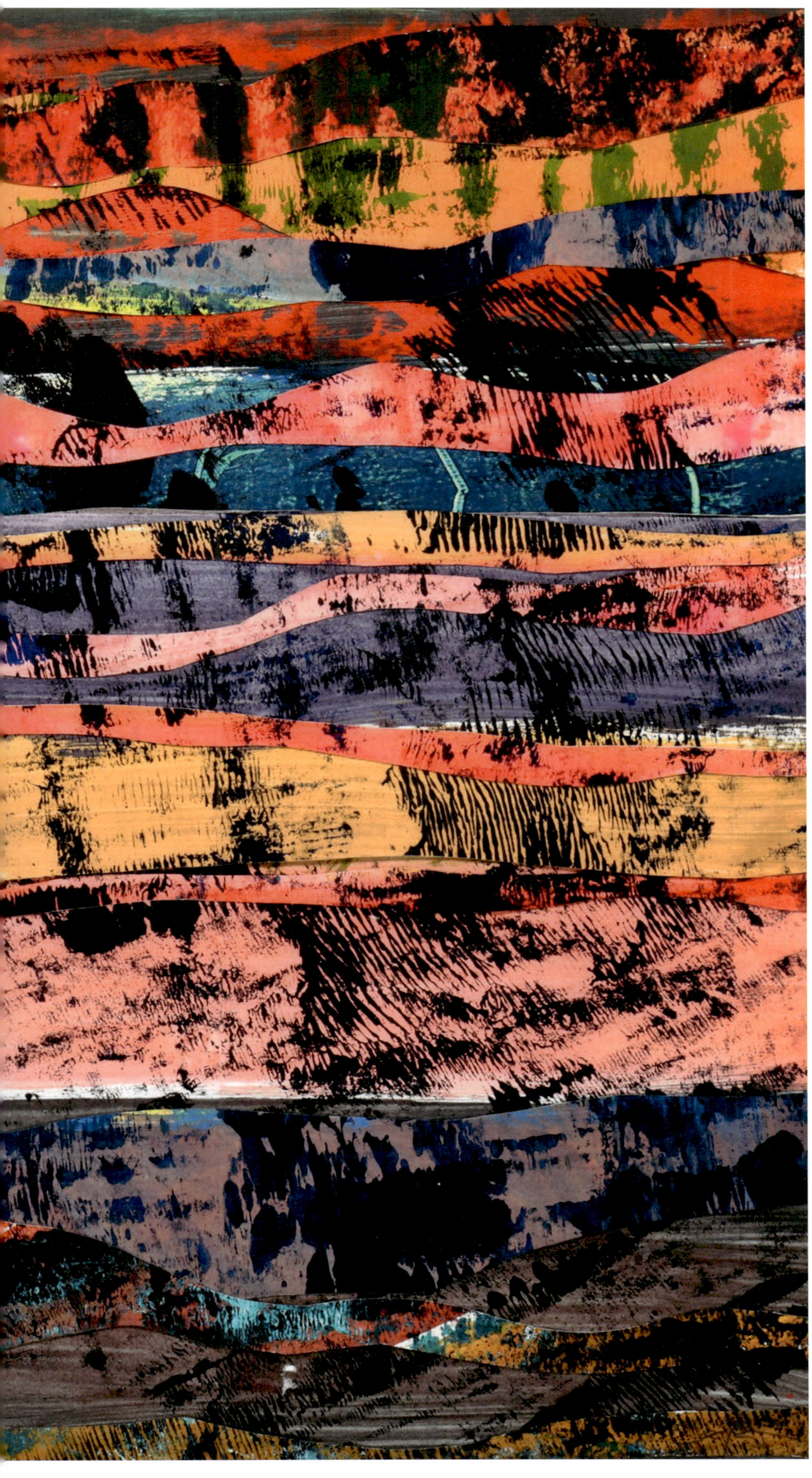

Refracted Red, 1995

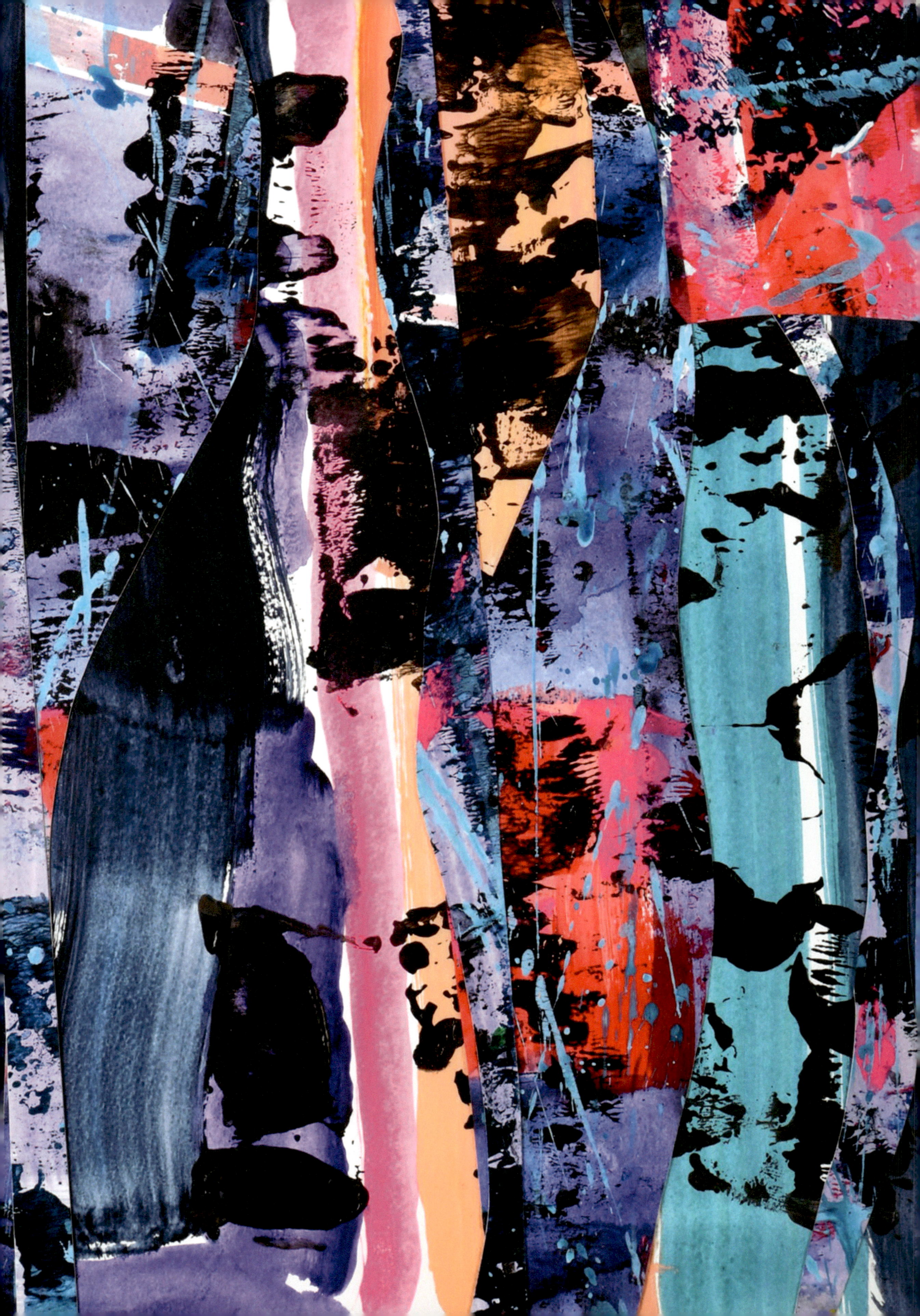

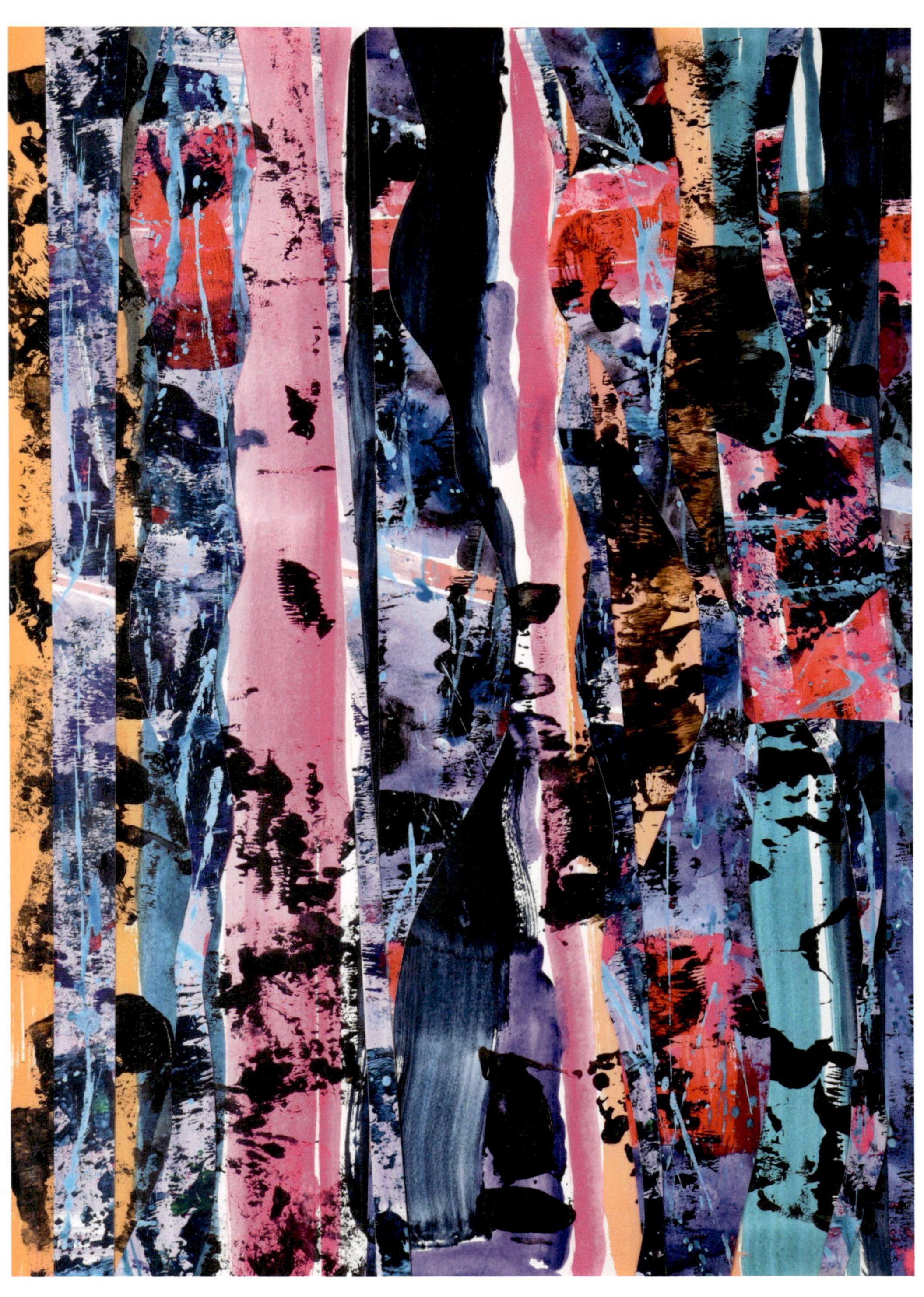

After the Rain, 1995

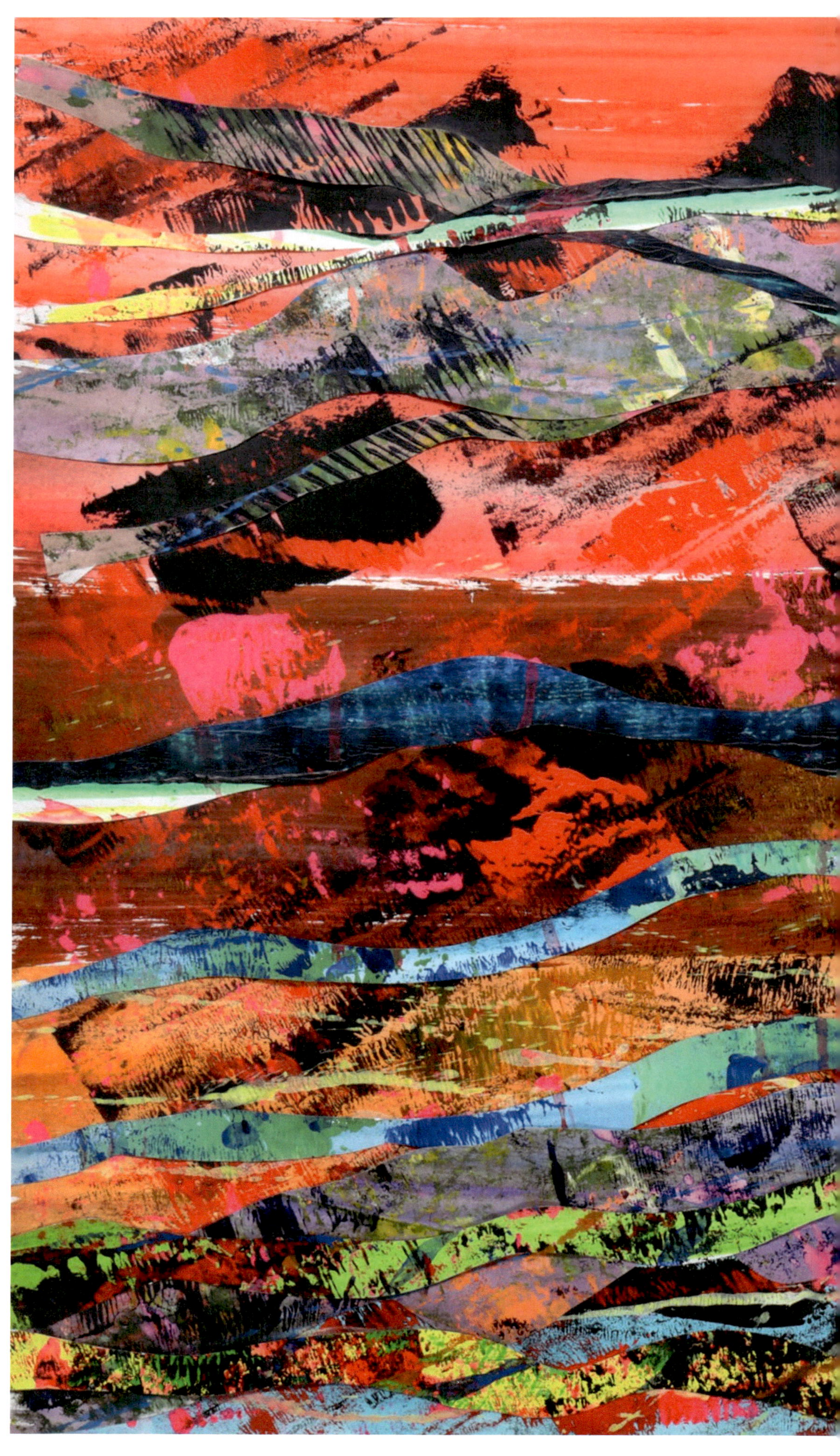

First Light, 1994

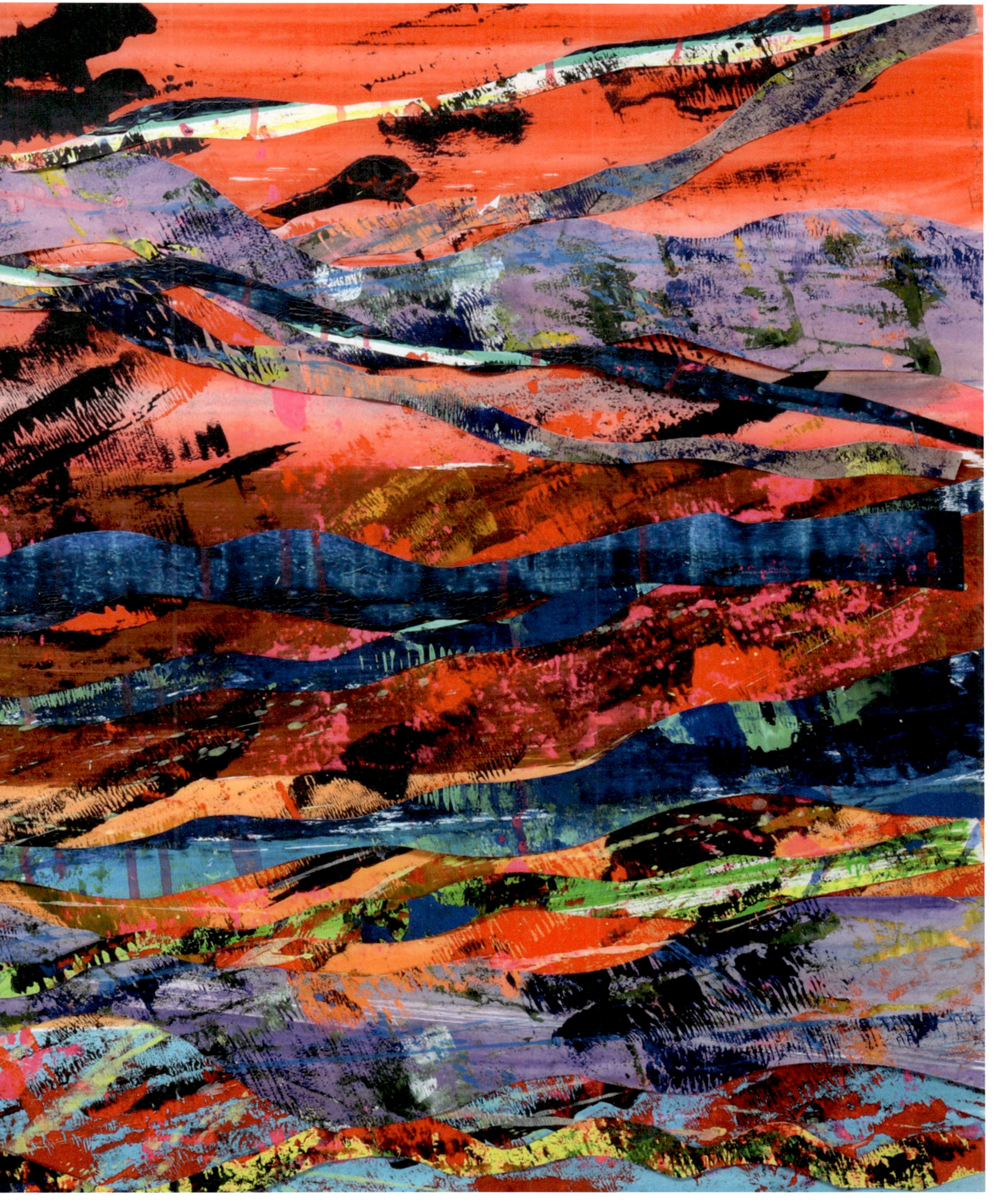

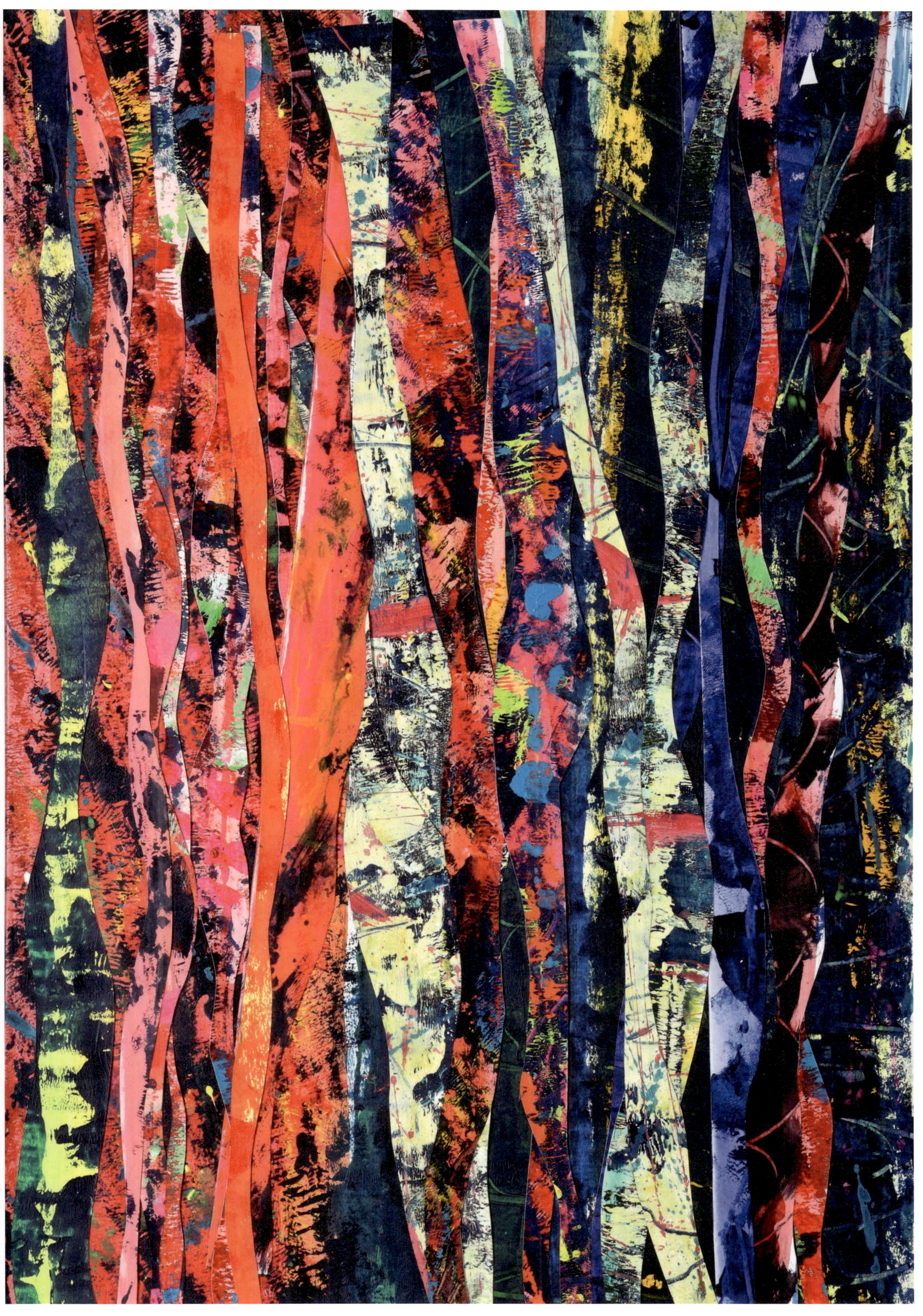

Night

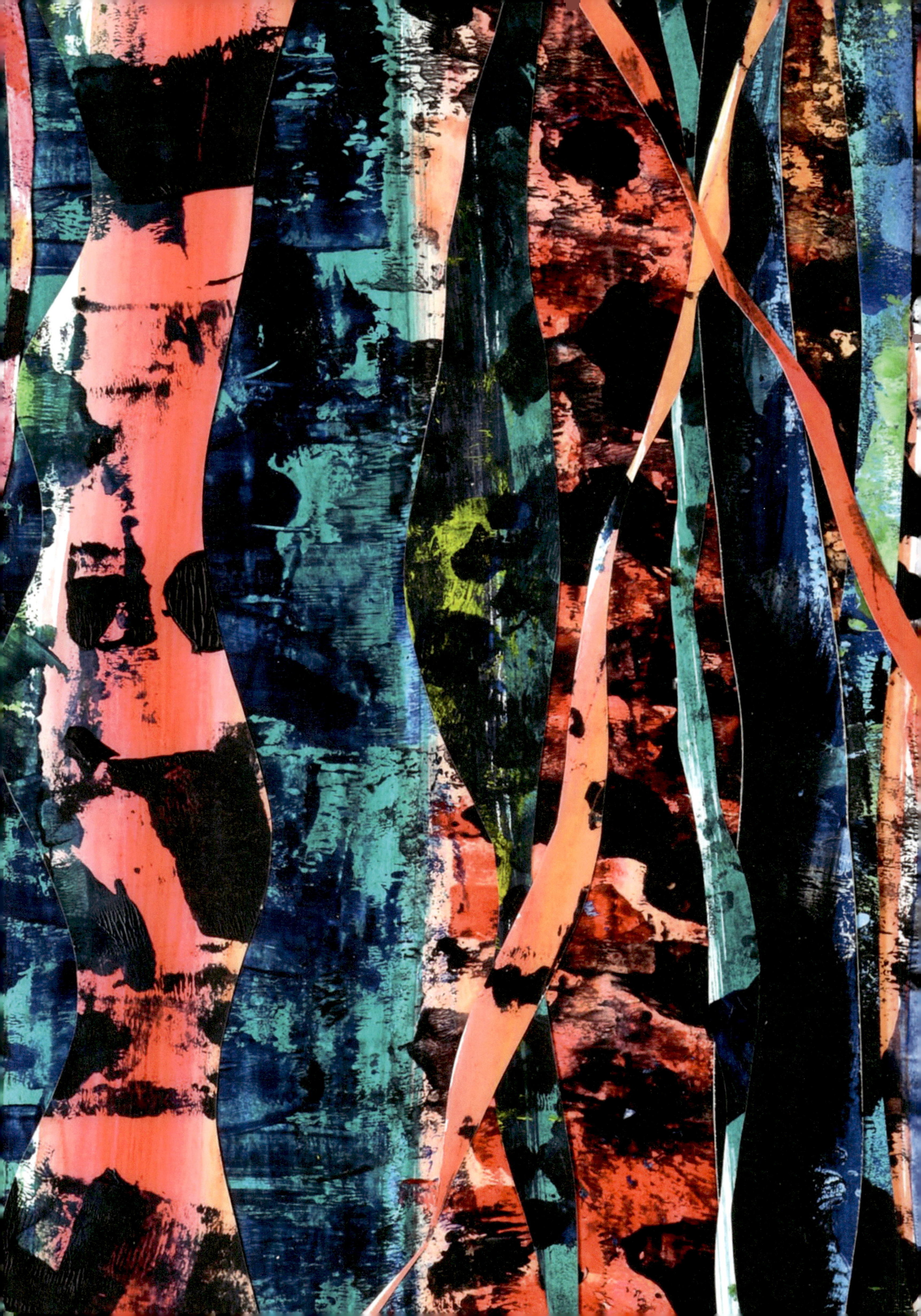

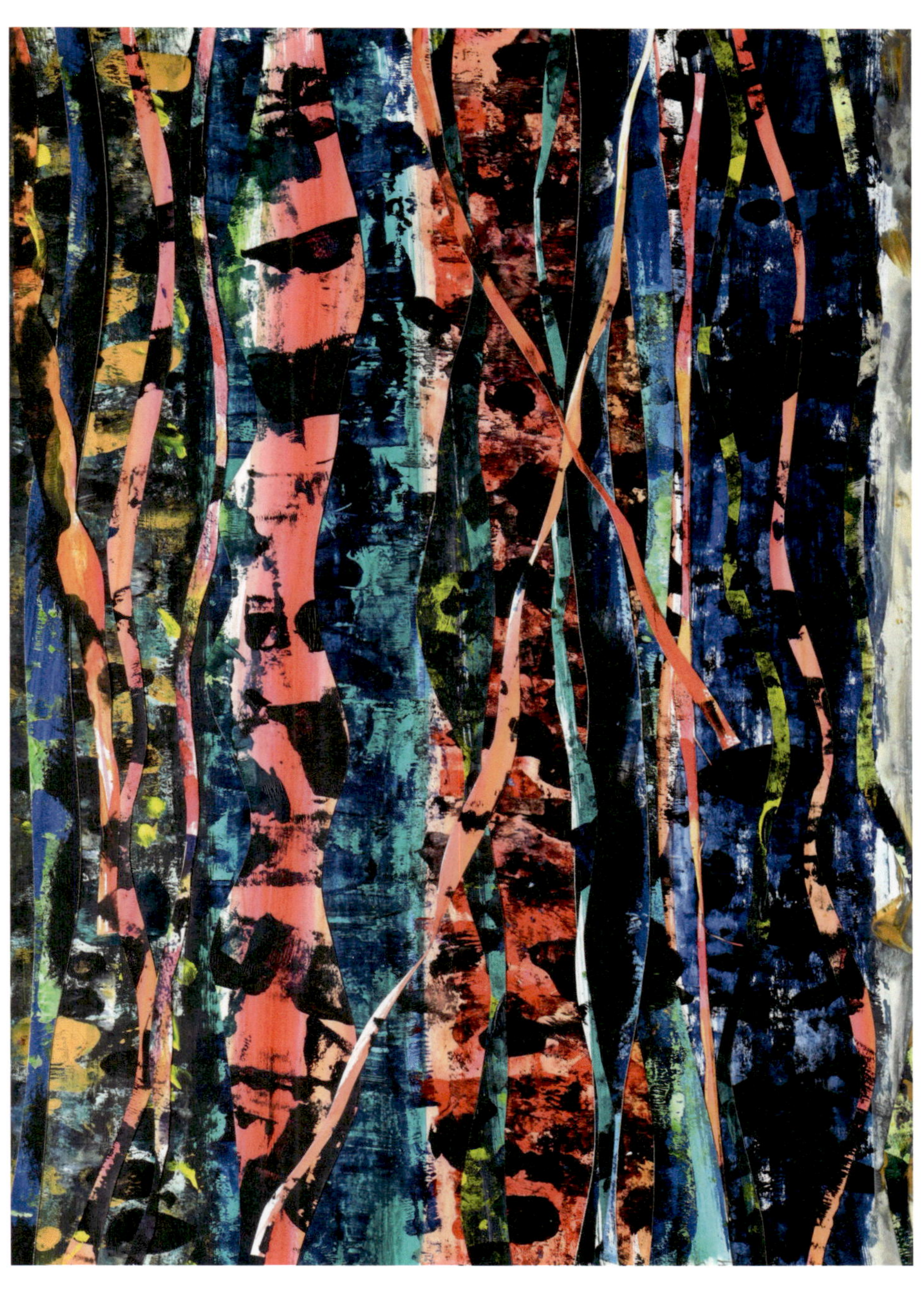

Lowering Sun Through Trees, 1996

The Long Night, 1994

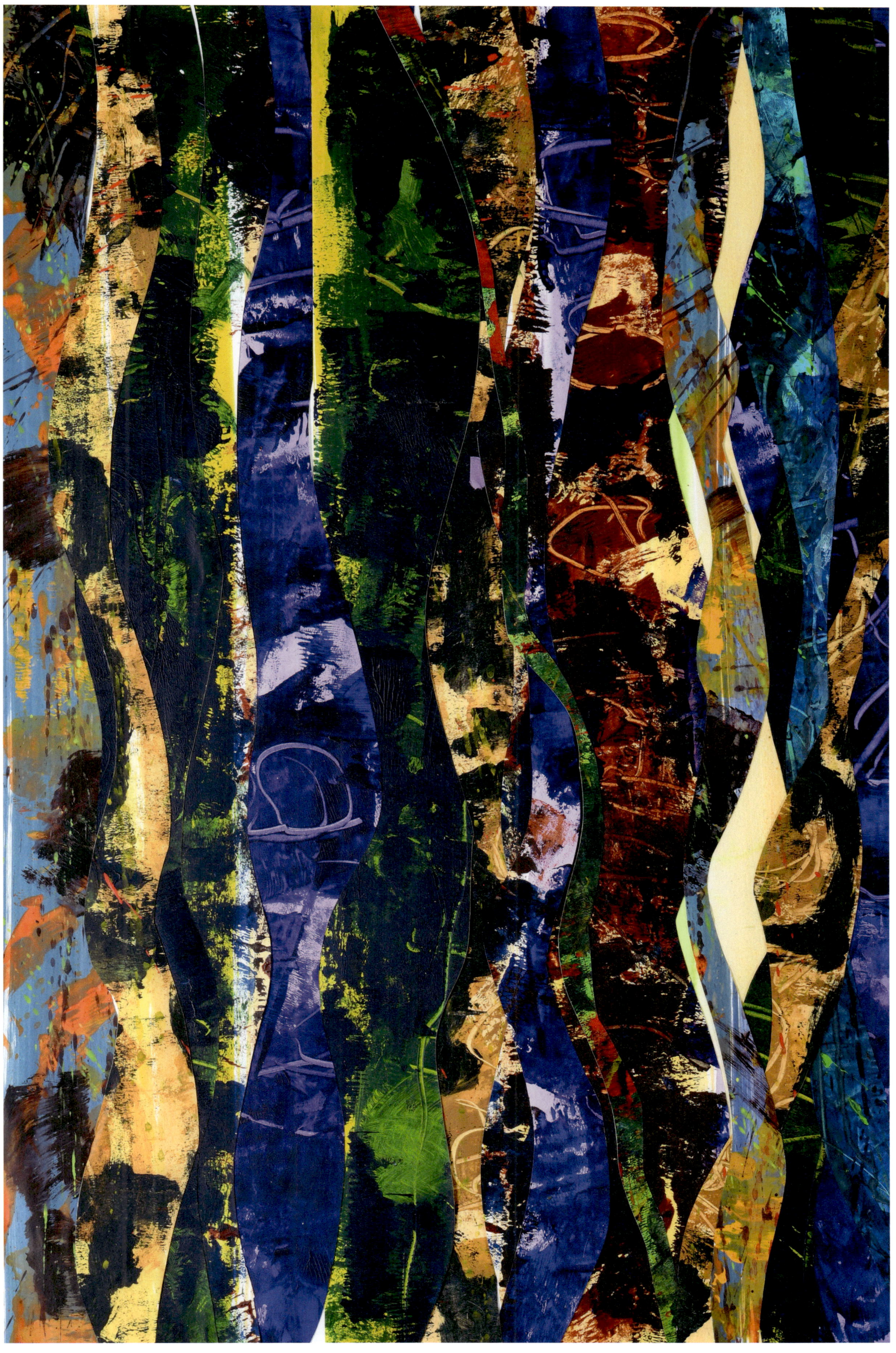

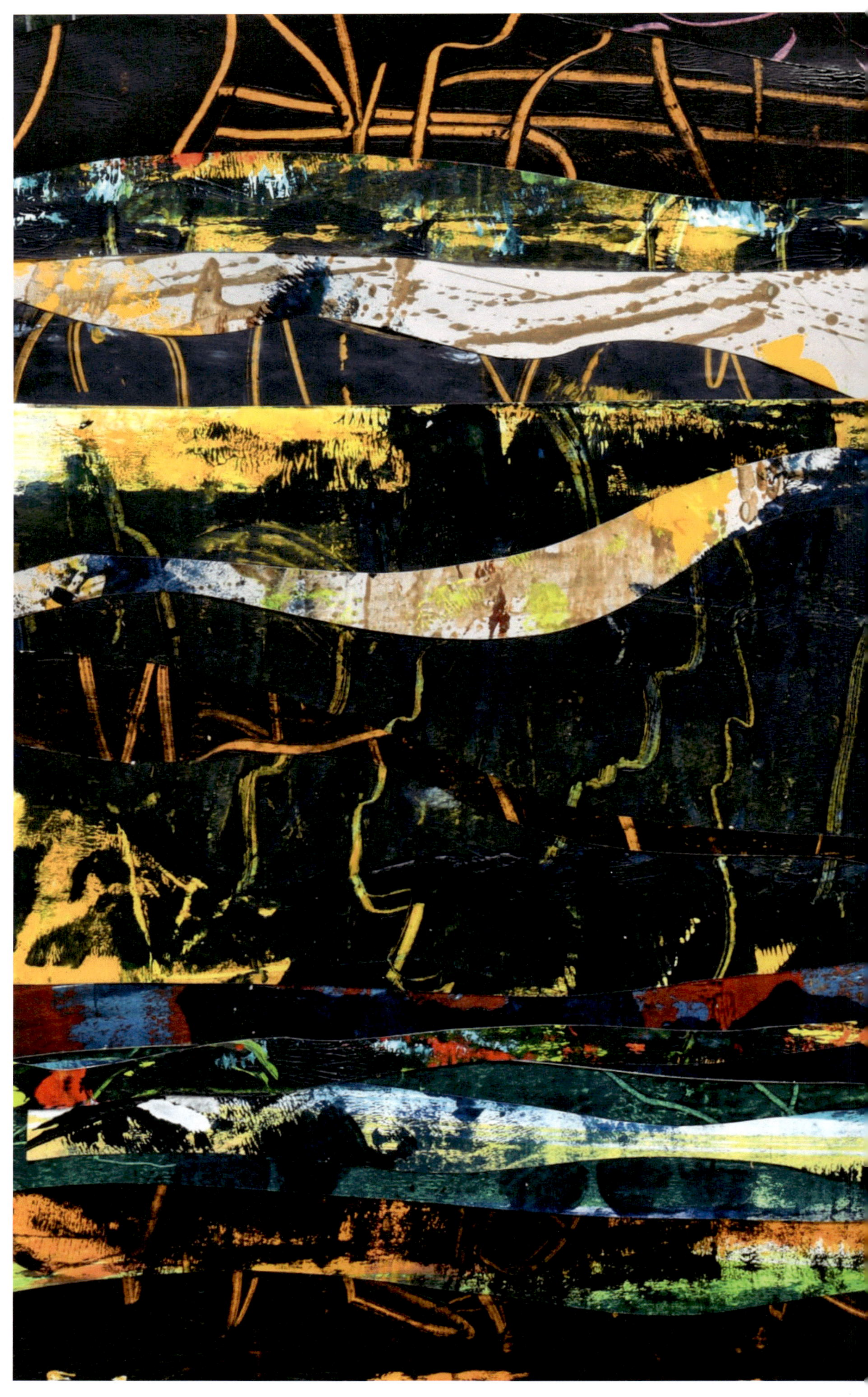

Storm Sky, 1995

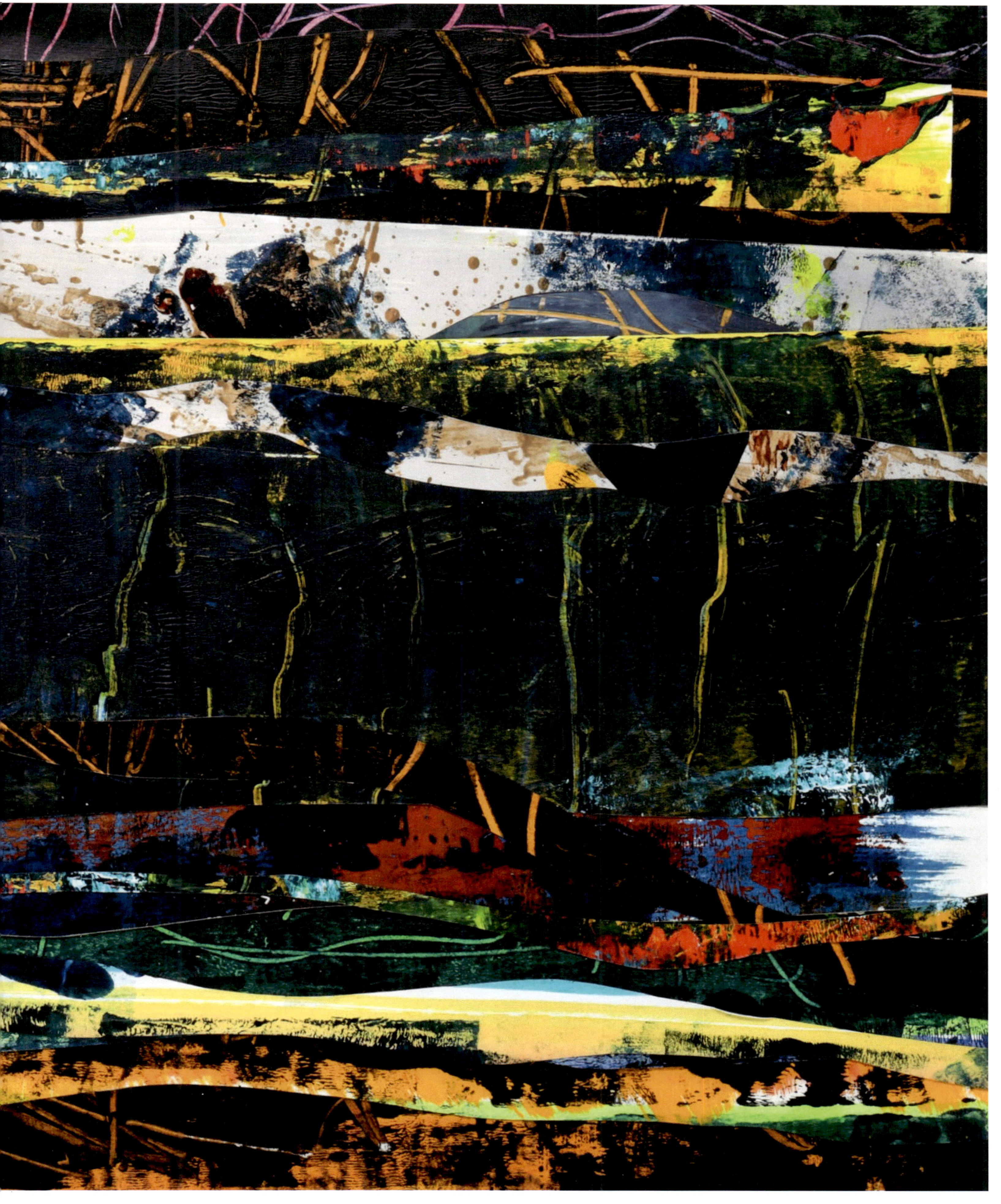

Bonfire Night, 1992

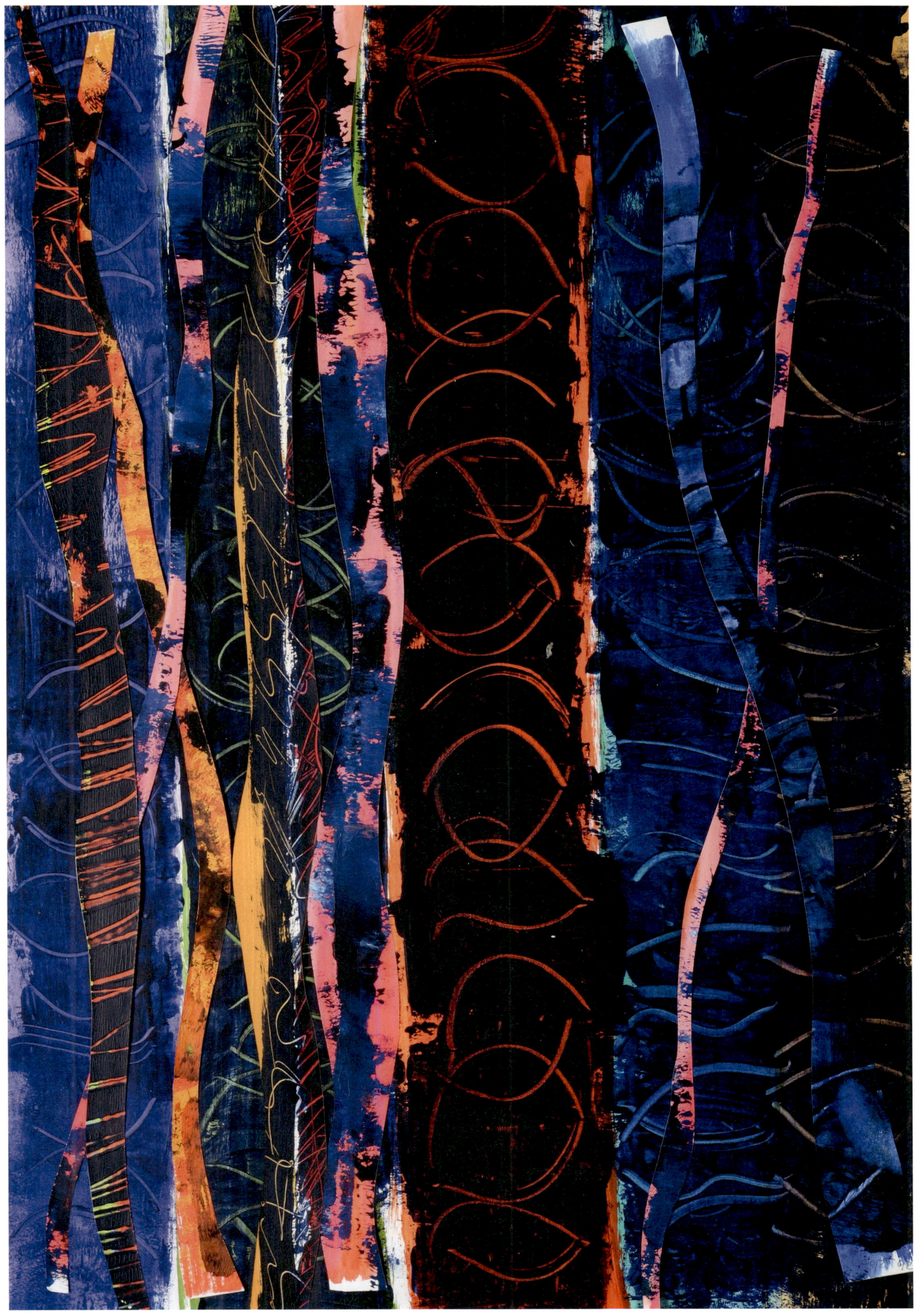

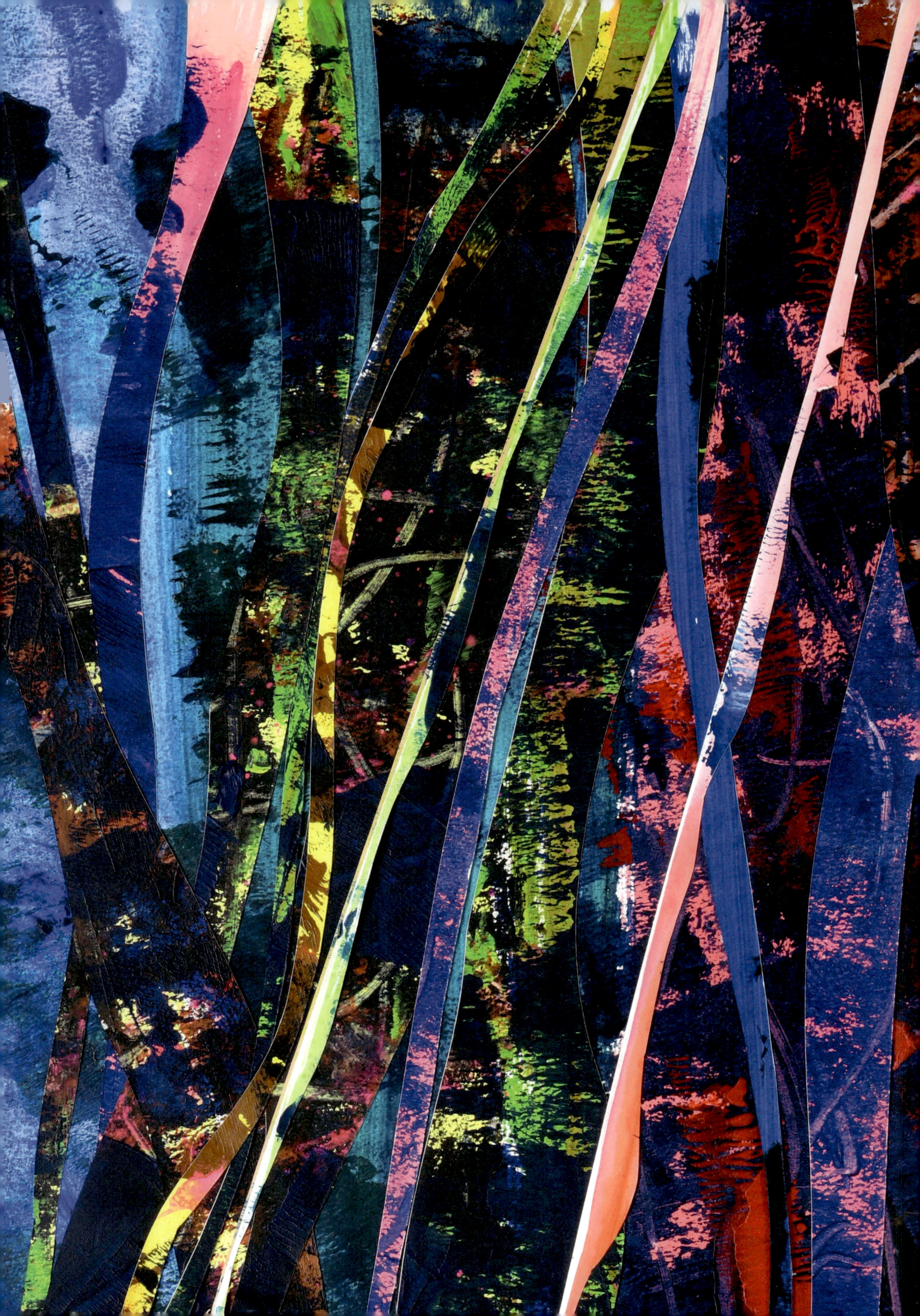

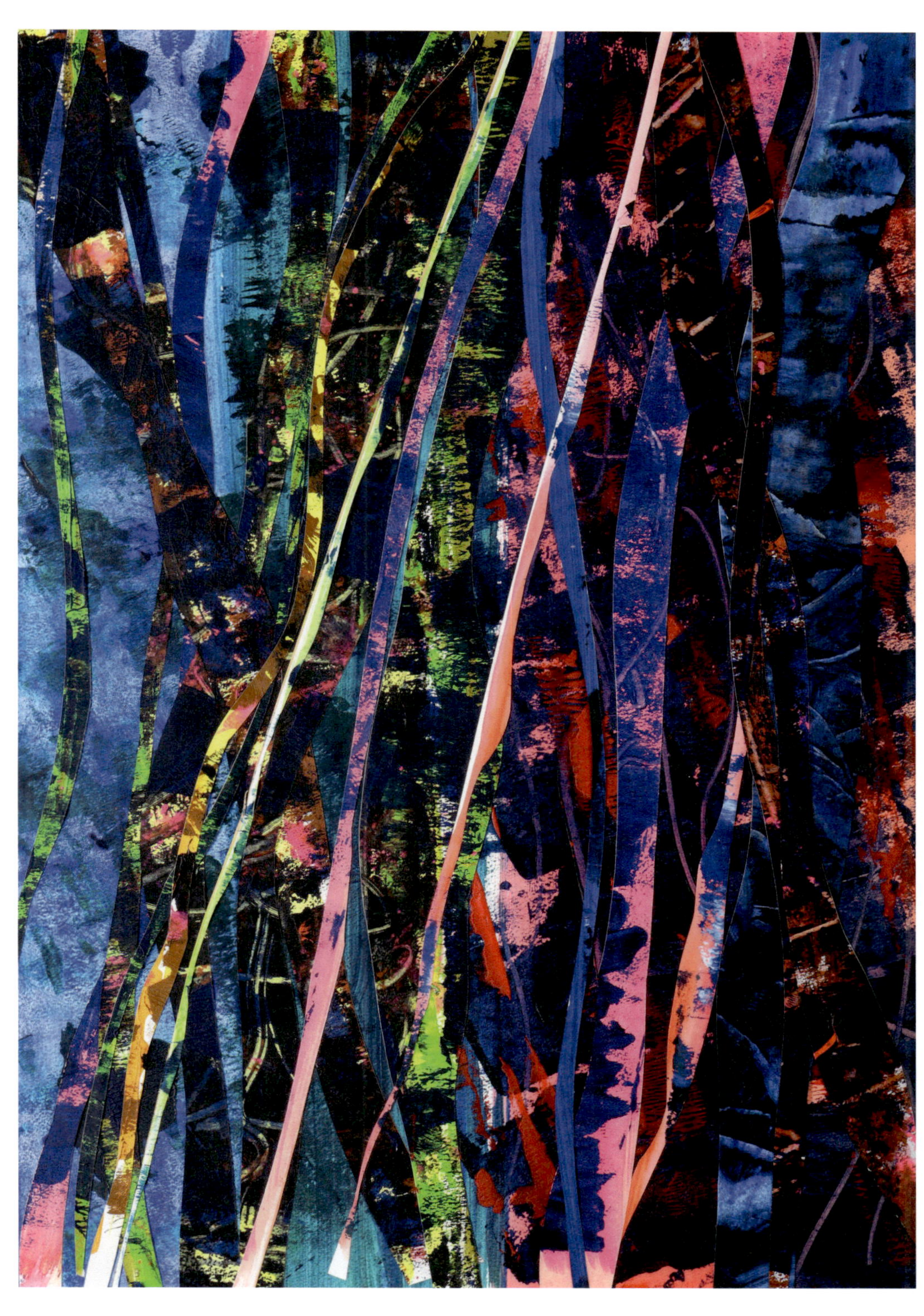

The Clearing, 1992

Bird Song, 1996

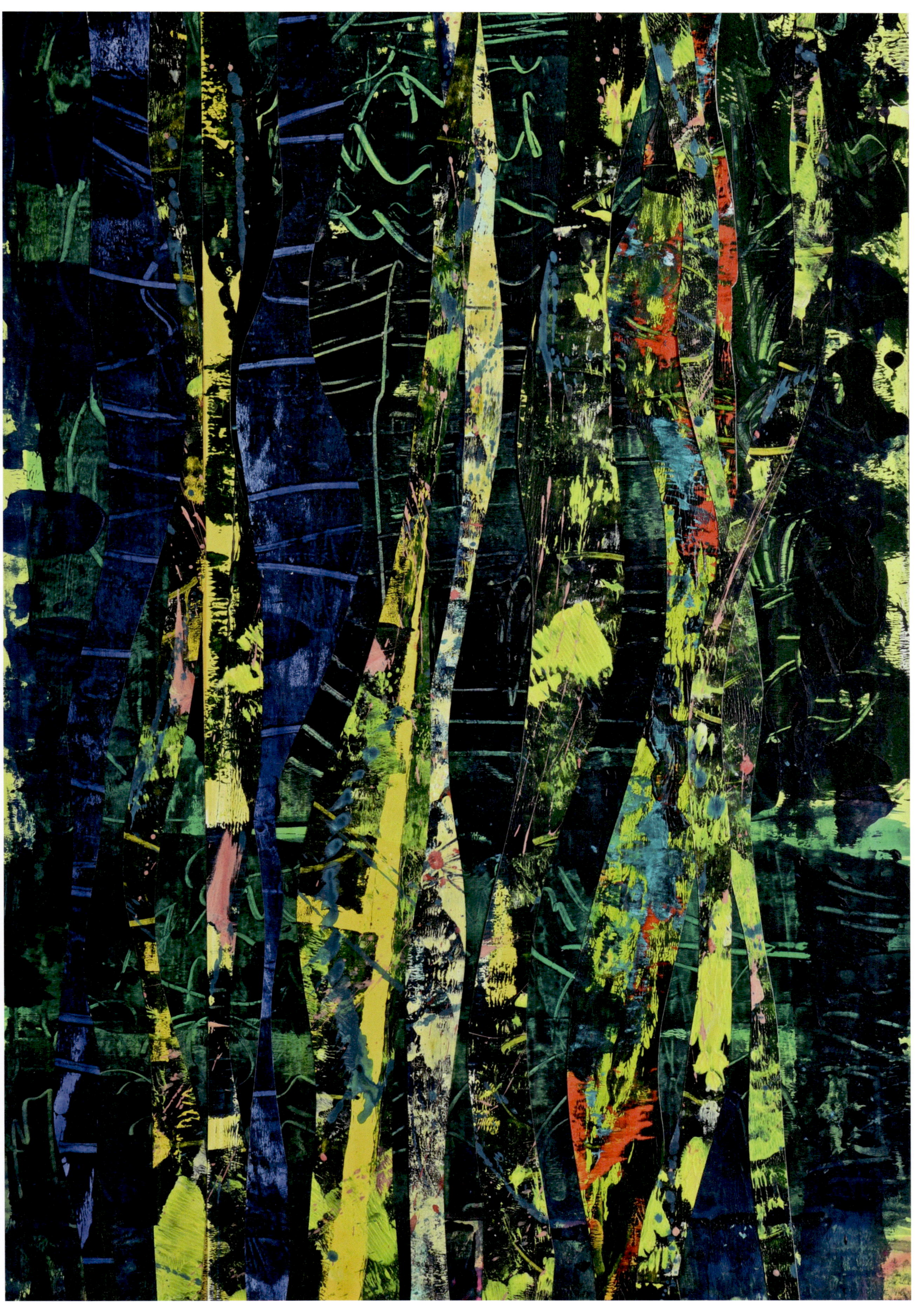

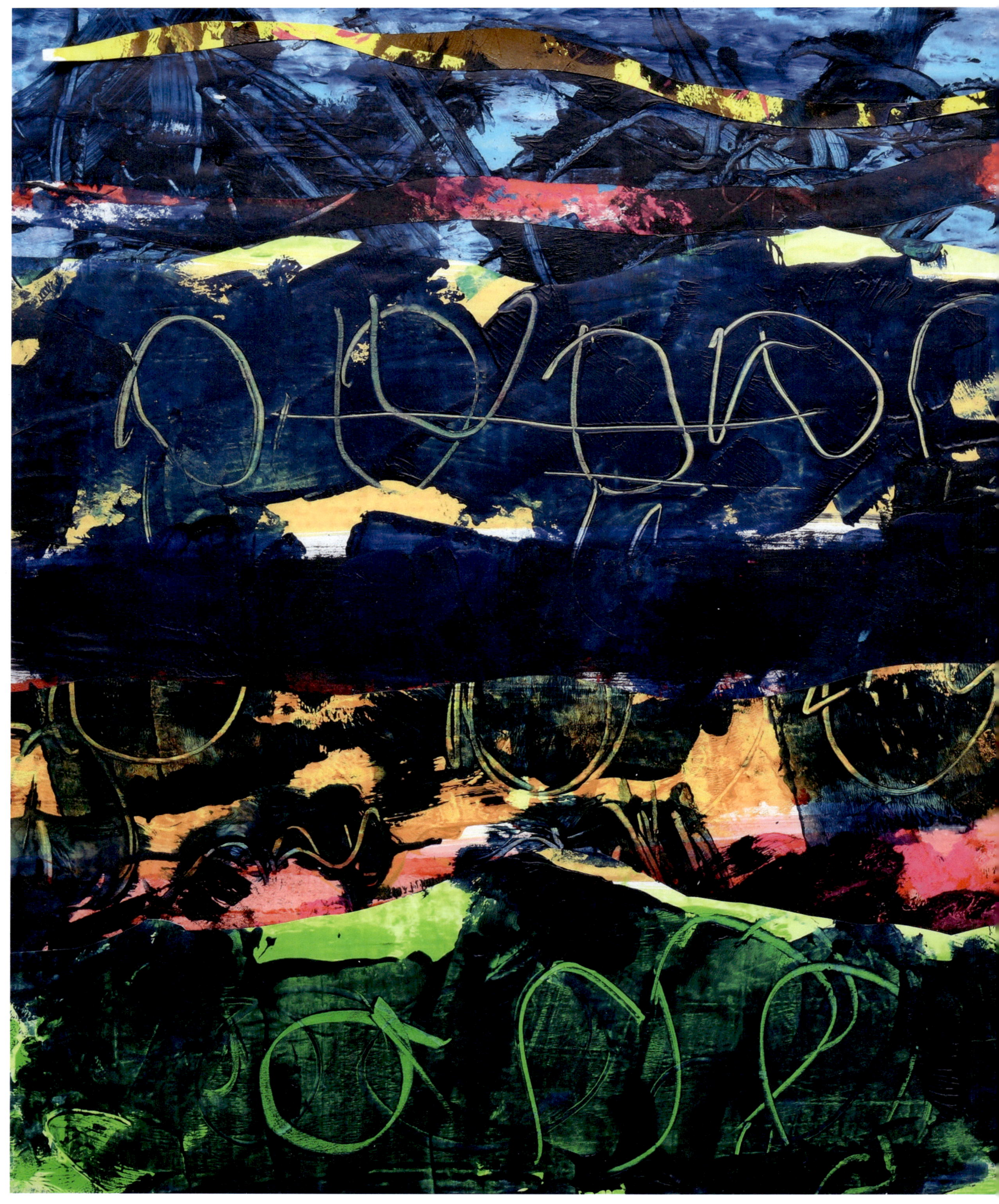

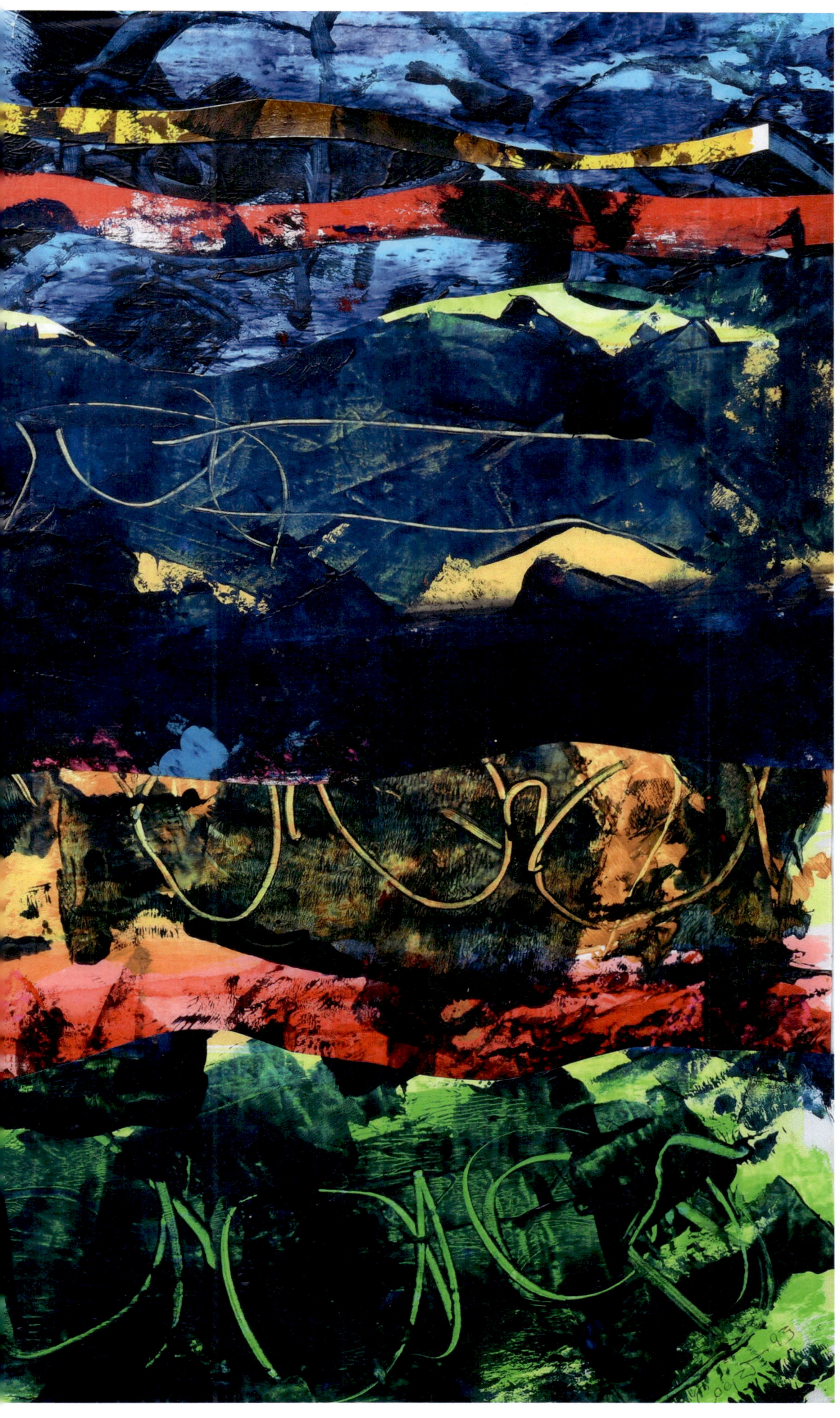

Thunder Sunset, 1993

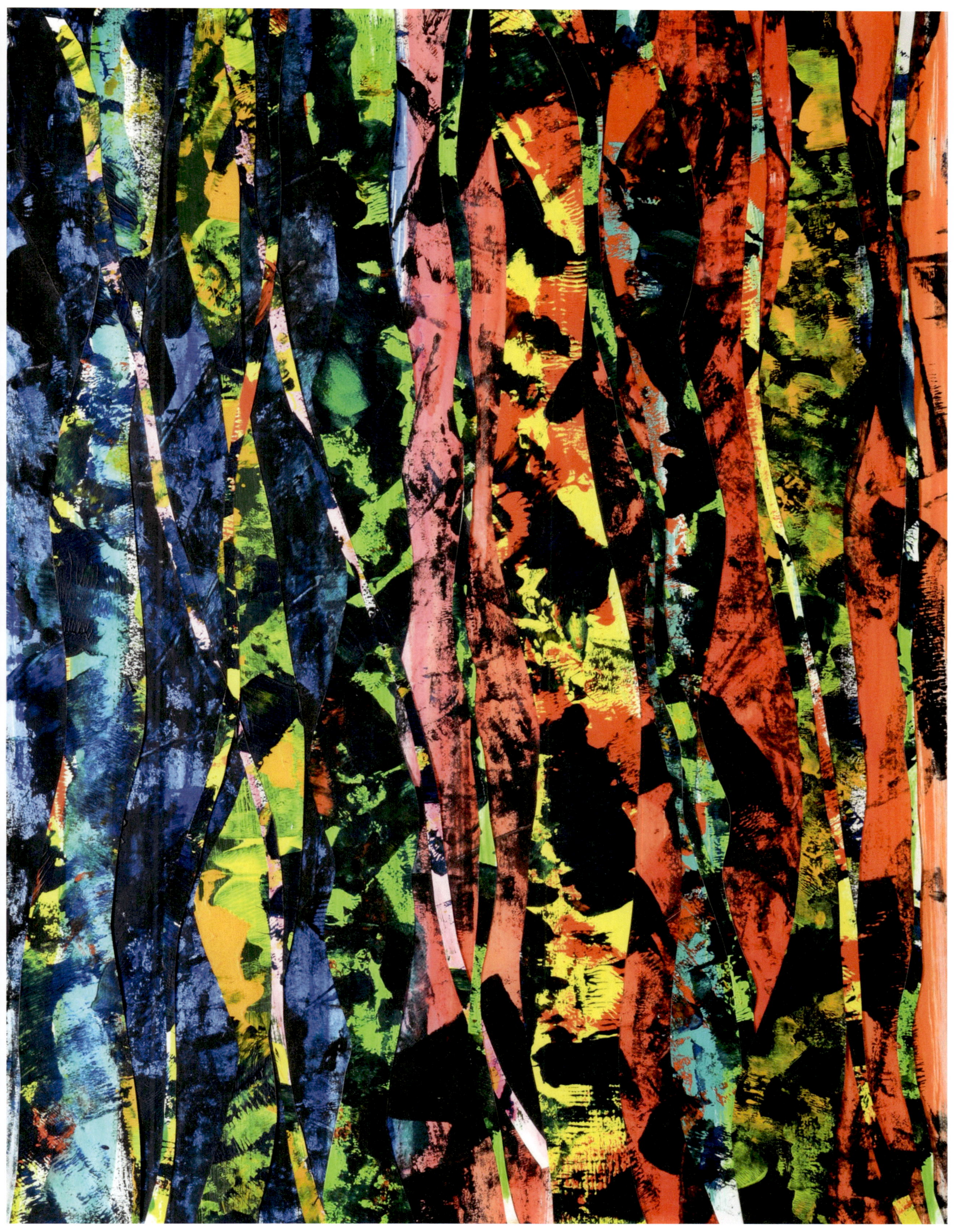

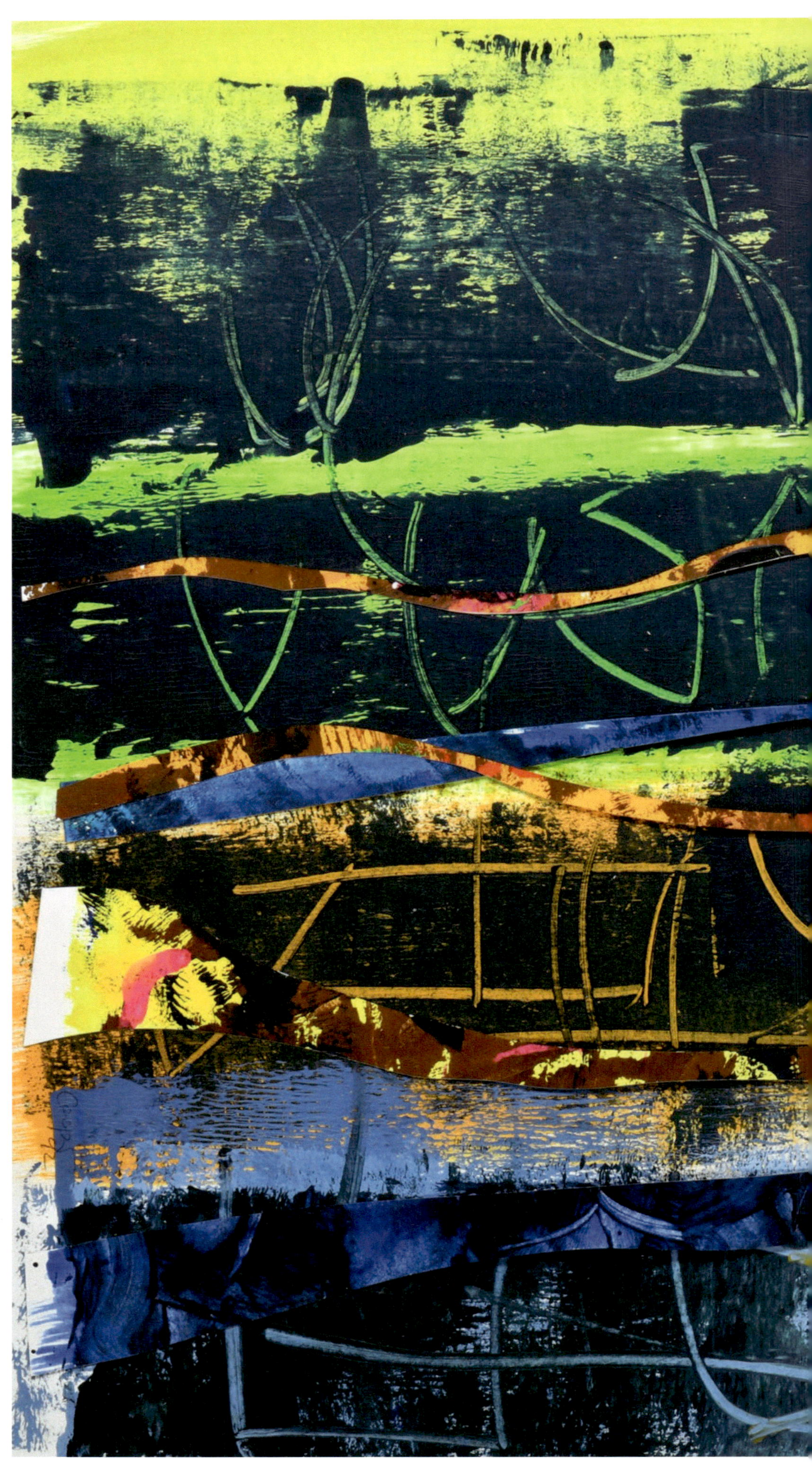

The Lane, 1992

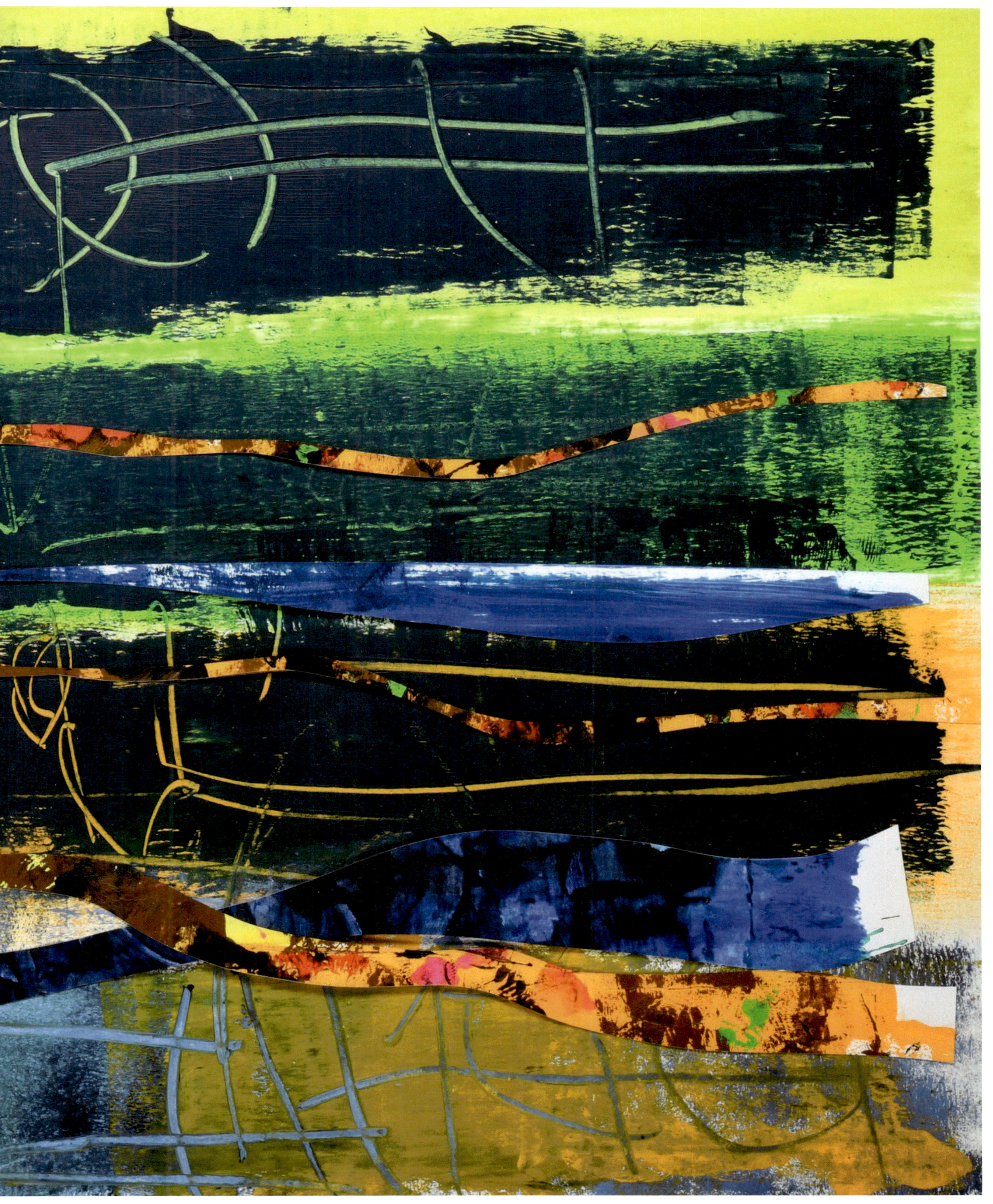

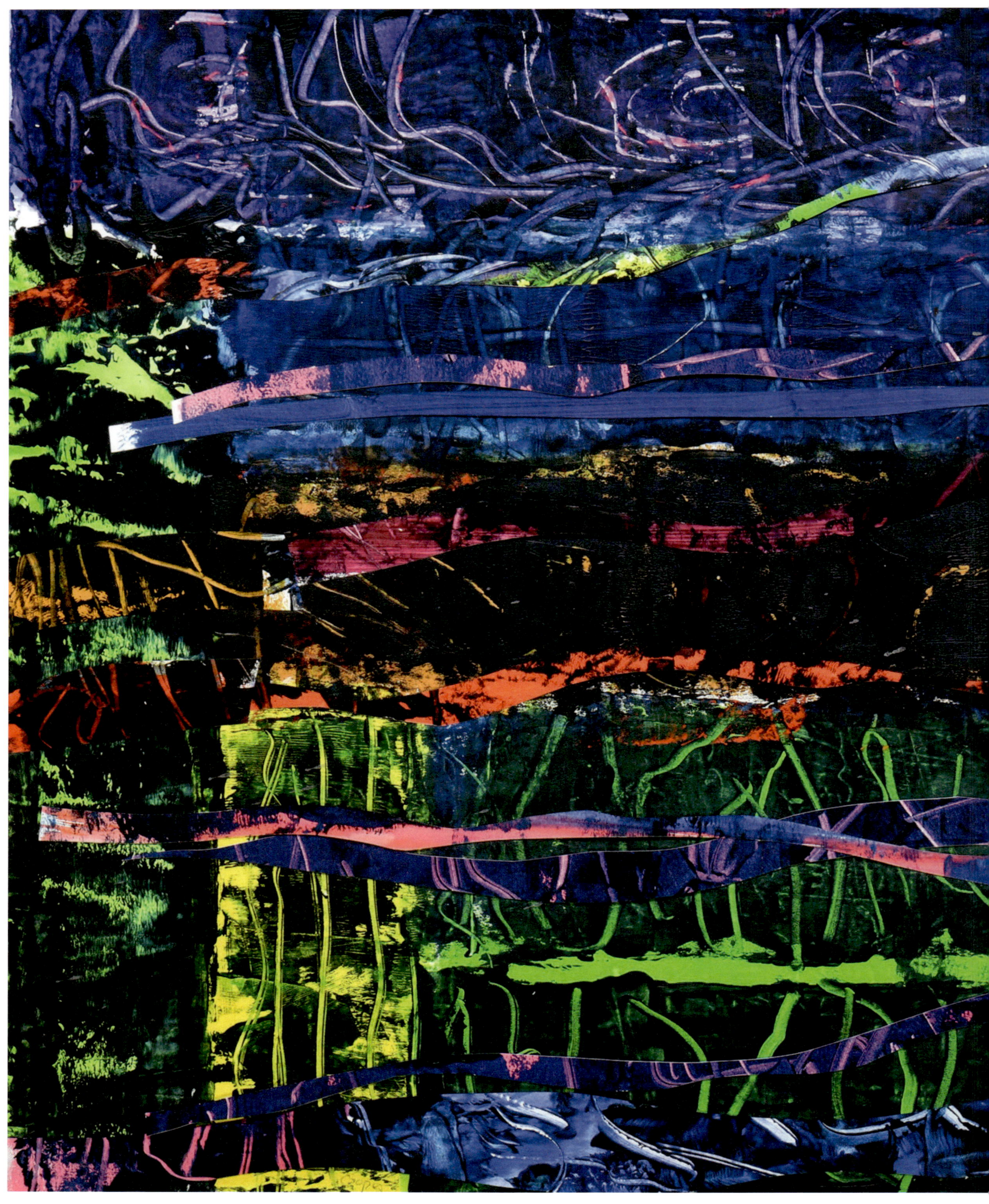

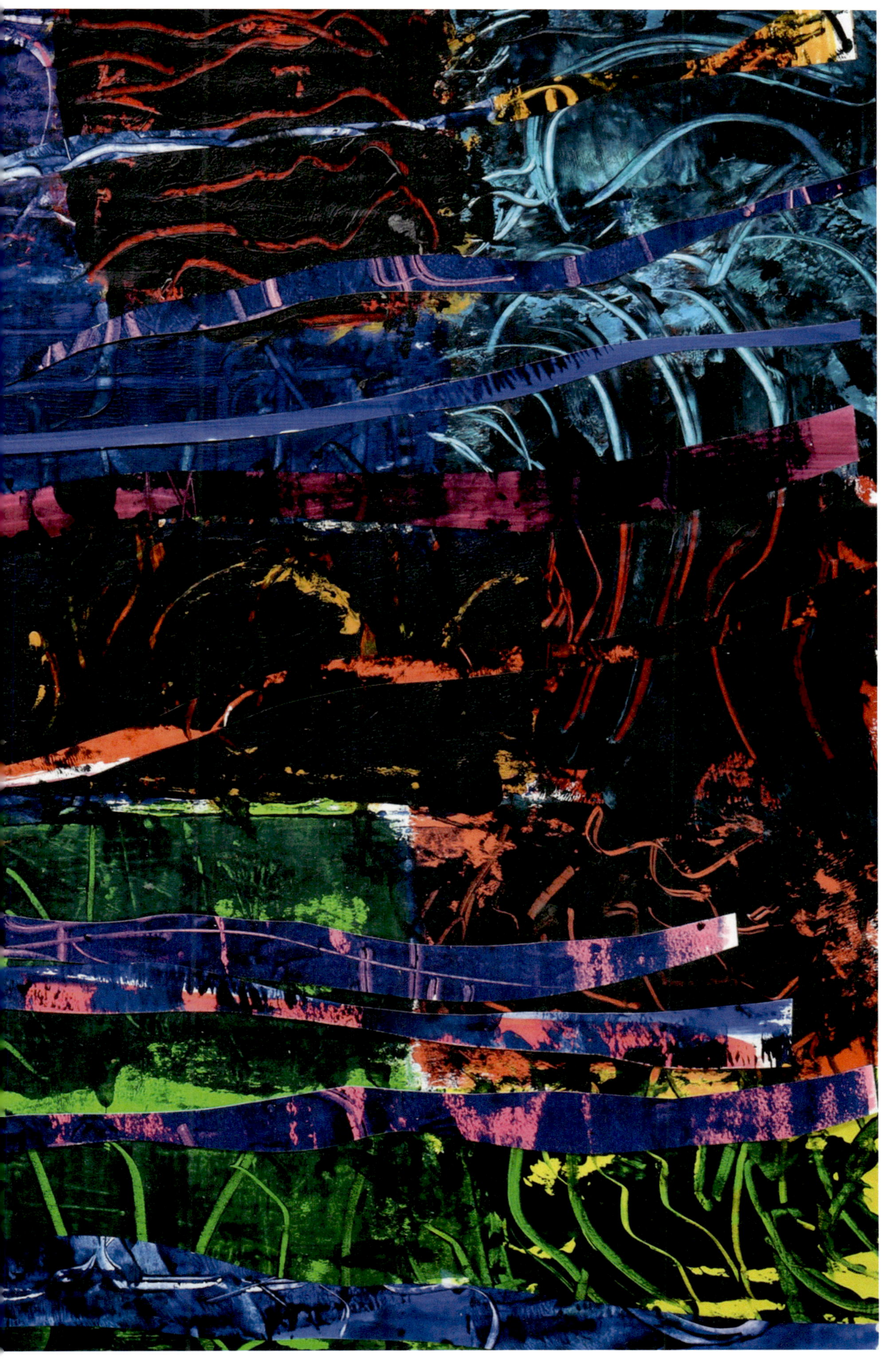

Pond at Dusk, 1992

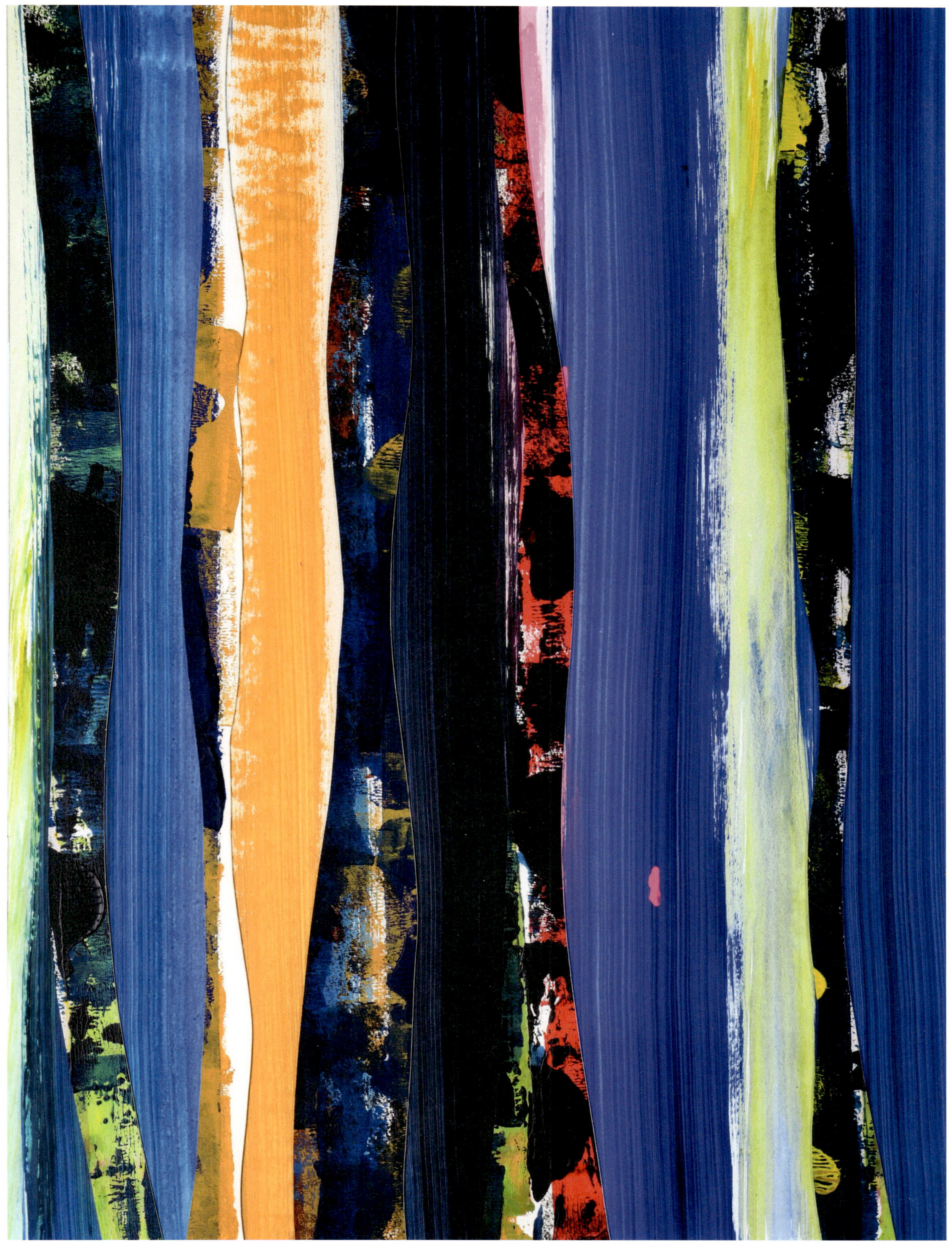

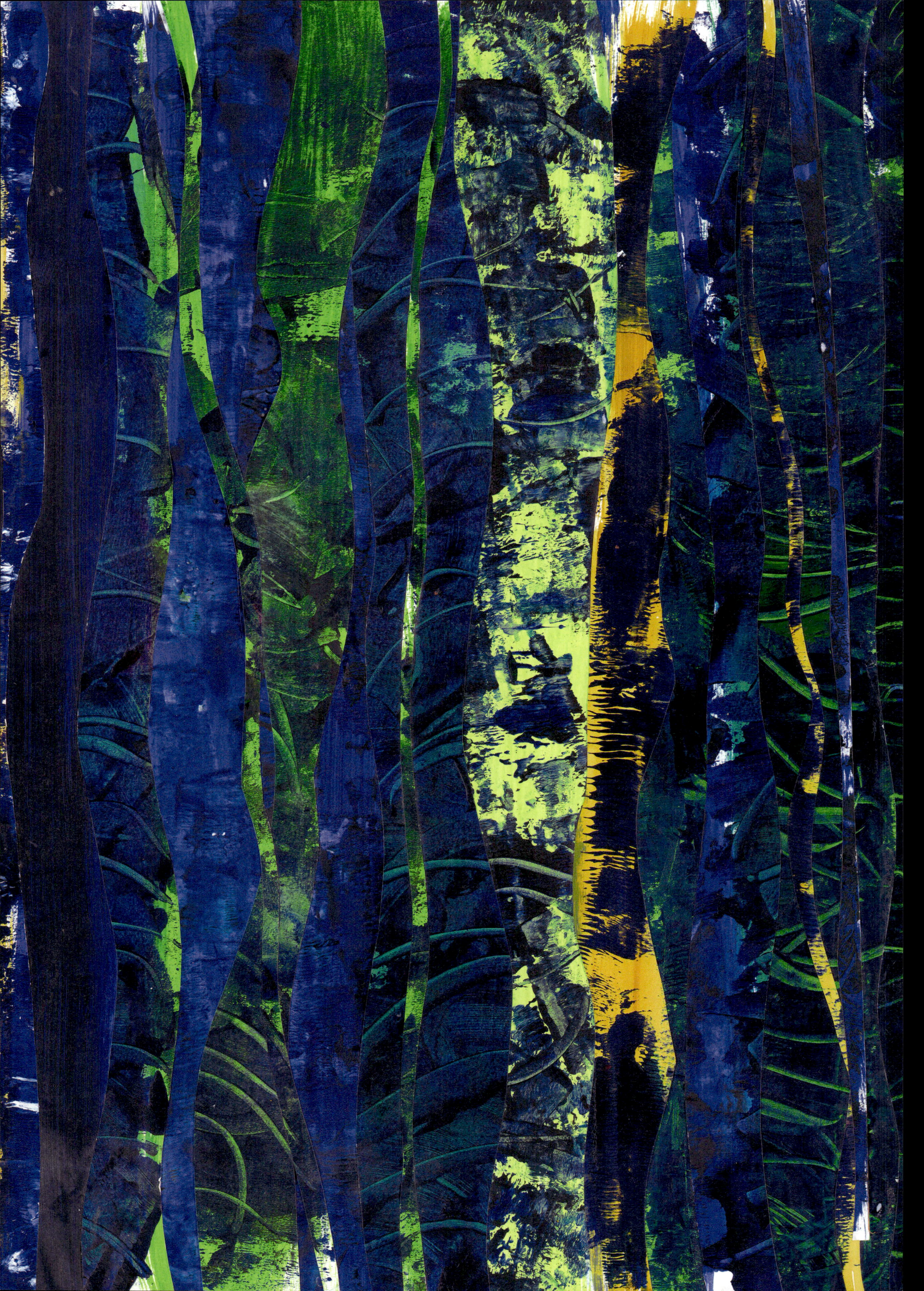

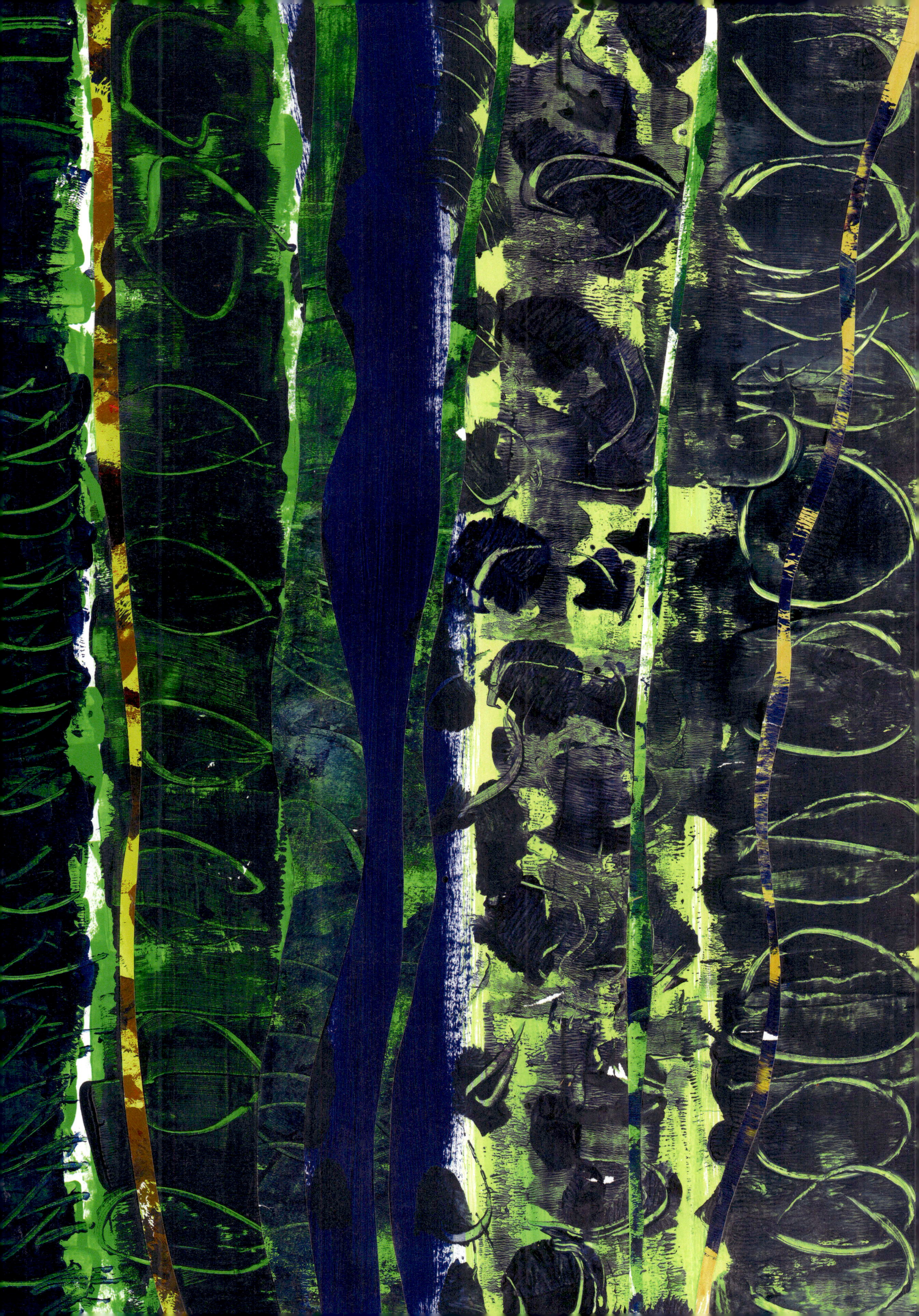

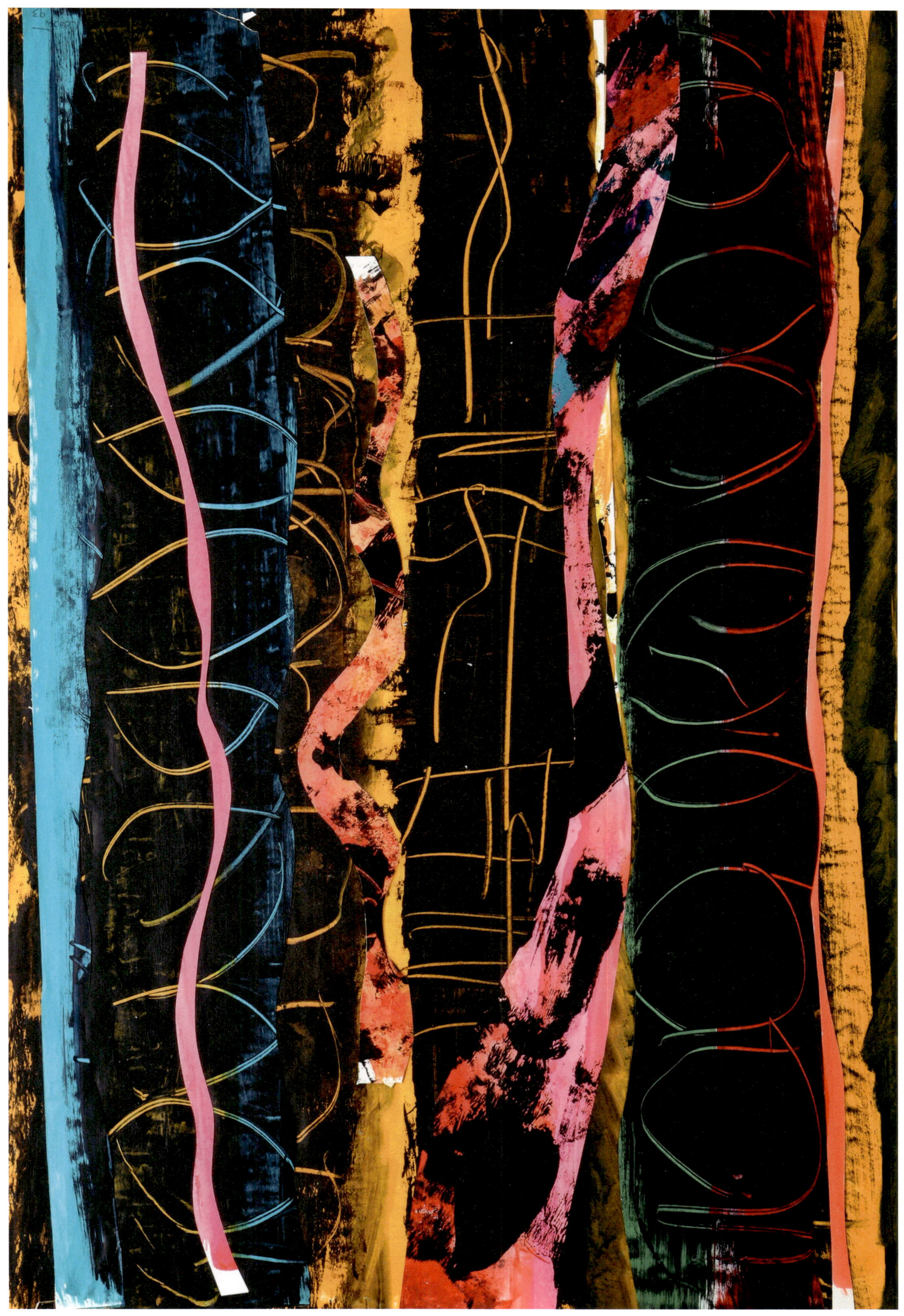

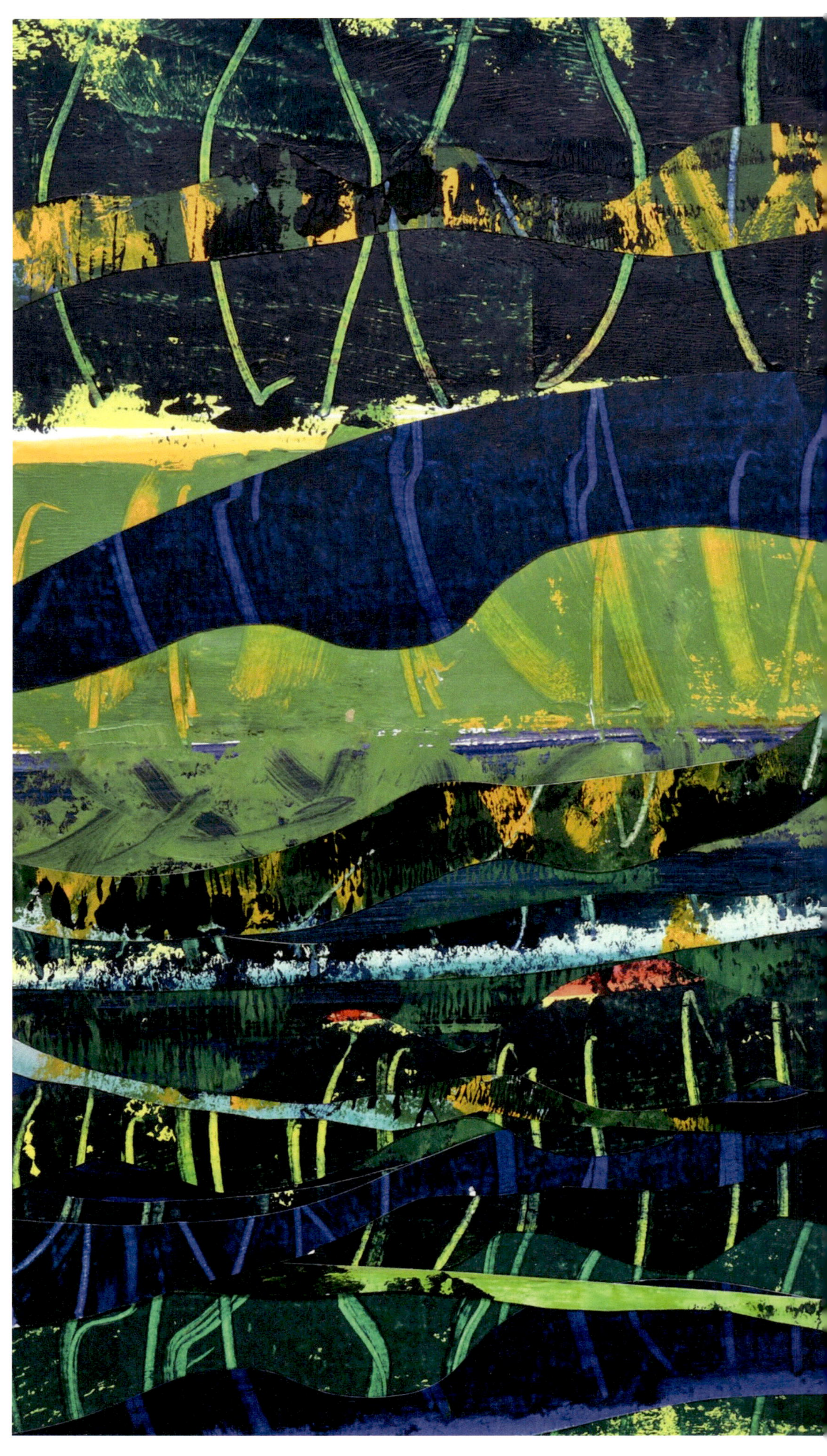

First Cut, 1995

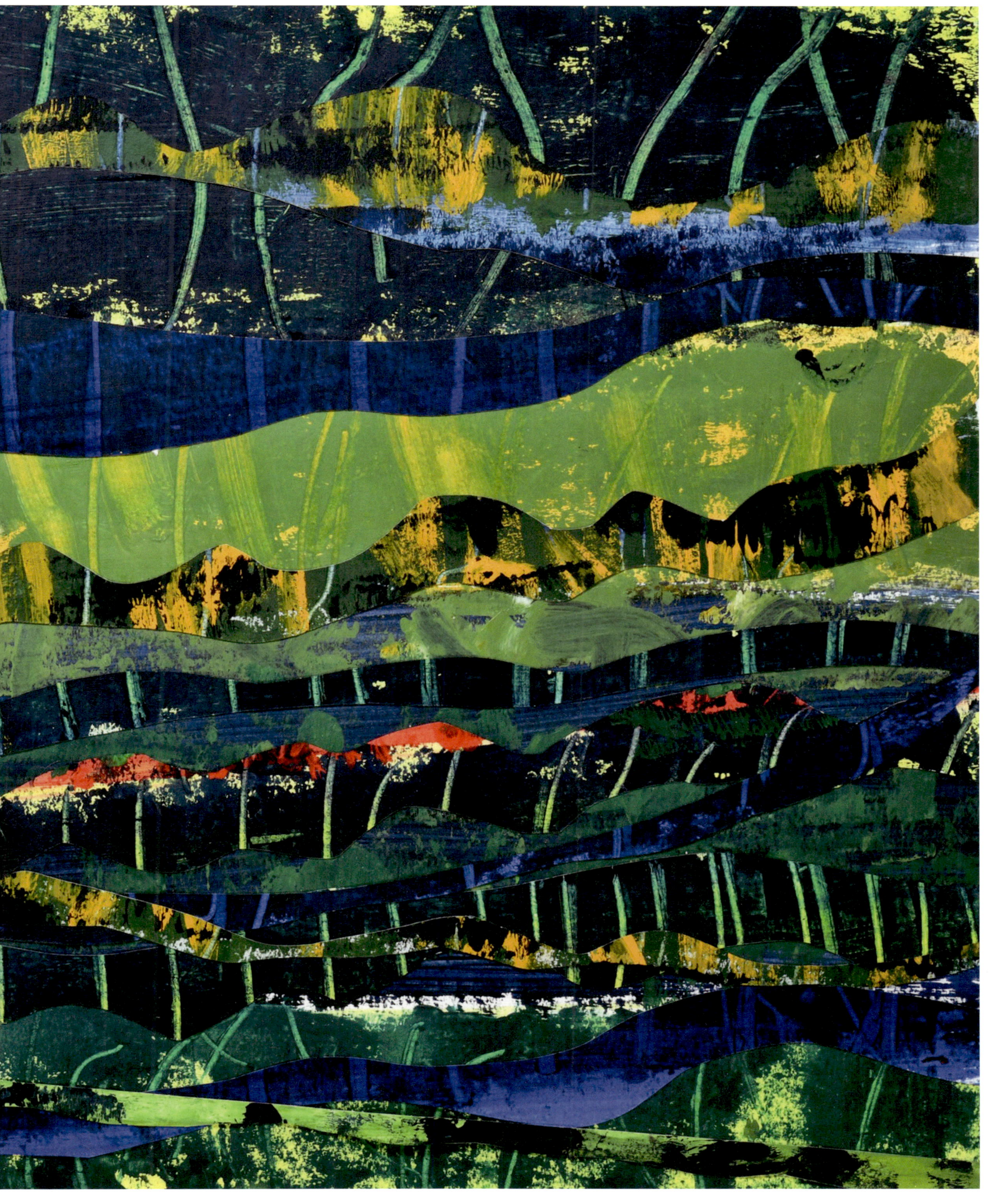

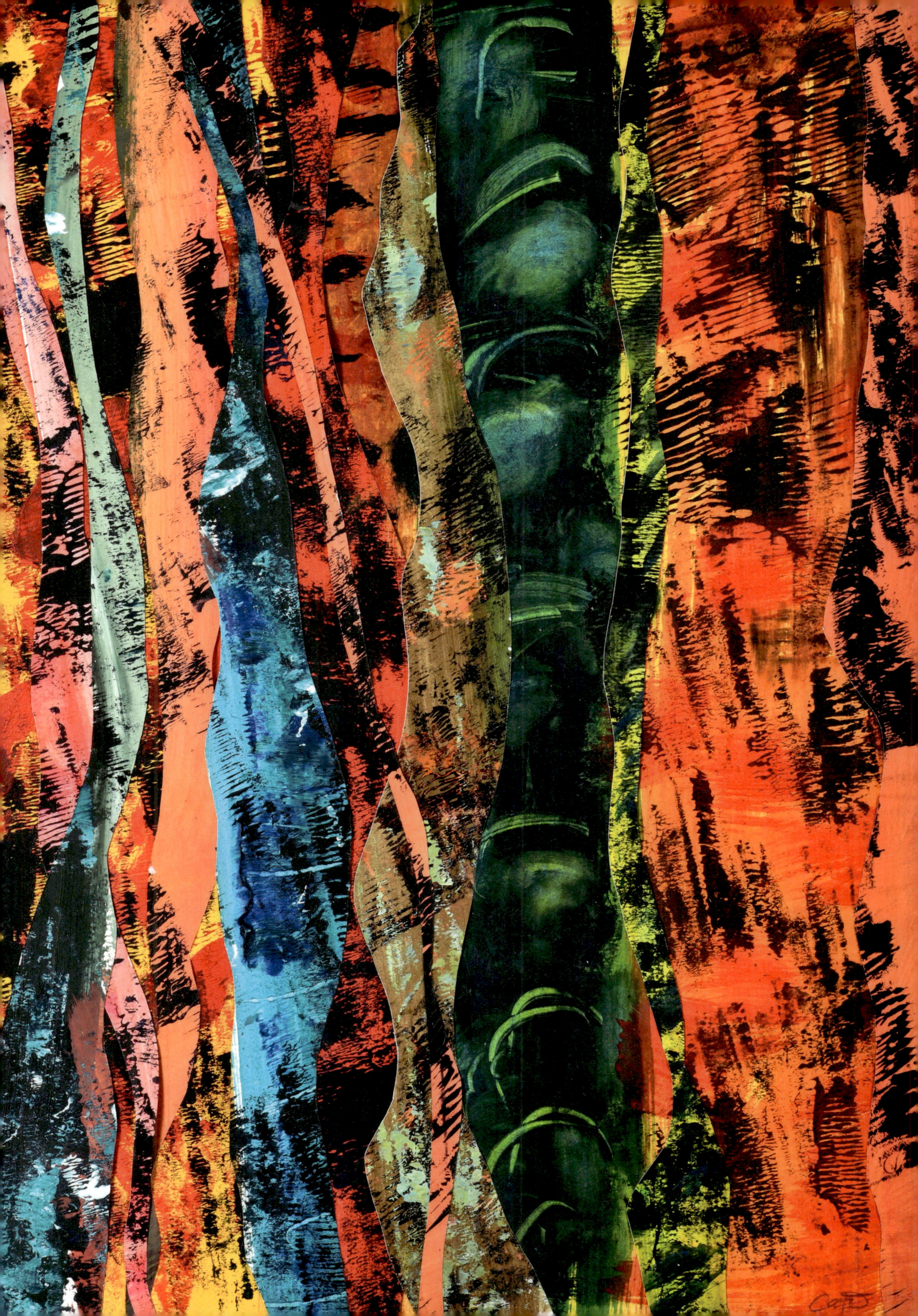

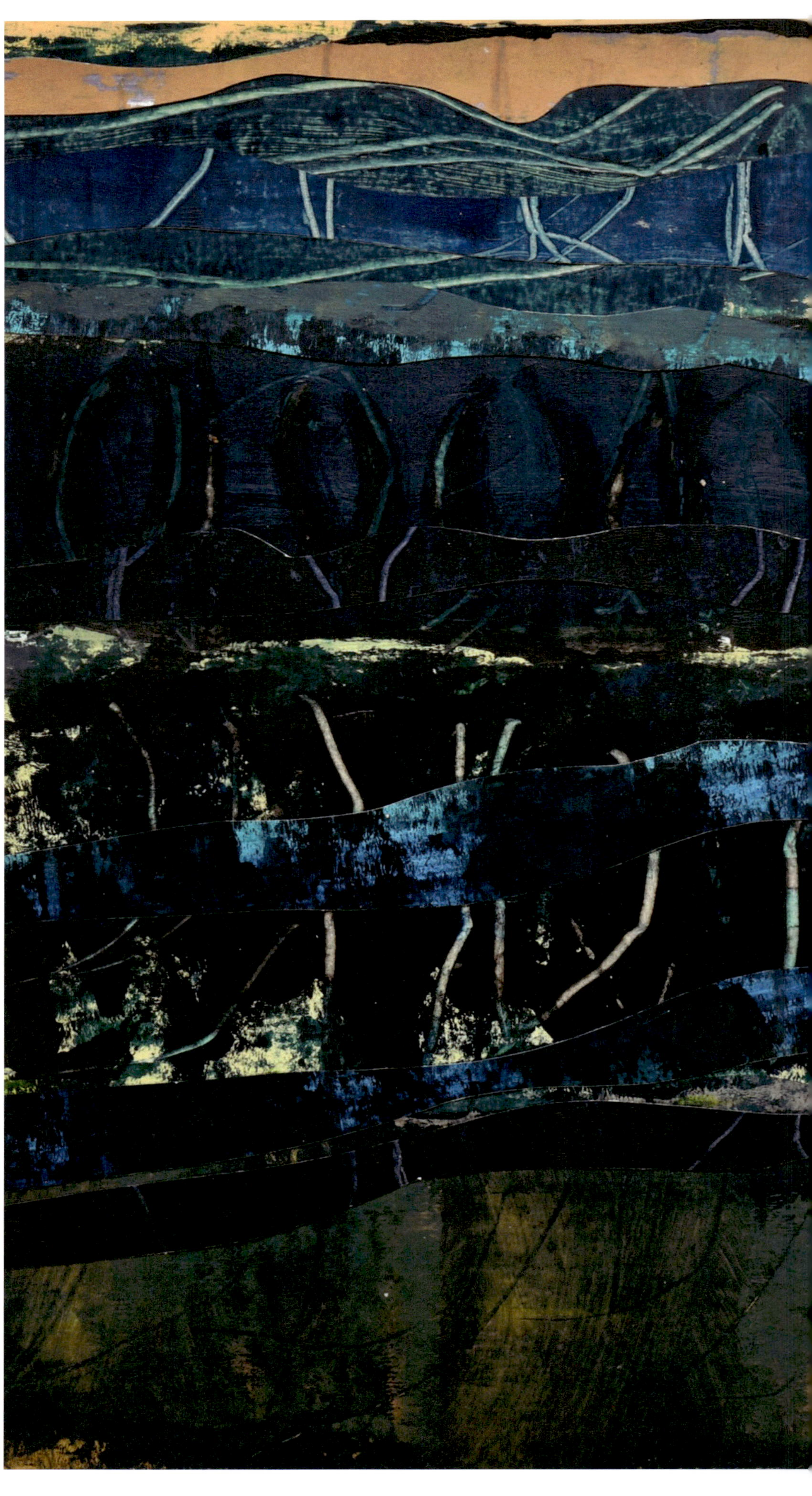

Toward Evening, 1996

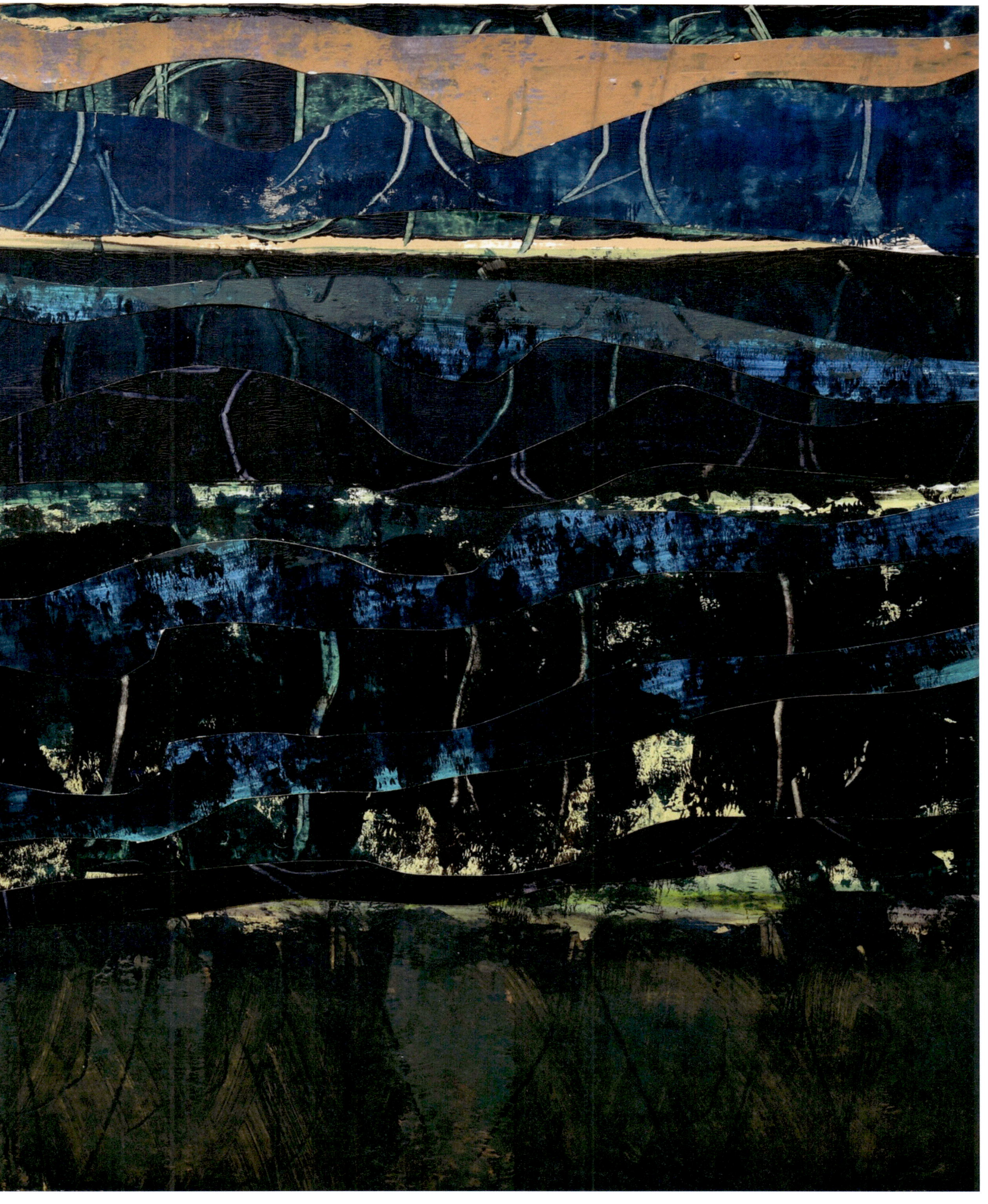

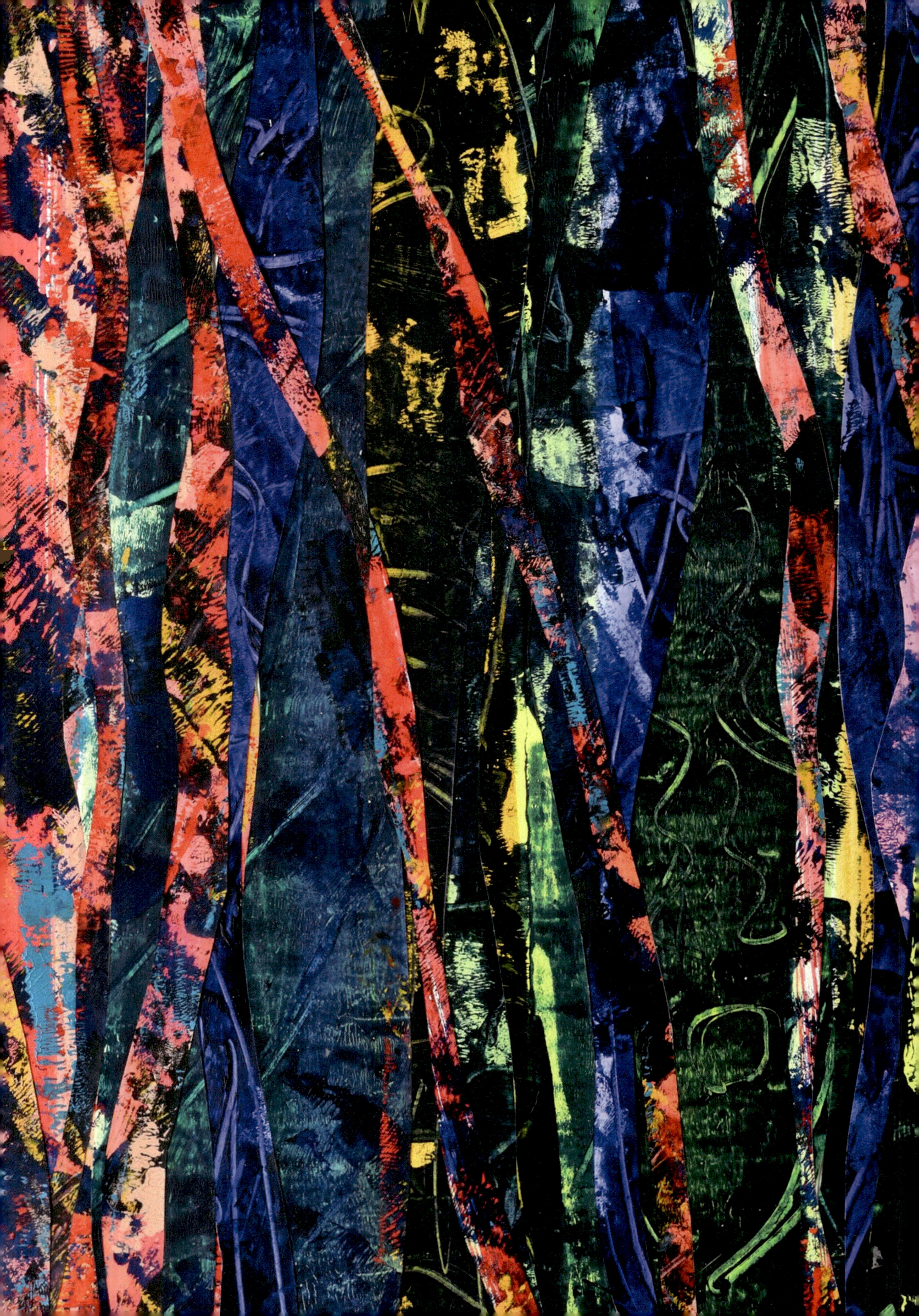

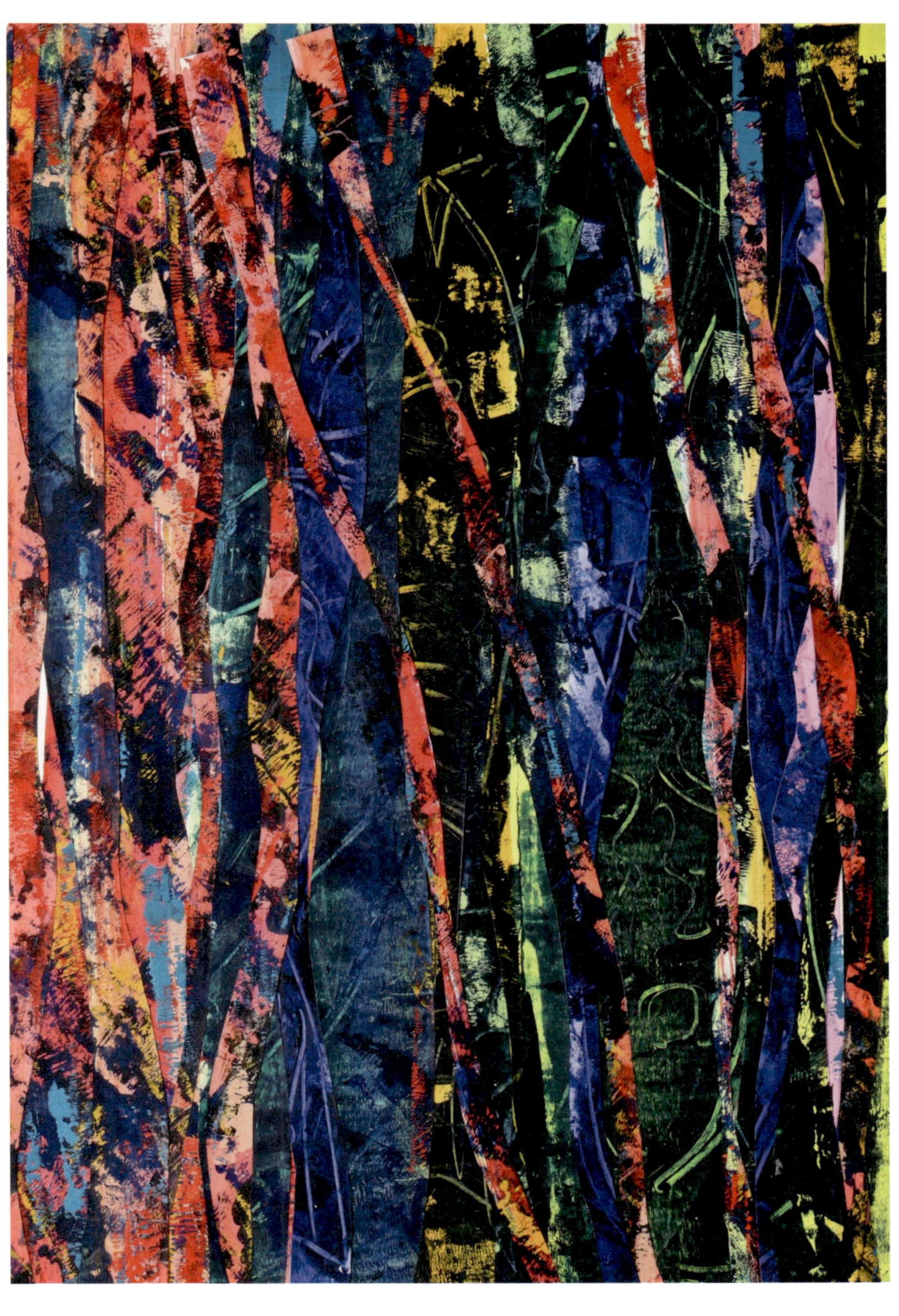

Big Sky, 1993

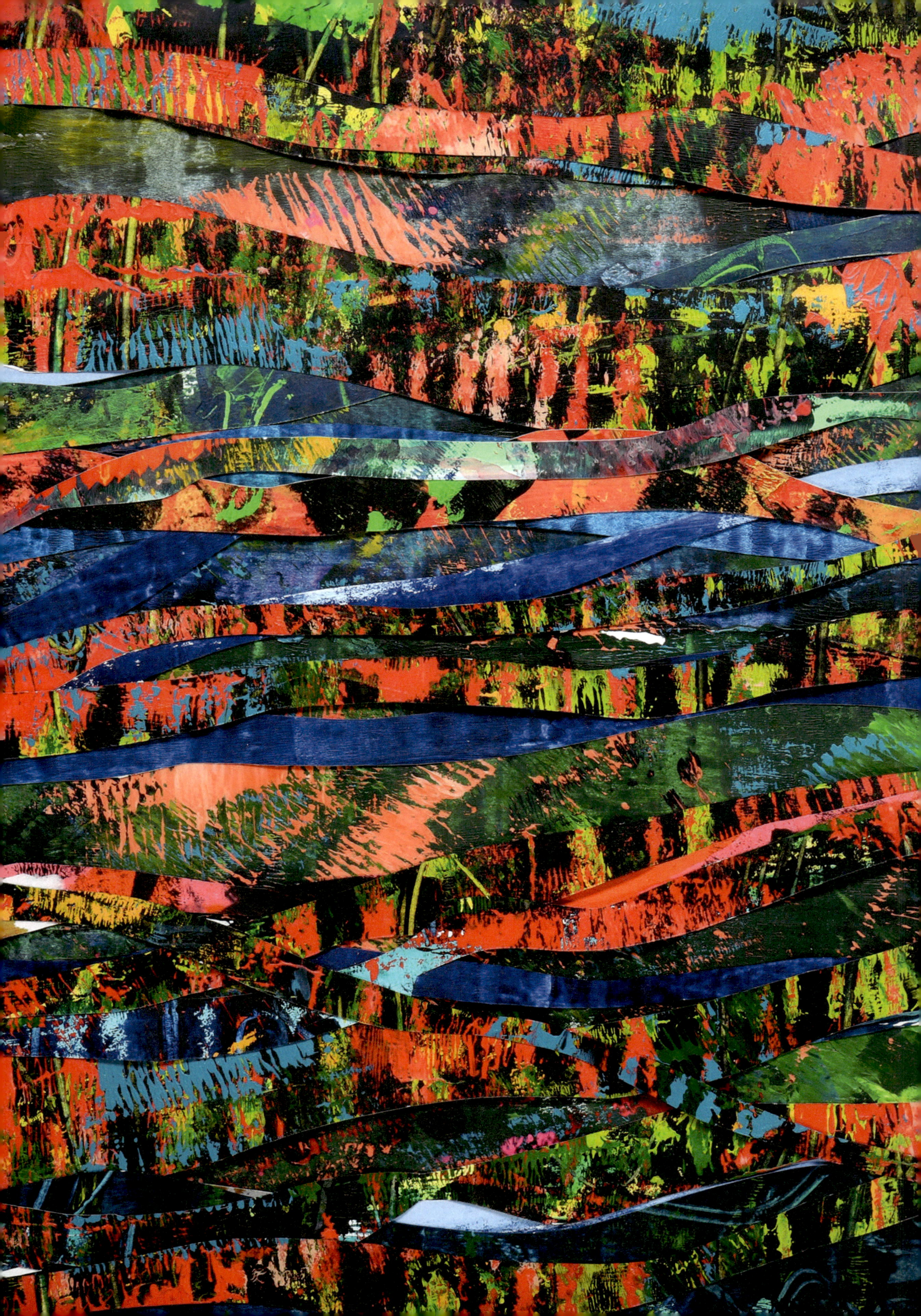

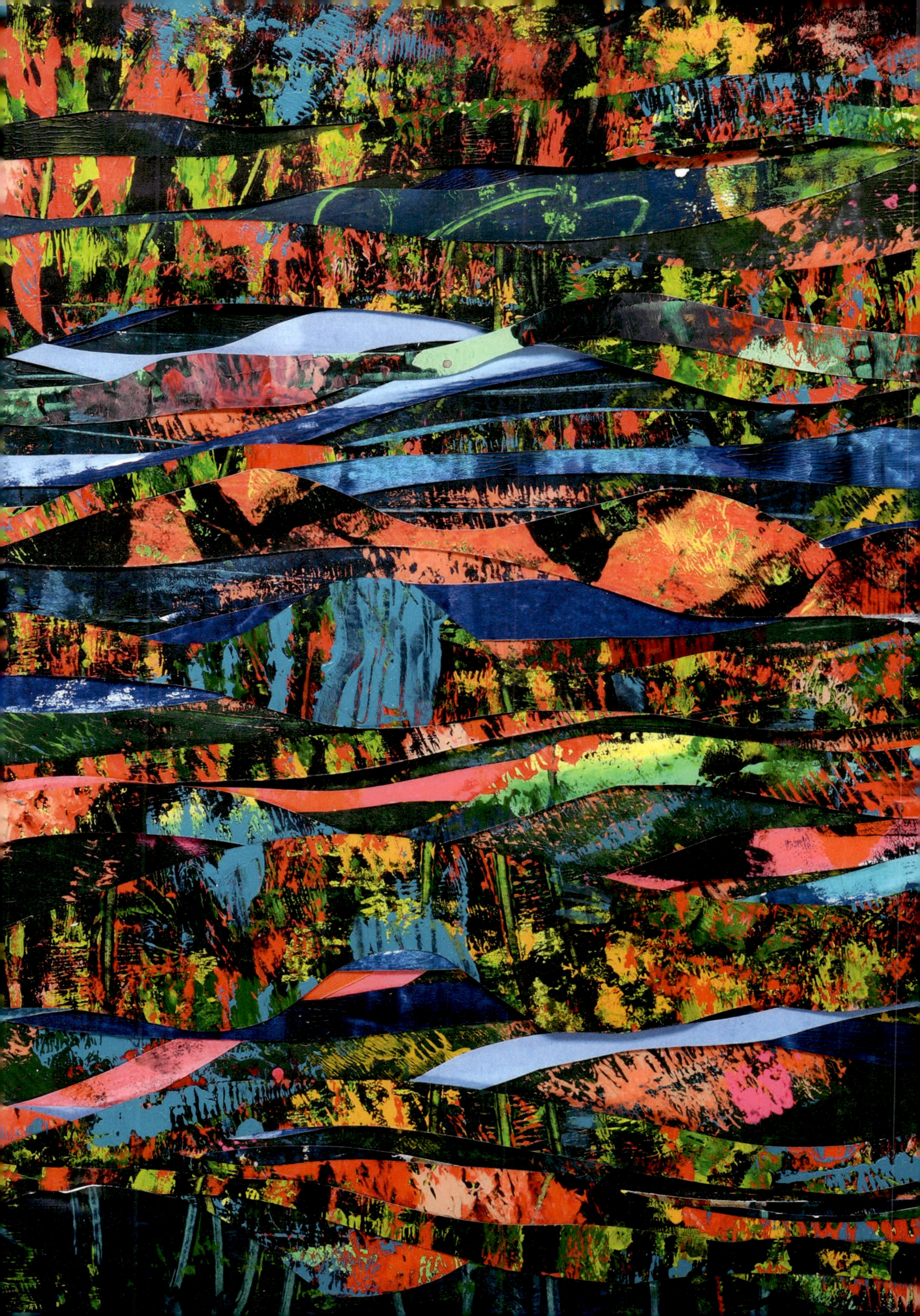

Previous pages **War Paint, 1993**   *Opposite* **Nocturnal Walk, 1993**

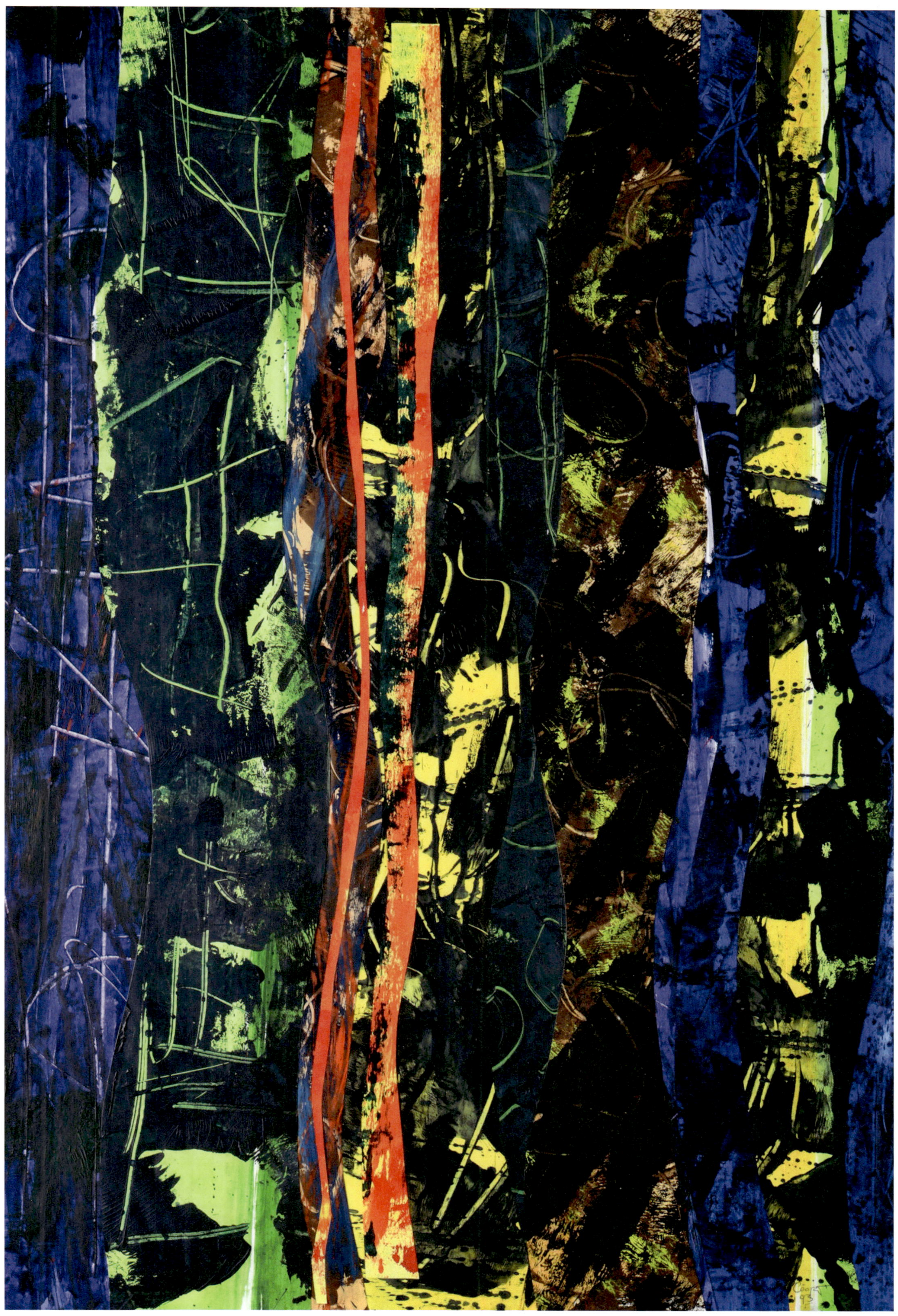

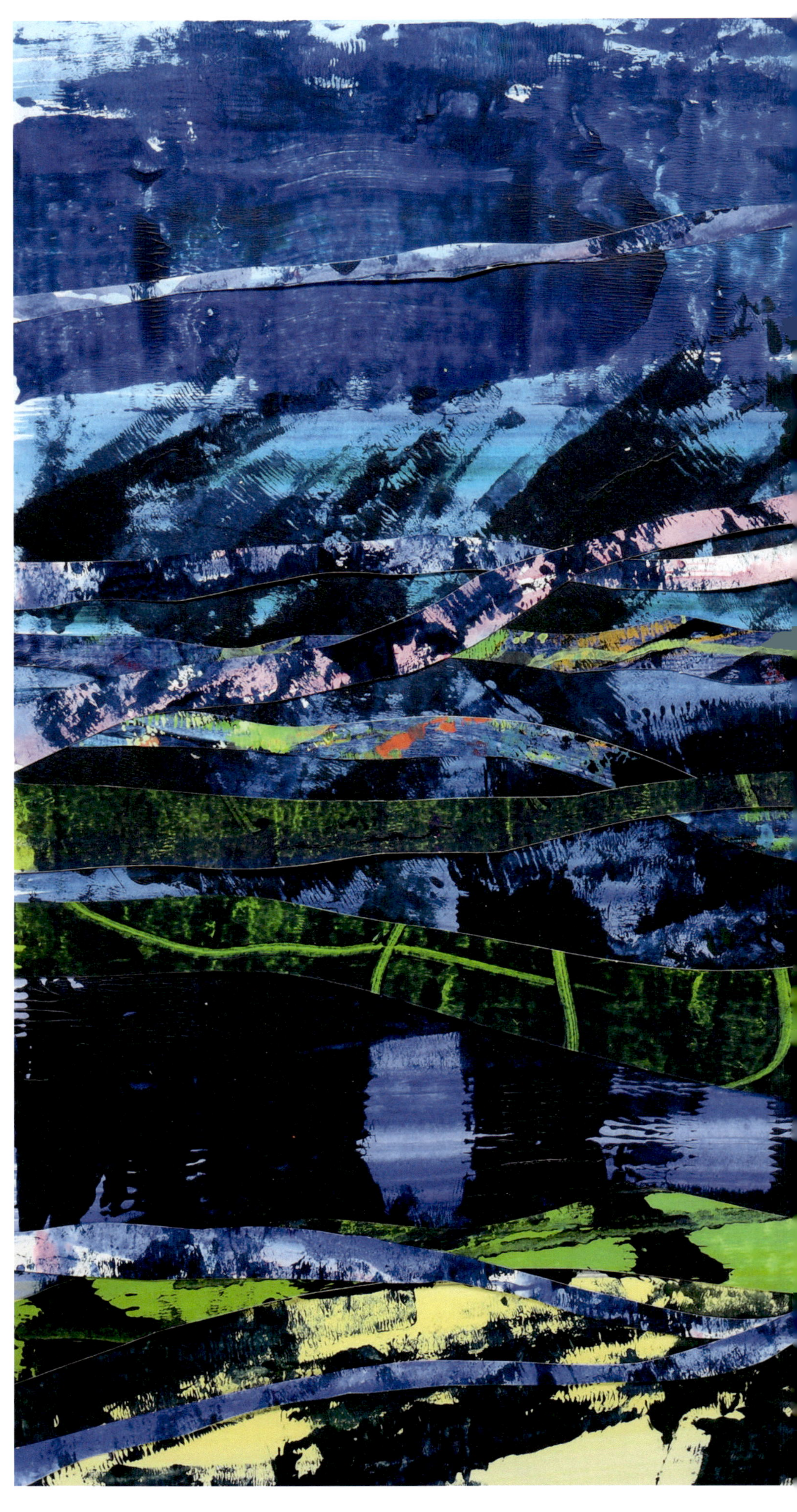

The Gate, 1993

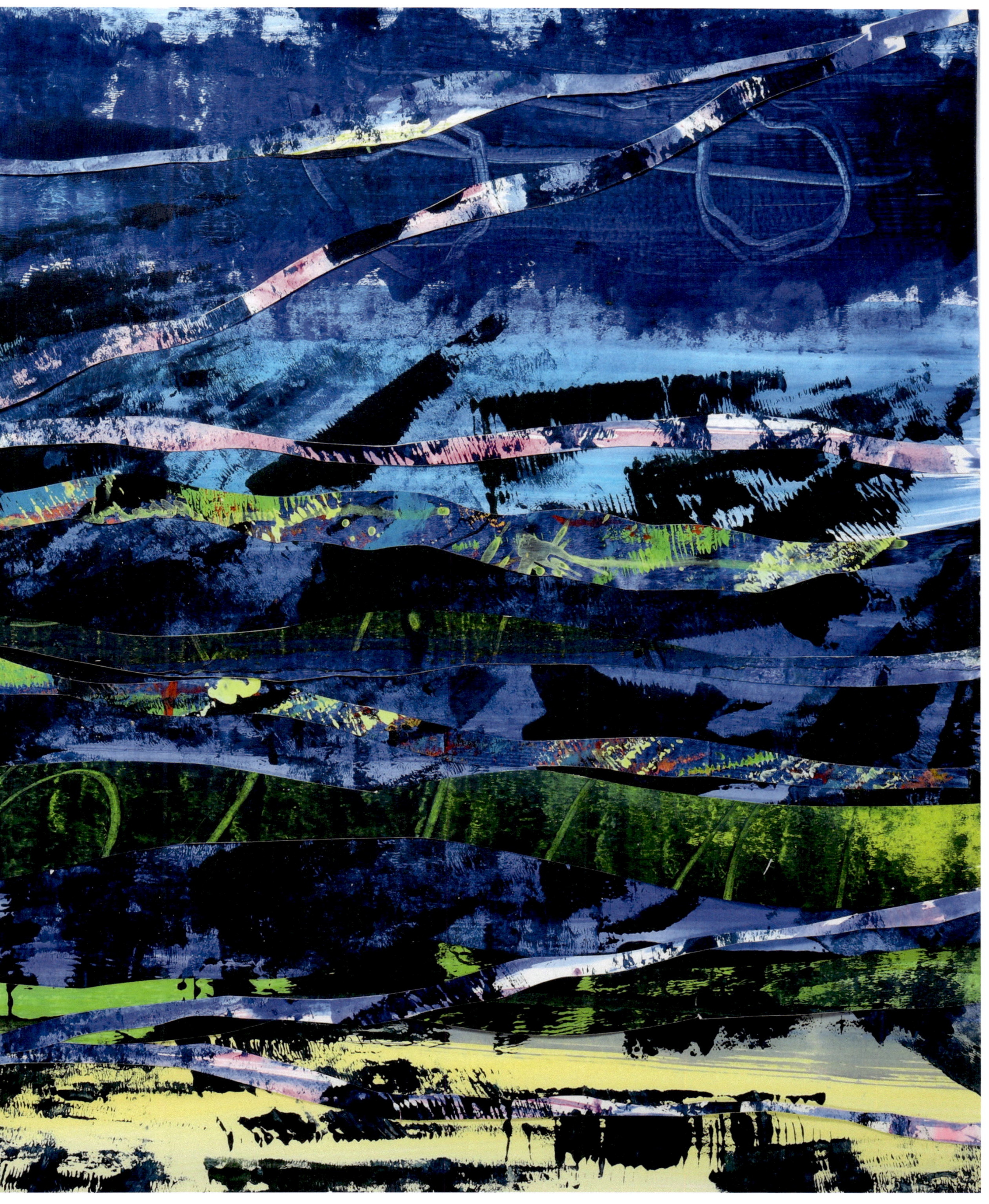

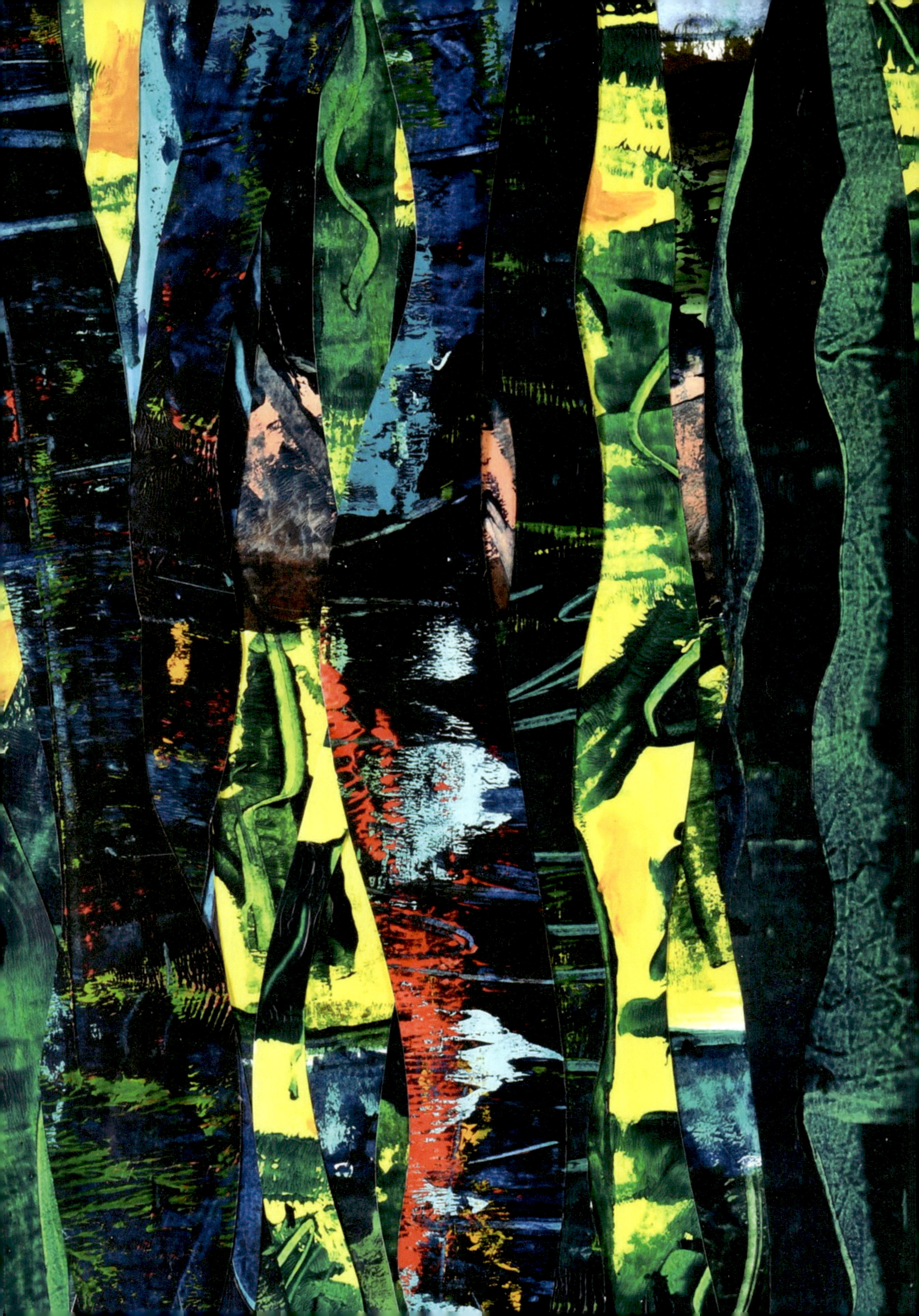

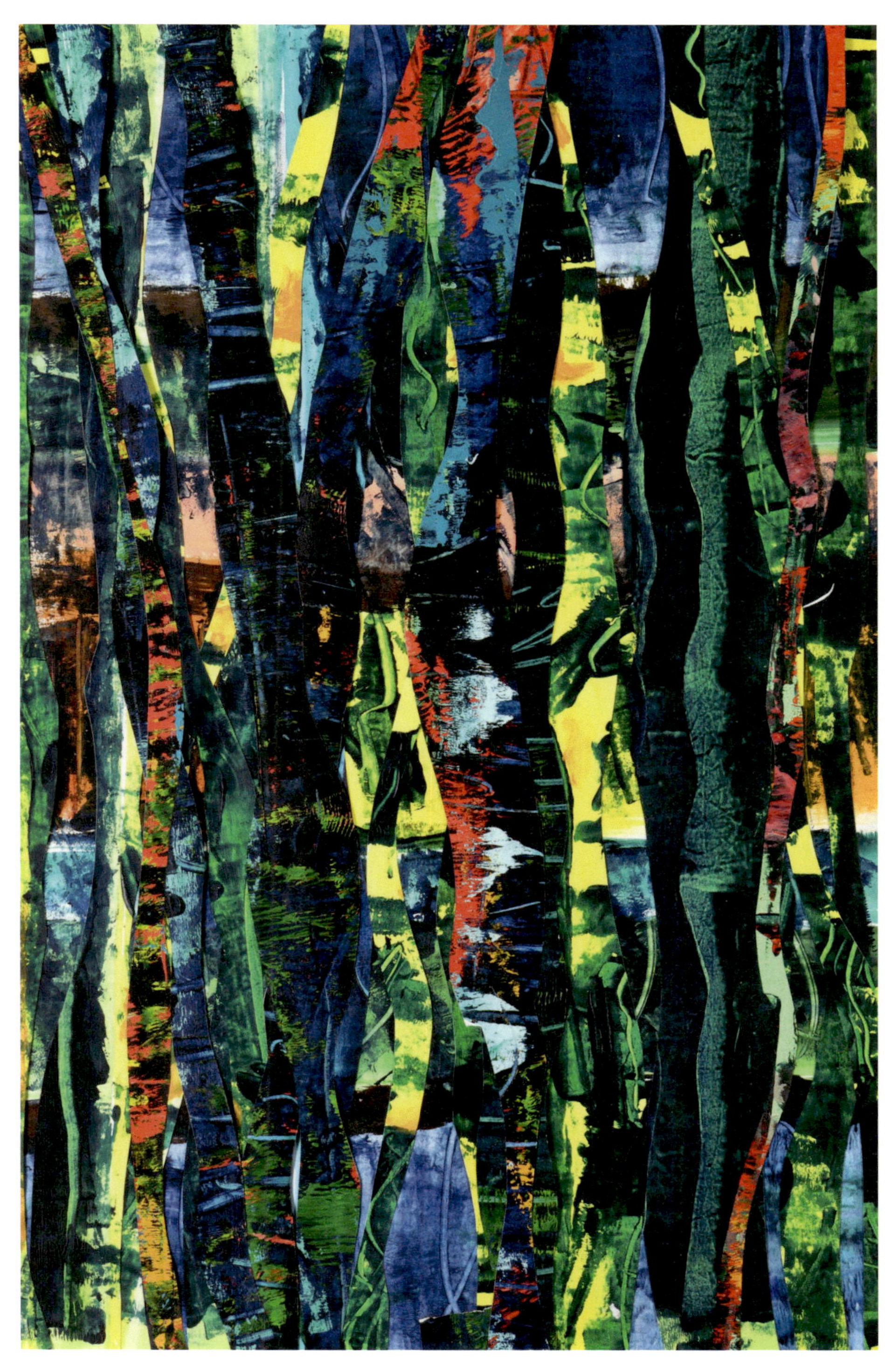

Green Shoots, 1992

Towards Lilac, 1992

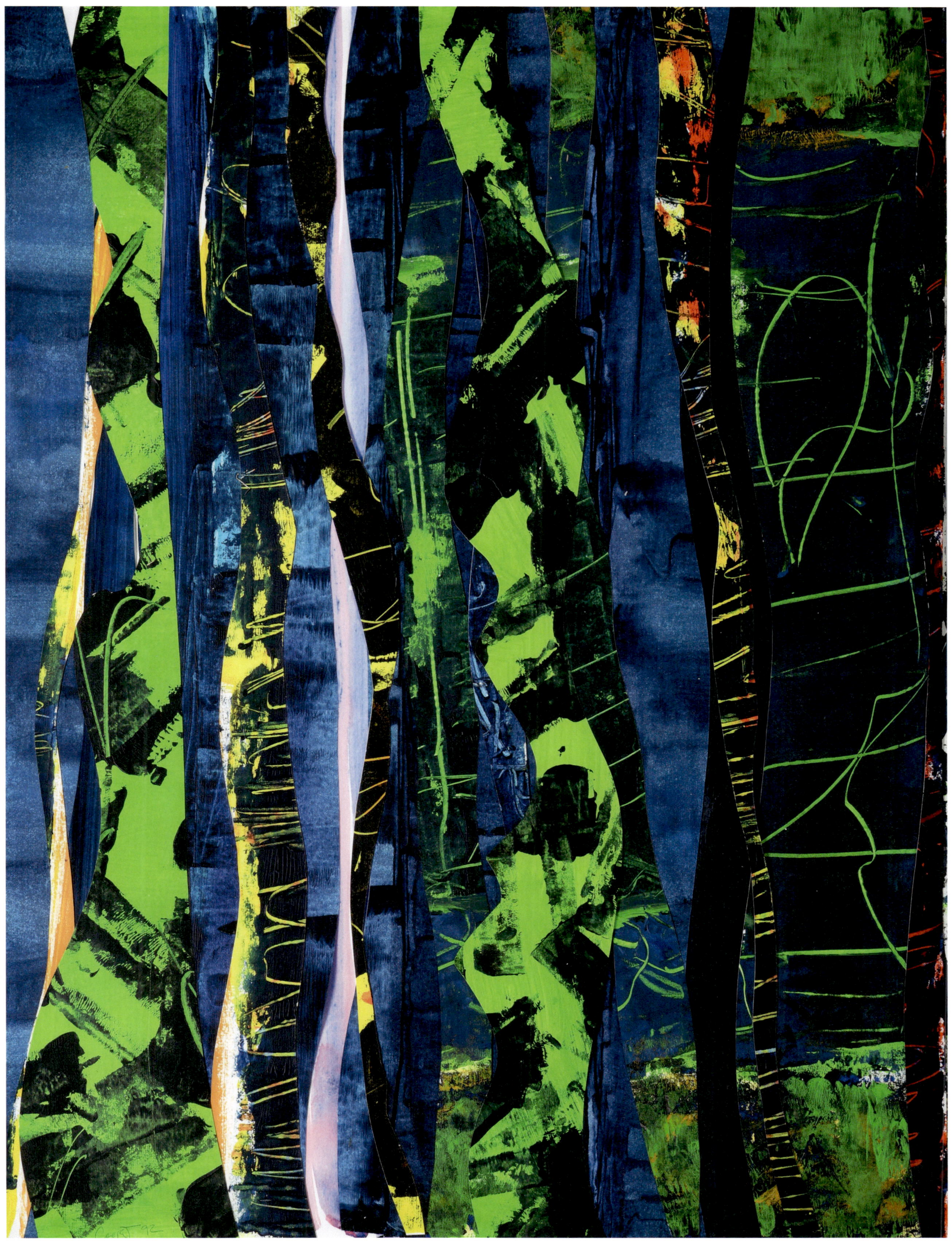

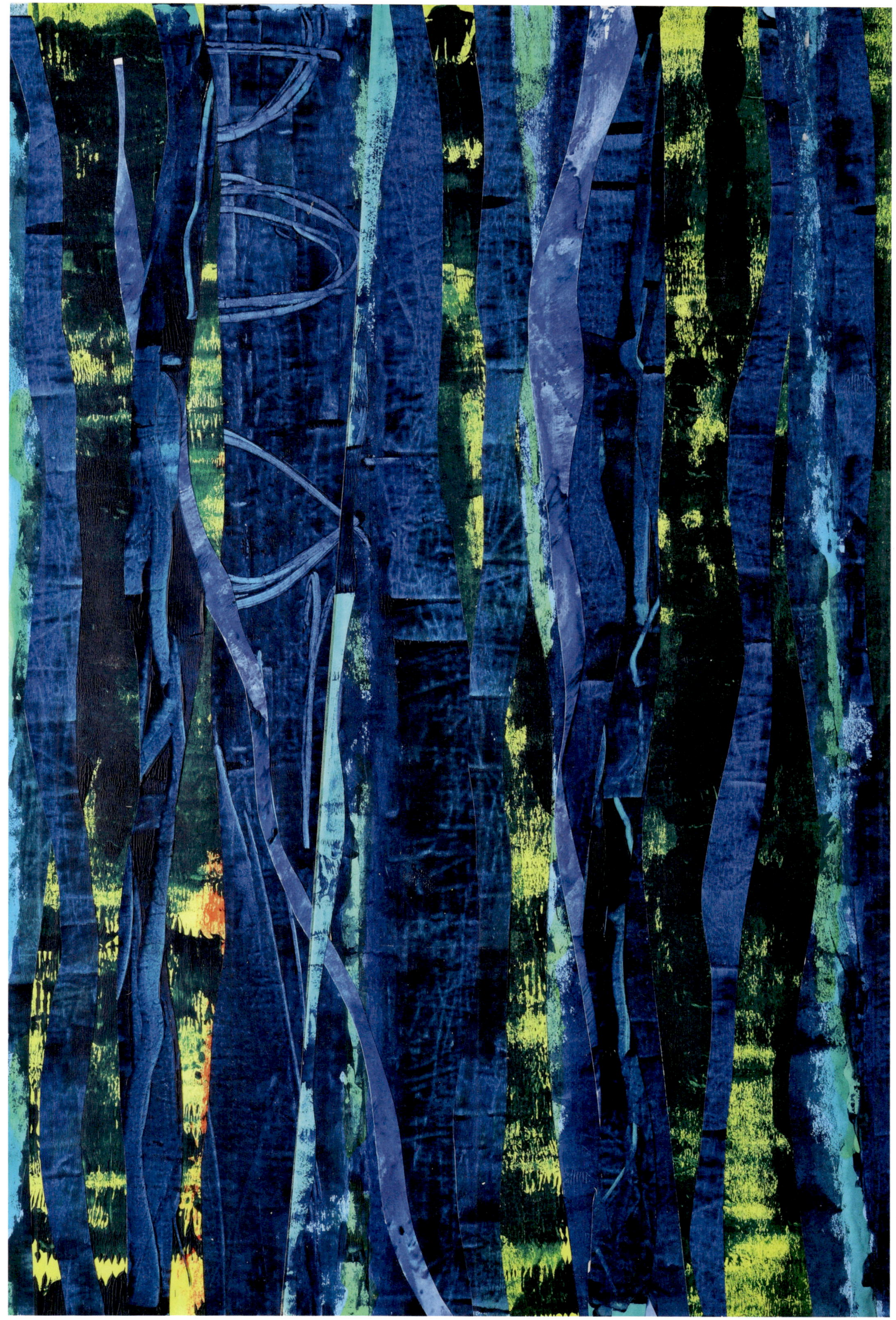

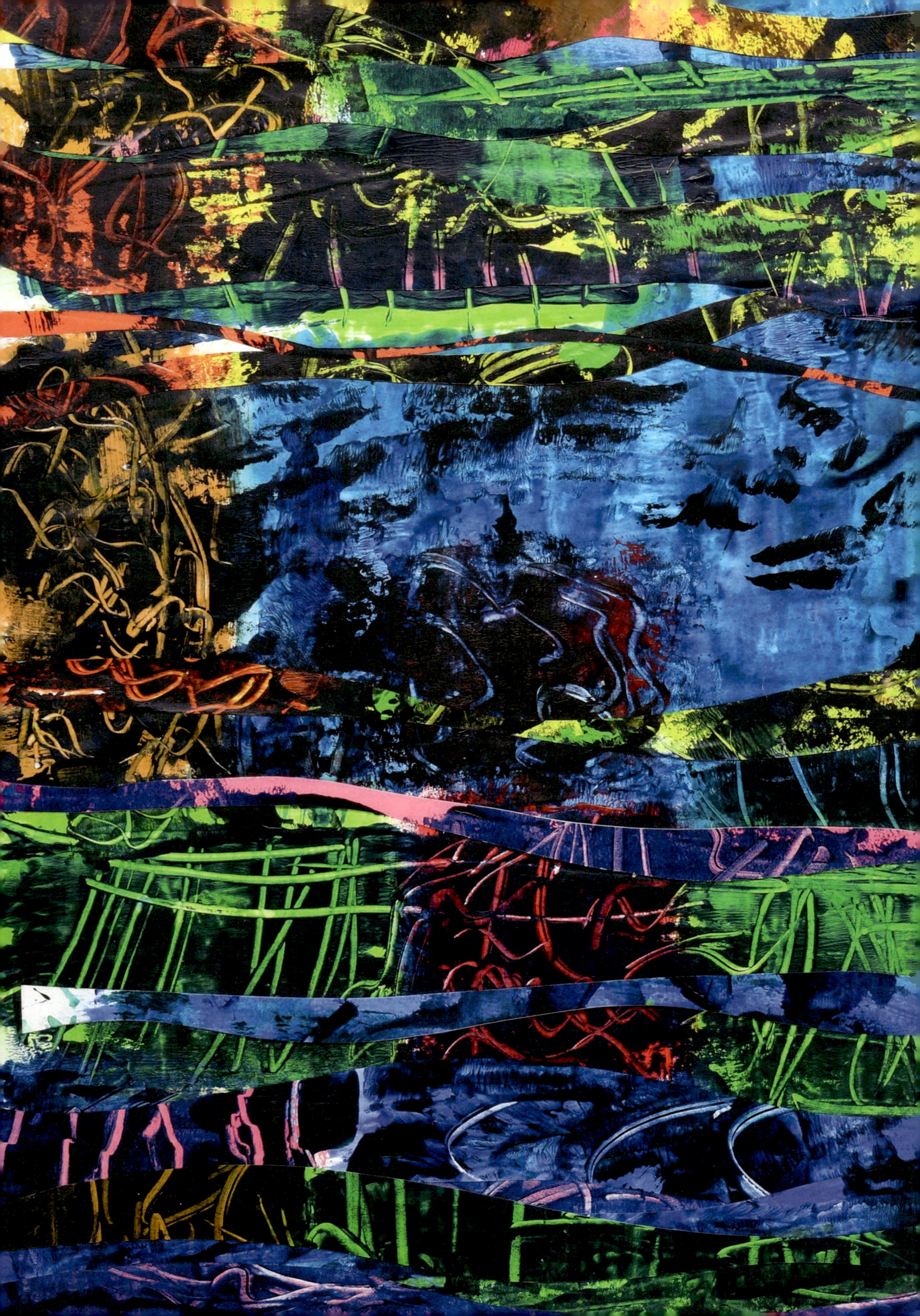

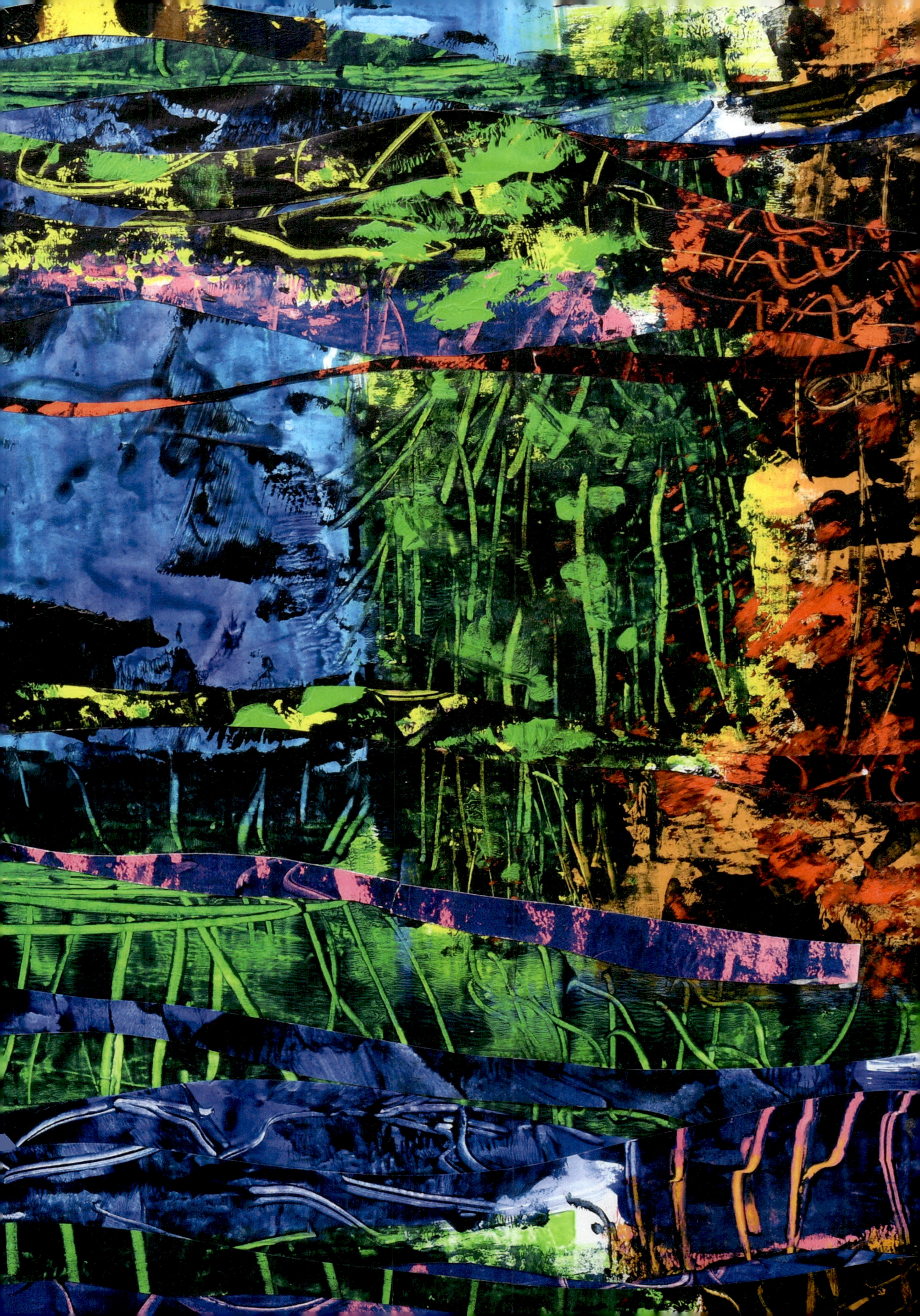

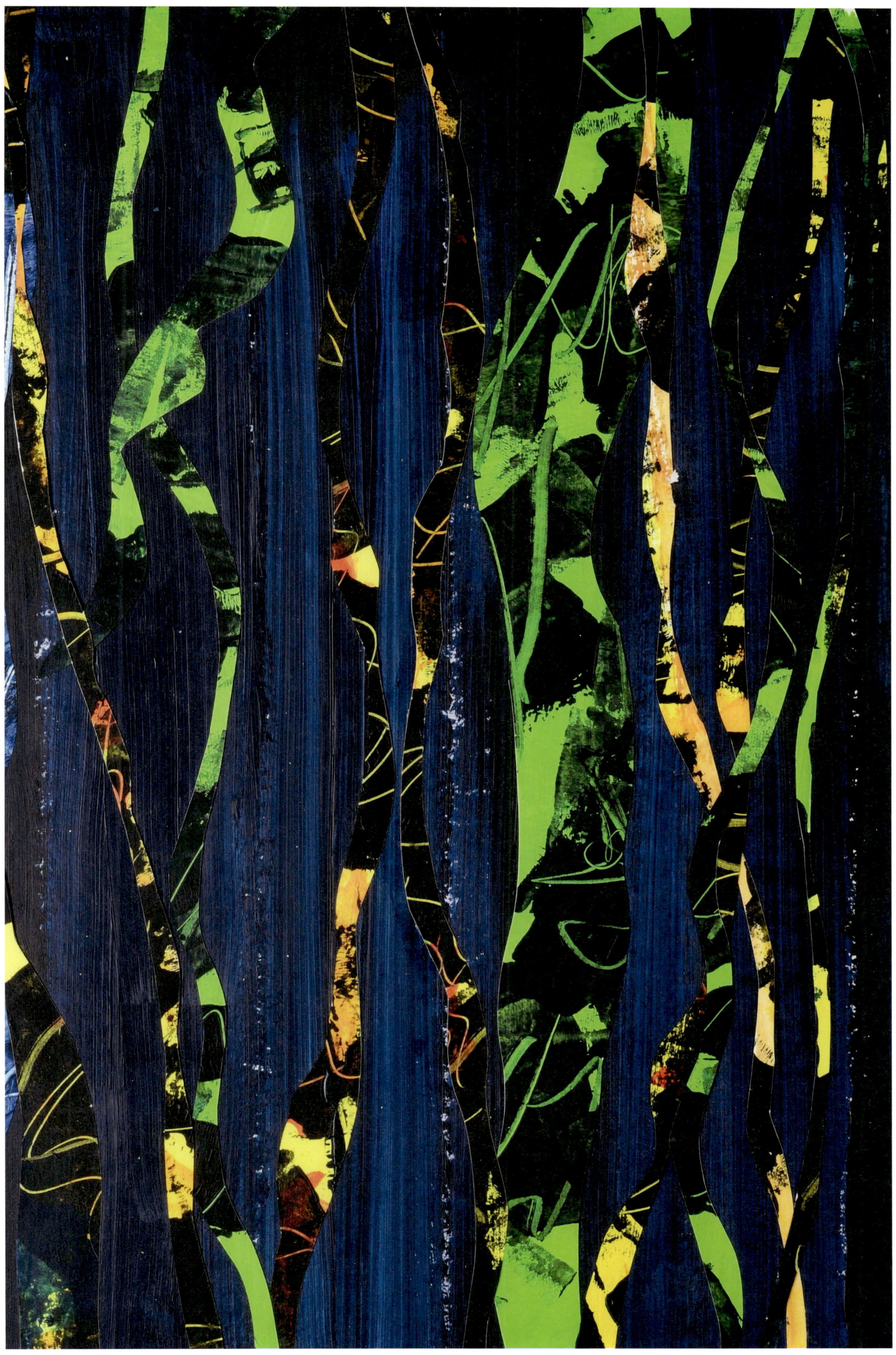

Strobe Dancer, 1997

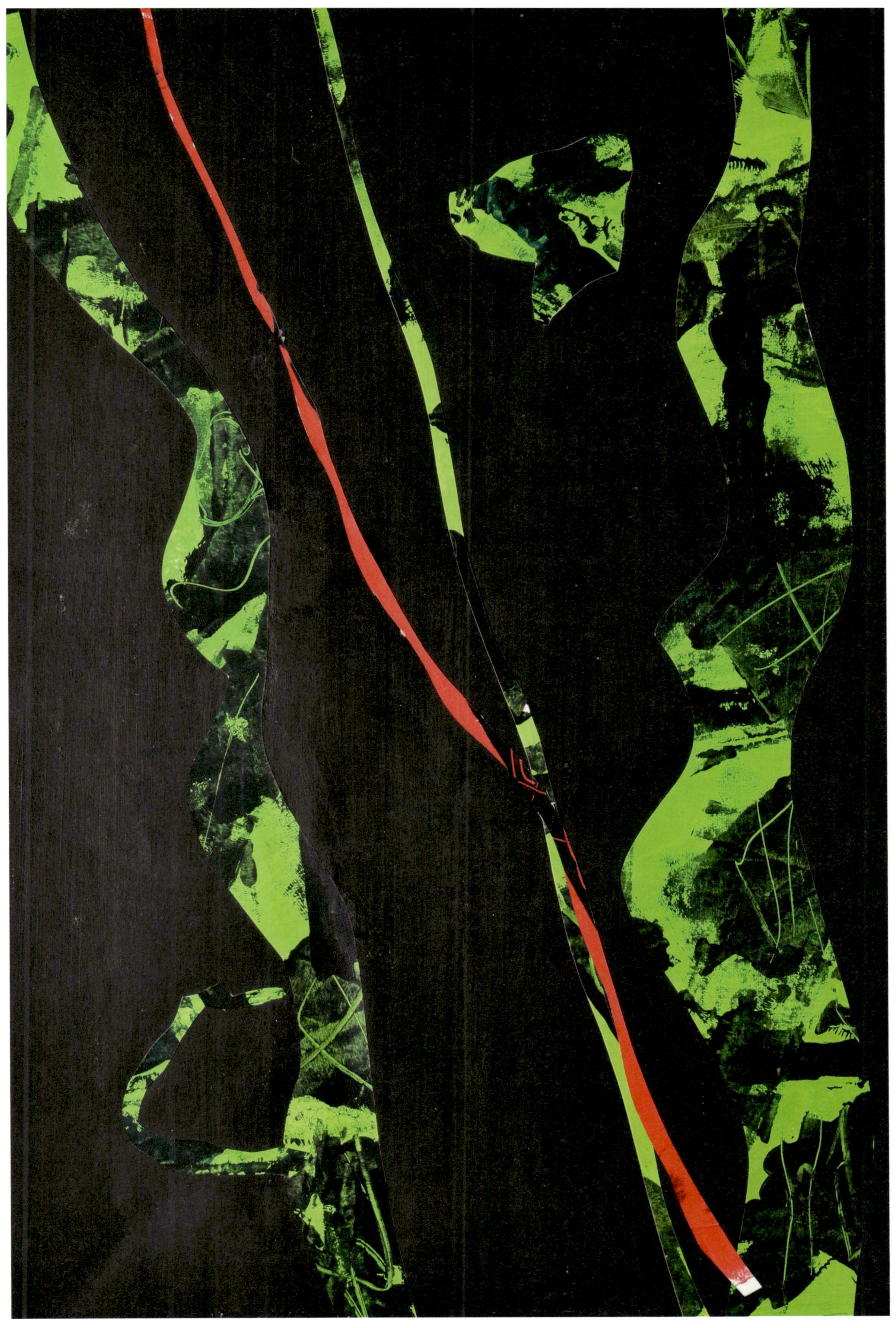

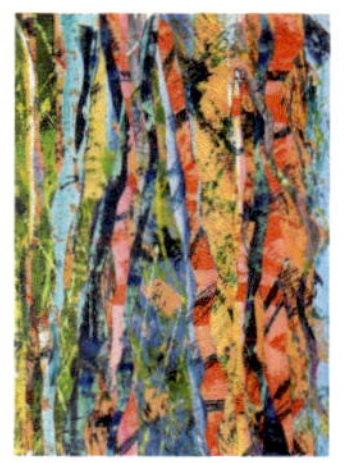

p. 19
Blue Orange, 1994
acrylic and collage on paper
80 x 55 cm

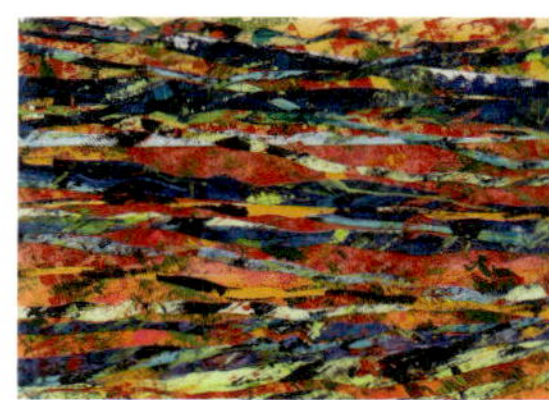

pp. 20–21
Gradations of Sunlight, 1996
acrylic and collage on paper
56 x 80 cm

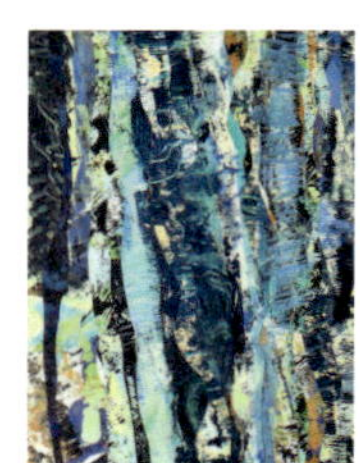

p. 23
A Misty Day, 1994
acrylic and collage on paper
72 x 50.5 cm

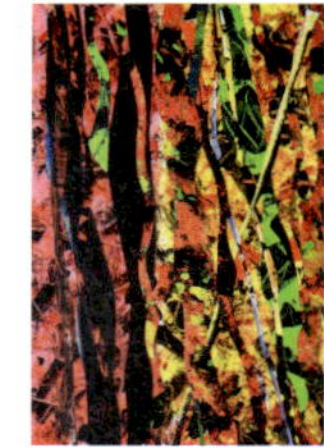

pp. 24–25
Afternoon Heat, 1992
acrylic and collage on paper
77 x 49.5 cm

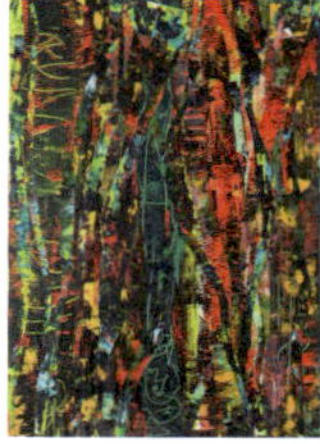

p. 27
Splintered Light, 1995
acrylic and collage on paper
81 x 56 cm

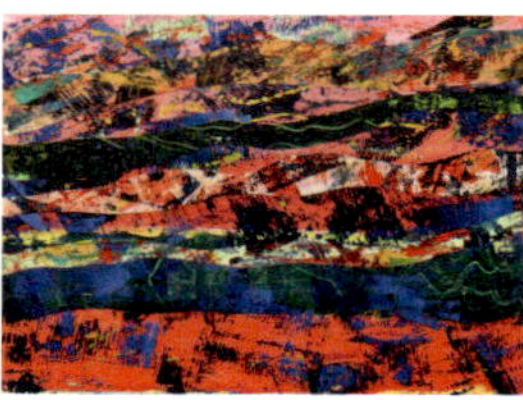

p. 28–29
Pink Sky, 1993
acrylic and collage on paper
49.5 x 74 cm

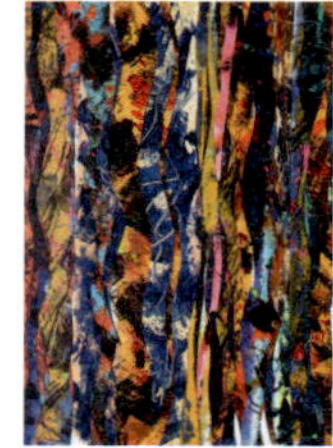

p. 31
Bridal Path in Autumn, 1994
acrylic and collage on paper
81 x 58 cm

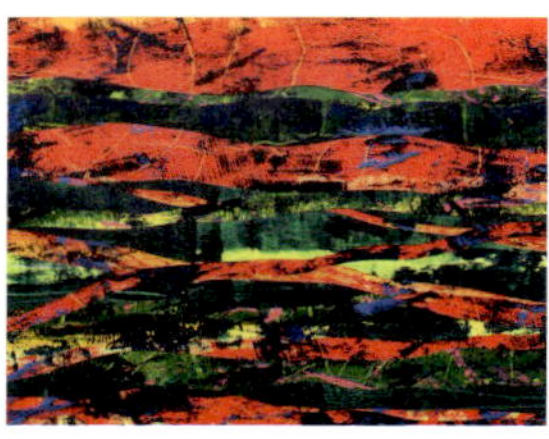

pp. 32–33
Parched Earth, 1996
acrylic and collage on paper
51 x 74 cm

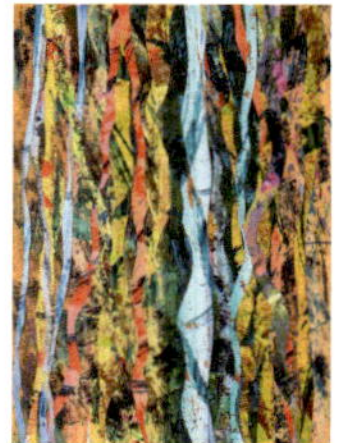

p. 35
Ice Capped, 1993
acrylic and collage on paper
78 x 55 cm

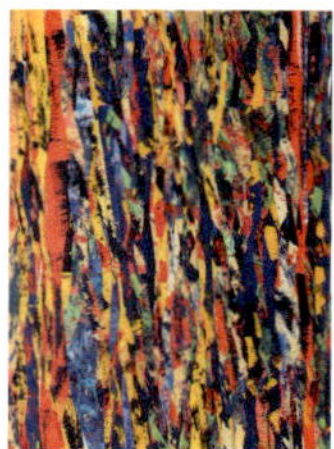

pp. 36–37
Dazzling Light, 1993
acrylic and collage on paper
84 x 59.5 cm

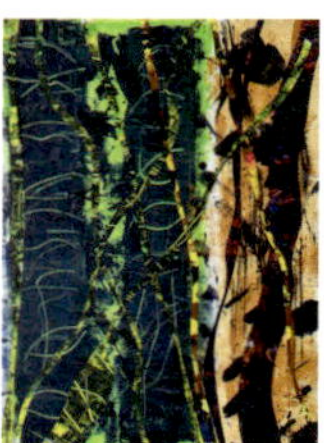

p. 39
Fallen Bough, 1995
acrylic and collage on paper
73 x 53 cm

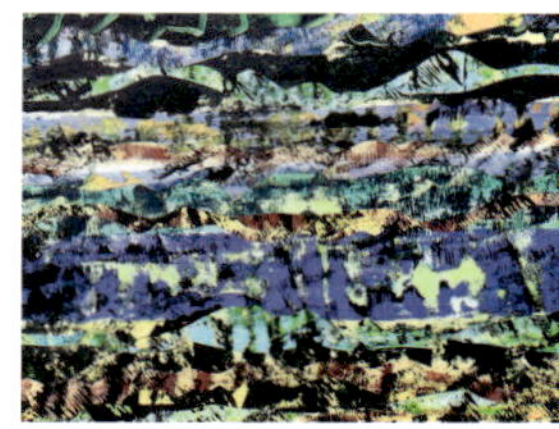

pp. 40–41
Leaves on the Path, 1995
acrylic and collage on paper
51.5 x 71.5 cm

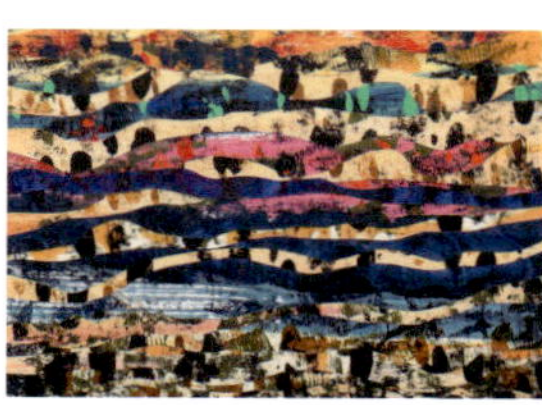

pp. 42–43
Stoney Beach, 1994
acrylic and collage on paper
51 x 72 cm

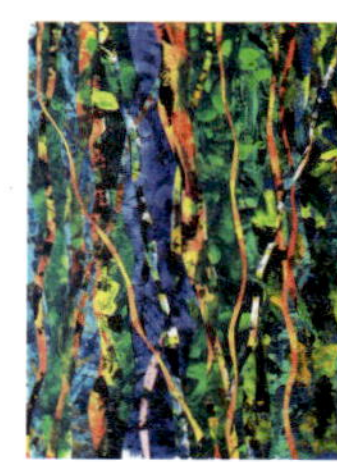

p. 45
Morning Light, 1995
acrylic and collage on paper
72 x 51 cm

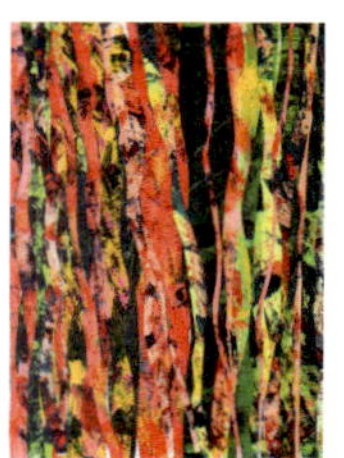

p. 47
Summer Solstice, 1994
acrylic and collage on paper
76 x 52 cm

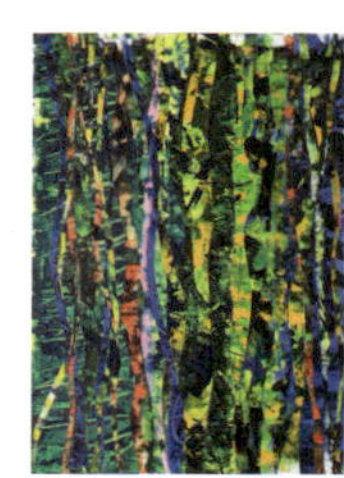

p. 49
The Green Man, 1992
acrylic and collage on paper
73 x 51 cm

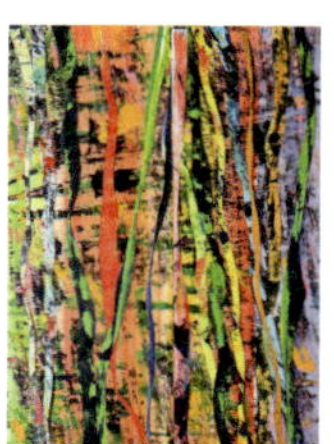

pp. 50–51
Rainbow, 1994
acrylic and collage on paper
80 x 55 cm

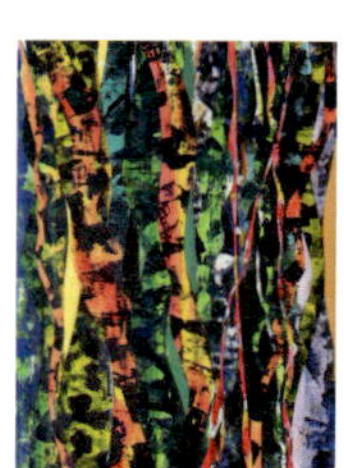

p. 53
Woodland Glade, 1992
acrylic and collage on paper
73 x 54 cm

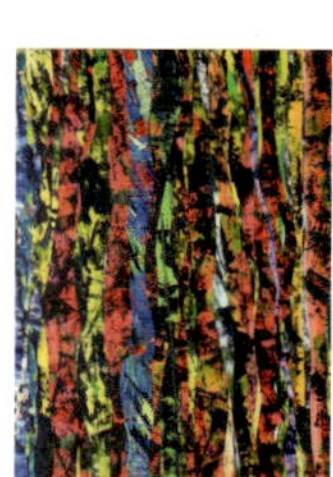

pp. 54–55
Fractured Light, 1993
acrylic and collage on paper
84 x 59 cm

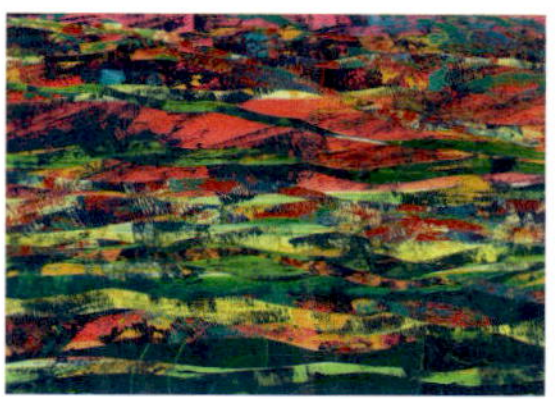

pp. 58–59
Sky Lark, 1994
acrylic and collage on paper
51 x 75 cm

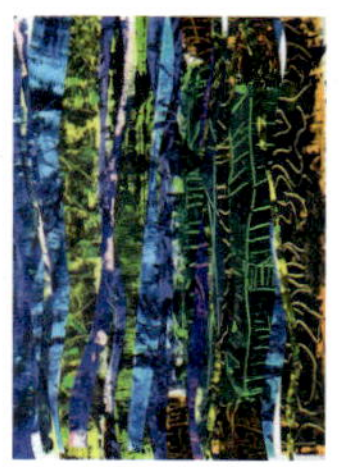

p. 61
The Paddock, 1994
acrylic and collage on paper
84 x 59 cm

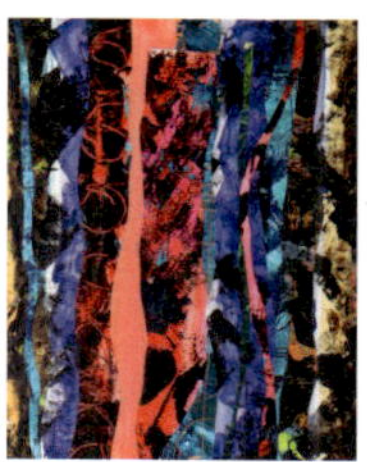

pp. 62–63
Lightening, 1994
acrylic and collage on paper
82 x 58 cm

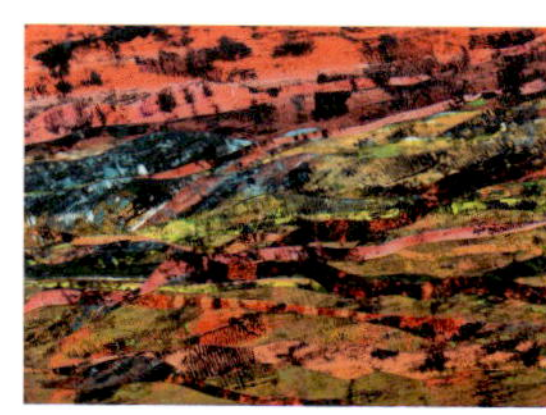

pp. 64–65
Cloud Strata, 1995
acrylic and collage on paper
56 x 80 cm

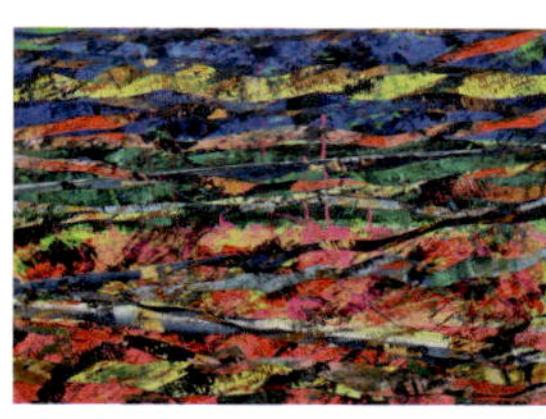

pp. 66–67
A Good Month, 1993
acrylic and collage on paper
56 x 80 cm

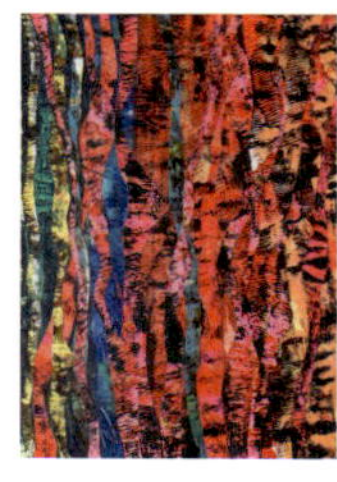

p. 69
Adder in the Grass, 1993
acrylic and collage on paper
71 x 51 cm

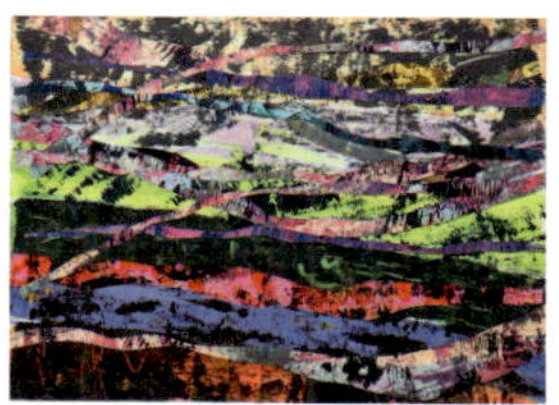

pp. 70–71
Plough Sky, 1994
acrylic and collage on paper
51.5 x 72 cm

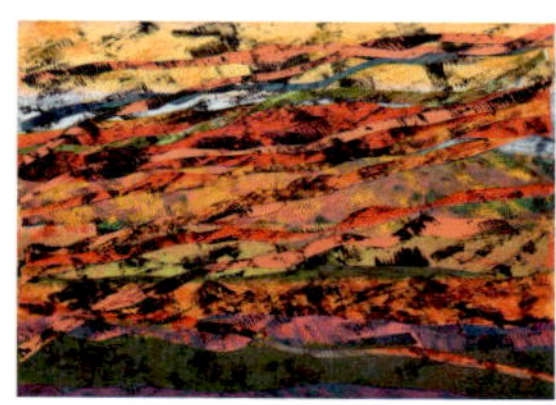

pp. 72–73
Cameo Sunset, 1994
acrylic and collage on paper
56 x 81 cm

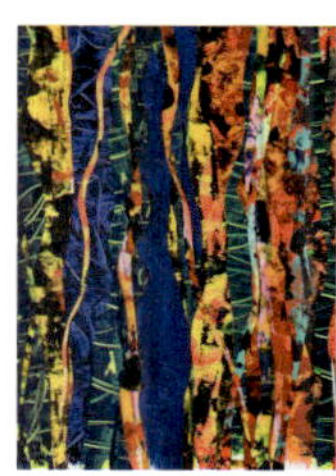

pp. 74–75
August Afternoon, 1995
acrylic and collage on paper
73.5 x 54 cm

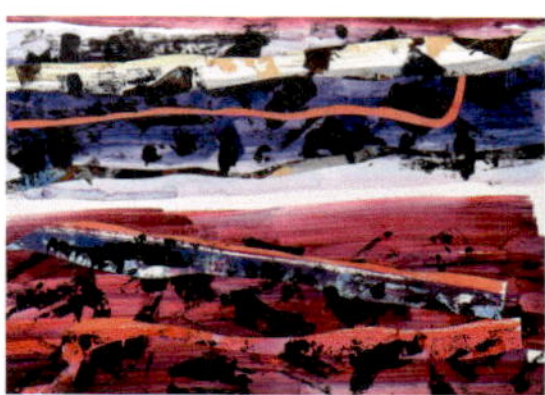

pp. 76–77
Silver Birch Shadow, 1995
acrylic and collage on paper
58 x 82 cm

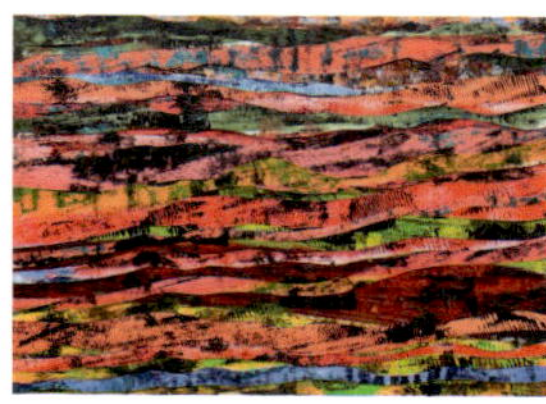

pp. 78–79
Solar Stream, 1996
acrylic and collage on paper
55.5 x 80 cm

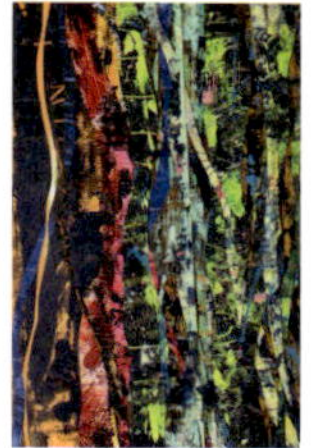

p. 81
Bull Rush Pond, 1993
acrylic and collage on paper
74.5 x 48.5 cm

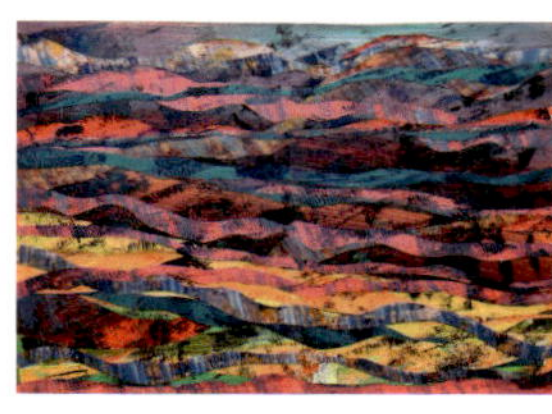

pp. 82–83
Cinders, 1996
acrylic and collage on paper
55 x 80 cm

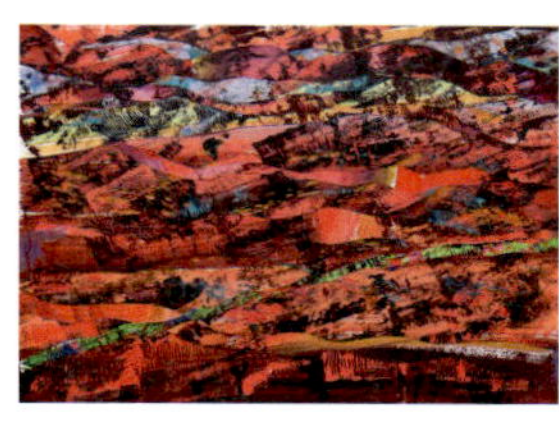

pp. 84–85
Burnished Woodland, 1994
acrylic and collage on paper
55 x 81 cm

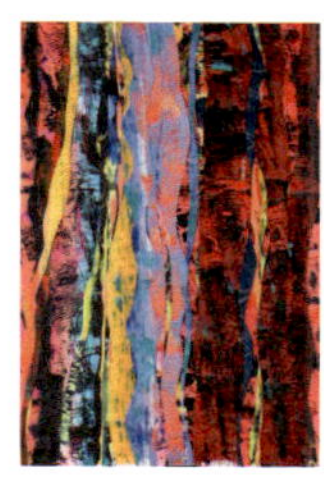

p. 87
West Country, 1996
acrylic and collage on paper
81 x 56 cm

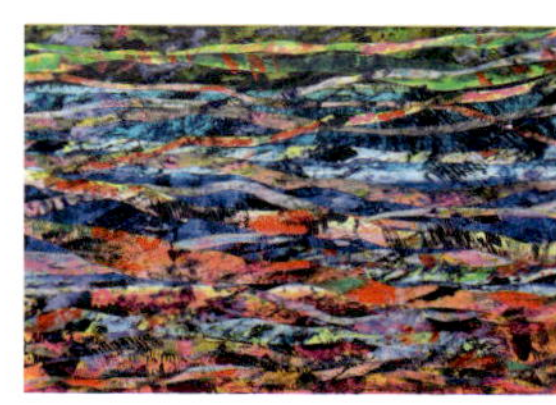

pp. 88–89
Ribbon Cloud, 1993
acrylic and collage on paper
55 x 80cm

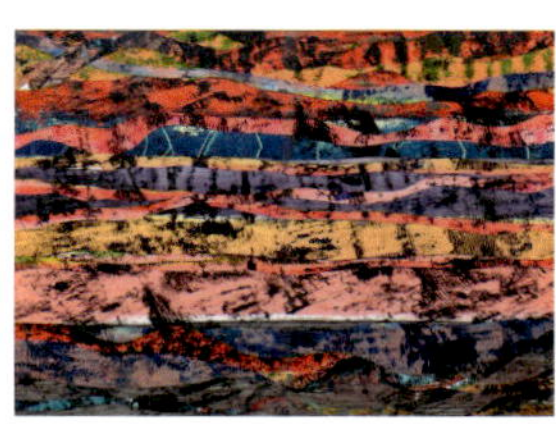

pp. 90–91
Refracted Red, 1995
acrylic and collage on paper
55 x 80 cm

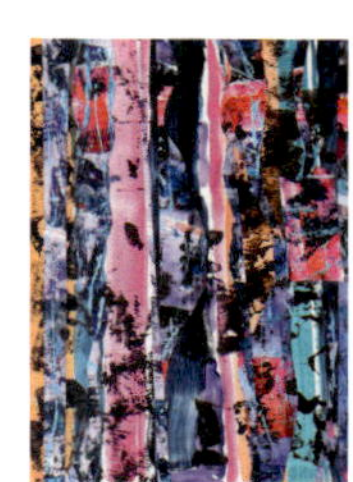

pp. 92–93
After the Rain, 1995
acrylic and collage on paper
74 x 53 cm

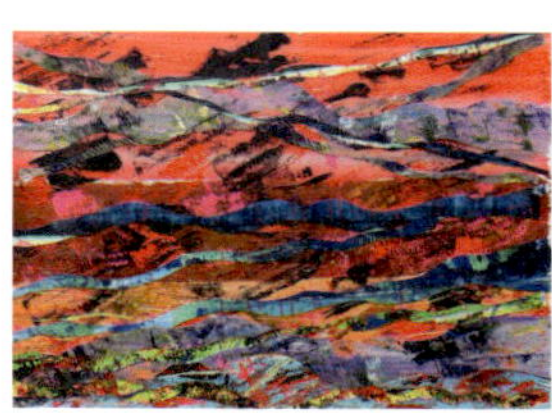

pp. 94–95
First Light, 1994
acrylic and collage on paper
51 x 81.5 cm

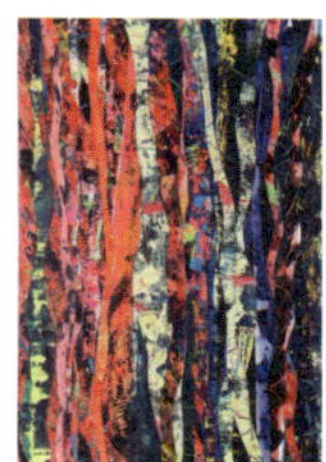

p. 97
Beech Trees, 1993
acrylic and collage on paper
49 x 74 cm

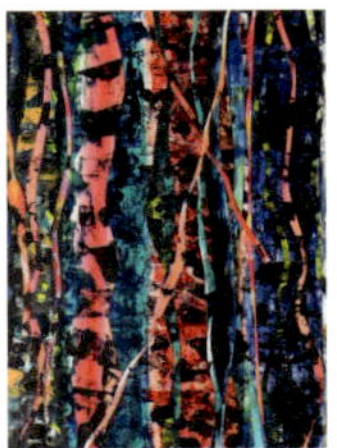

pp. 100–101
Lowering Sun Through Trees, 1996
acrylic and collage on paper
73 x 53 cm

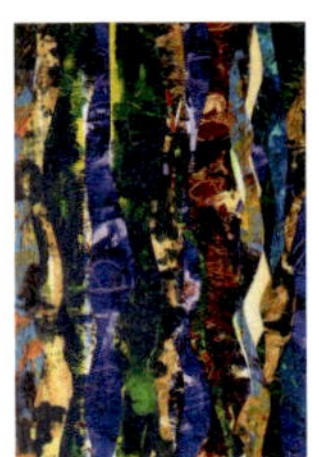

p. 103
The Long Night, 1994
acrylic and collage on paper
80 x 52 cm

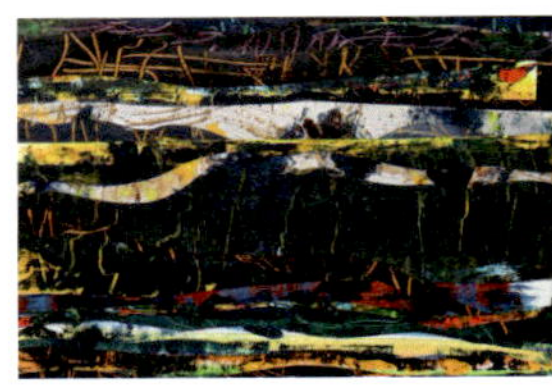

pp. 104–105
Storm Sky, 1995
acrylic and collage on paper
52 x 81 cm

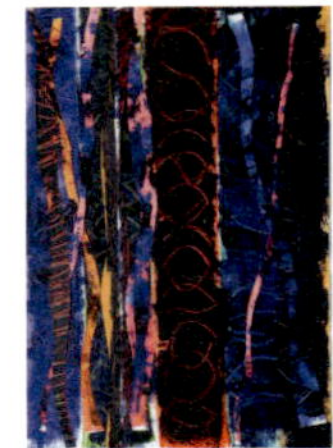

p. 107
Bonfire Night, 1992
acrylic and collage on paper
79.5 x 56 cm

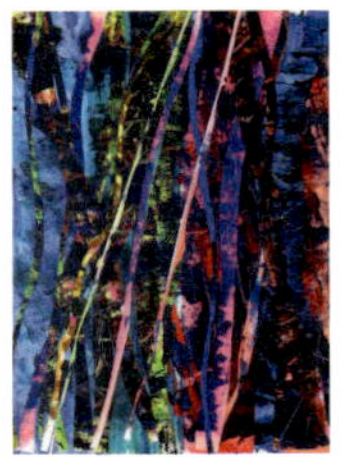

pp. 108–109
The Clearing, 1992
acrylic and collage on paper
73 x 53 cm

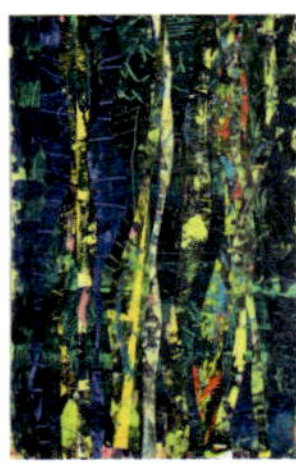

p. 111
Bird Song, 1996
acrylic and collage on paper
74.5 x 48 cm

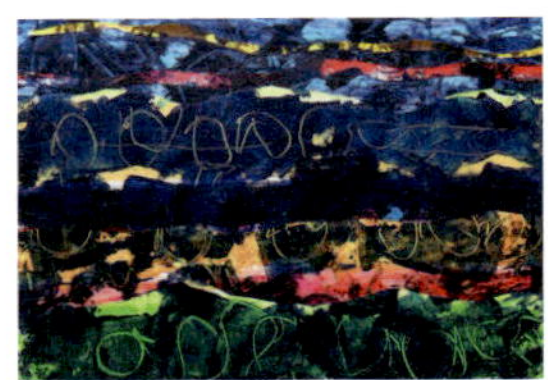

pp. 112–113
Thunder Sunset, 1993
acrylic and collage on paper
56 x 80 cm

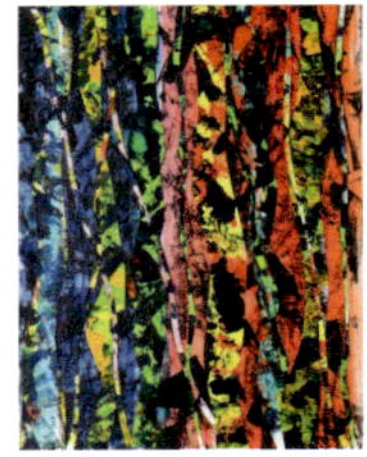

p. 115
Evening, 1993
acrylic and collage on paper
69.5 x 54 cm

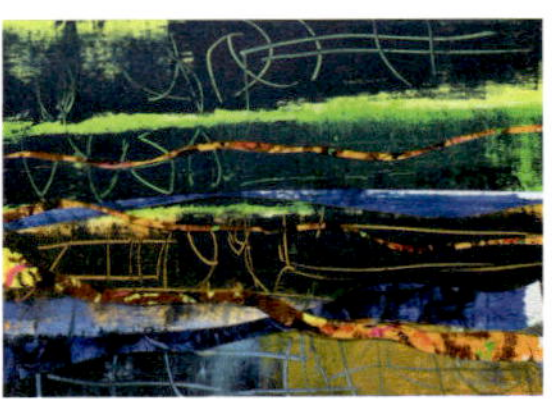

pp. 116–117
The Lane, 1992
acrylic and collage on paper
56.5 x 79 cm

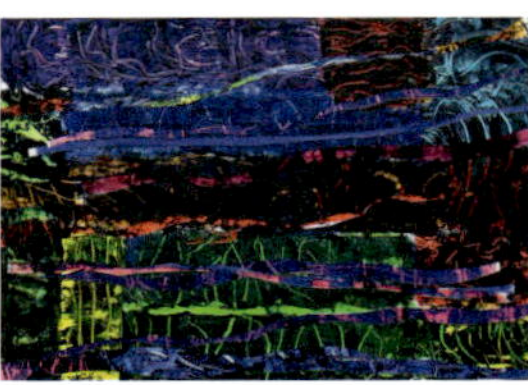

pp. 118–119
Pond at Dusk, 1992
acrylic and collage on paper
55 x 79.5 cm

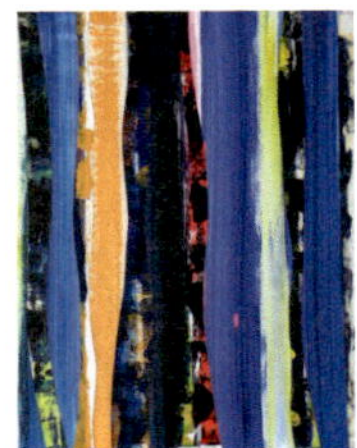

p. 121
From the Bridge, 1992
acrylic and collage on paper
67 x 51.5 cm

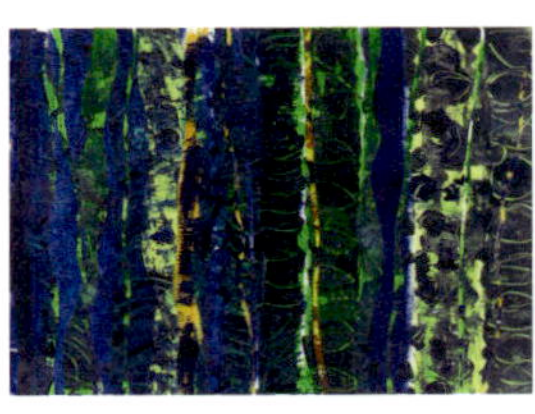

pp. 122–123
Garden Walk, 1993
acrylic and collage on paper
79 x 105 cm

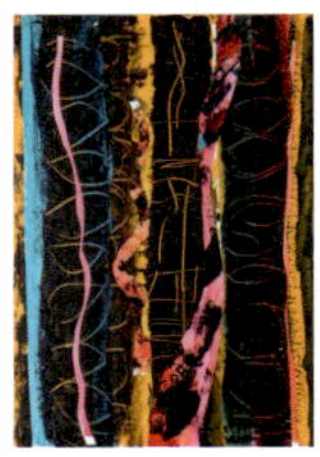

p. 125
The Long View, 1993
acrylic and collage on paper
80 x 56 cm

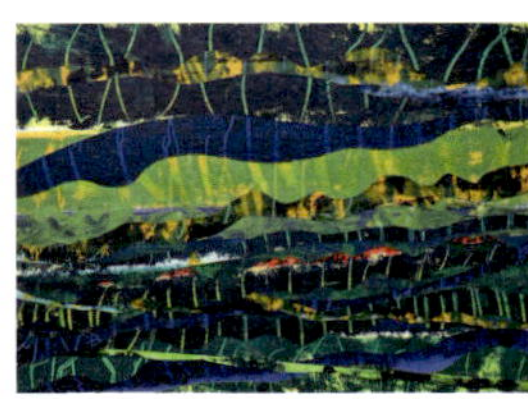

pp. 126–127
First Cut, 1995
acrylic and collage on paper
56 x 80.5 cm

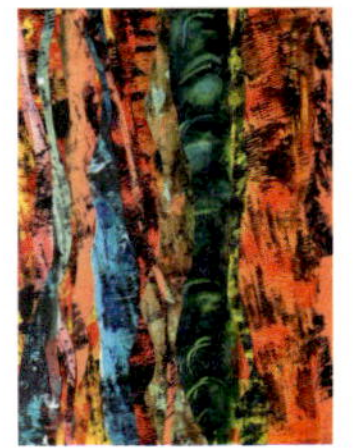

p. 129
Peacock, 1996
acrylic and collage on paper
70 x 50 cm

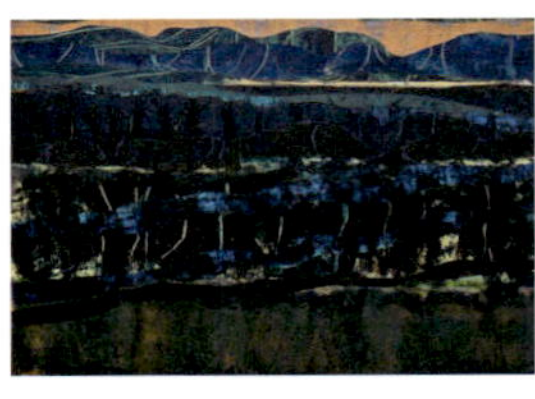

p. 130–131
Toward Evening, 1996
acrylic and collage on paper
56 x 81 cm

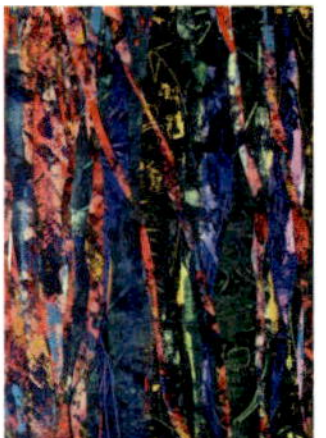

pp. 132–133
Big Sky, 1993
acrylic and collage on paper
78 x 52 cm

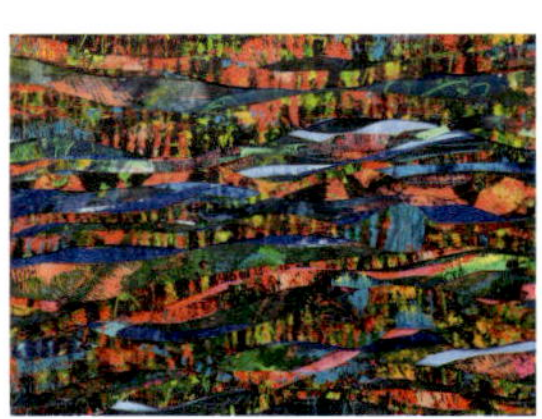

pp. 134–135
War Paint, 1993
acrylic and collage on paper
49 x 74 cm

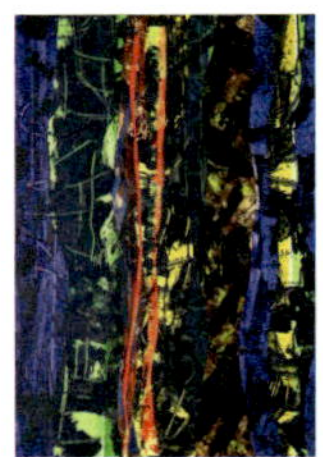

p. 137
Nocturnal Walk, 1993
acrylic and collage on paper
80.5 x 55 cm

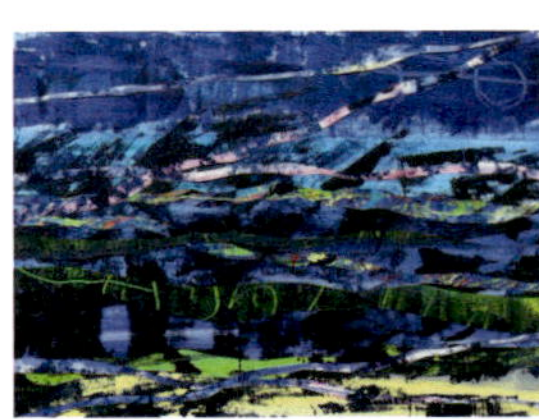

pp. 138–139
The Gate, 1993
acrylic and collage on paper
57 x 80 cm

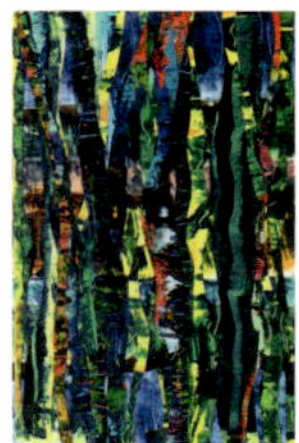

pp. 140–141
Green Shoots, 1992
acrylic and collage on paper
80 x 56 cm

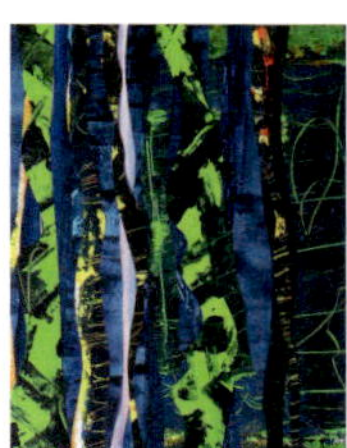

p. 143
Towards Lilac, 1992
acrylic and collage on paper
76 x 56 cm

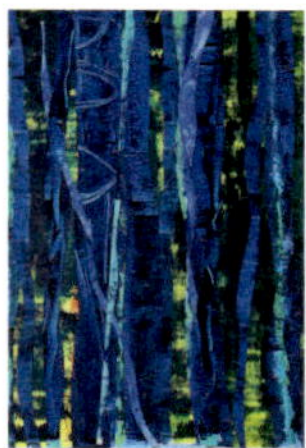

p. 145
Blue Day, 1996
acrylic and collage on paper
80 x50 cm

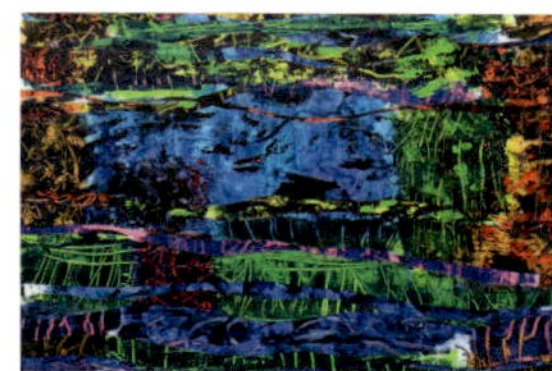

pp. 146–147
The Pond, 1995
acrylic and collage on paper
55 x 81 cm

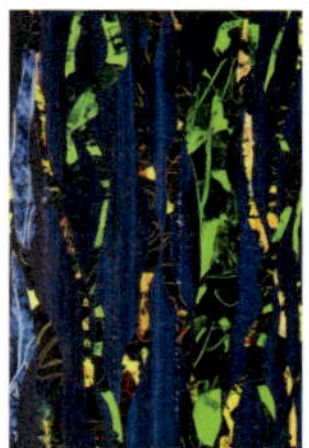

p. 149
Mayfly, 1992
acrylic and collage on paper
74 x 50 cm

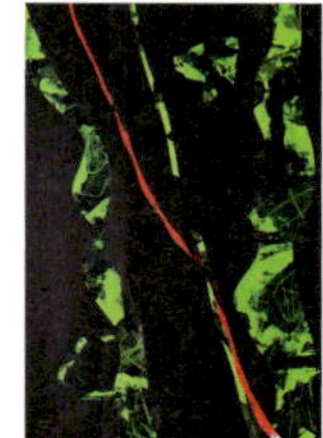

p. 151
Strobe Dancer, 1997
acrylic and collage on paper
75 x 50 cm

Mel Gooding

Mel Gooding is an art critic, writer and curator. He received his MA in English
at the University of Sussex in 1966, was Senior Research Fellow at Edinburgh
College of Art (1998-2005), and Research Professor at Wimbledon School
of Art, University of the Arts, London (2006-2008). He has written many
catalogue texts and essays, and contributed extensively to the art press,
including magazines and newspapers. Mel Gooding has written monographs
on artists including: Bruce McLean (1990), Patrick Heron (1994), Gillian Ayres
(2001), Ceri Richards (2001), John Hoyland (2006), Herman de Vries (2006),
Merlyn Evans (2010) and Frank Bowling (2011).

Gabriella Pounds

Gabriella Pounds is an art critic, writer and editor. She received her MA in
History of Art from The Courtauld Institute of Art in 2016. Her writing
has appeared in many publications including *Frieze* and *Artforum*.

Acknowledgements

Firstly, profound thanks to my son Maximillion, without whom this project
would never have happened.

Huge thanks to Anna Danby, Aniela Gil and Daphne Fordham-Smith
at Black Dog Press for their passion and commitment to the production
of this book, my second to be published by Black Dog. Many thanks also
extended to Richard Freed at the SJH Group.

Special thanks to the writers; Mel Gooding, for his interest in this
project and for the sensitive and poetic foreword text, and Gabriella Pounds
for contributing an engaging and insightful essay to accompany the book.
As ever, thank you to my studio manager, Maudie Gibbons, for the
coordination of this project and her support throughout.

Thanks too, of course, are due to all who helped with production:
Gibson Blanc Photography, Octopus Print, Idea Digital Imaging Ltd and
Prom Print Cheltenham for reproductions of the artworks featured, and to
Darbyshire Ltd for framing all works for the 'Fractured Light' exhibition.

Dedicated to

My wife Cynthia

Our son, Maximillion, for his unstinting support, vision and passion

Our daughters, Lucinda, Kitty and Poppy

Johnnie Cooper

A note from the artist

During the period after I moved to Brook Farm in rural Gloucestershire in June 1992, I was interested in the juxtaposition of harmonious and contrasting colours that created an exciting stimulus on the retina; a vibration of colours. The surrounding woodland and fields provided the perfect inspiration.

When the morning sunlight lit the wood from the east it created a blaze of light that was refracted by the first line of trees, illuminating the dark interior and picking out individual shapes of muted shade. At noon and throughout the early afternoon, light poured through the canopy and set up a patchwork of shadows between pools of vivid colour. The setting of the sun behind the western horizon filled the wood with shafts of light that moved down the tree trunks, setting the whole wood on fire in an array of burnished shades of brown.

The wood next to the cottage became my muse. In response to the ever-changing quality of light and refracted hues, I decided to develop a series of paintings that would reflect the varying colour palettes that each time of day created.

The woodland restricted views of the countryside to the west, but as the sun moved past the midday point, the dense atmosphere of the wood was sliced by bright shafts of light. The effect of these beams on the tree trunks, branches, foliage and bushes was like looking into a kaleidoscope of thousands of shifting colours and shapes. Each gradient of light created a different atmosphere, from the sparkling of a jewellery box to the moody tones of melancholy.

Black Dog Press Limited
298 Regents Park Road
London N3 2SZ
United Kingdom

+44 (0)20 8371 4047
office@blackdogonline.com
www.blackdogonline.com

Project managed by Maudie Gibbons
Text written by Mel Gooding and Gabriella Pounds
Designed by Aniela Gil
Edited by Justin Lewis

Cover image: *Sky Lark*, 1994
© 2020 Johnnie Cooper Studio

British Library in Cataloguing Data. A CIP record for
this book is available from the British Library.

ISBN 978-1-912165-24-7

Printed in the United Kingdom by Pureprint Group.